CONGO ——

CONGO ———————————

Thomas Turner

polity

First published in 2013 by Polity Press

Polity Press
65 Bridge Street
Cambridge CB2 1UR, UK

Polity Press
350 Main Street
Malden, MA 02148, USA

ISBN-13: 978-0-7456-4843-9
ISBN-13: 978-0-7456-4844-6(pb)

A catalogue record for this book is available from the British Library.

Typeset in 10.5 on 12 pt Sabon
by Toppan Best-set Premedia Limited
Printed and bound in Great Britain by the MPG Printgroup

For further information on Polity, visit our website:
www.politybooks.com

Contents ————————————————

Maps

Abbreviations

ABAKO	Association des Bakongo pour l'Unification, la Conservation et l'Expansion de la Langue Kikongo/Association for the Maintenance, the Unity, and the Expansion of the Kikongo Language (1950); also Alliance des Bâtisseurs du Kongo/Alliance of Builders of Kongo (present day)
ABIR	Anglo-Belgian India Rubber Company
ADF	Allied Democratic Forces
ADP	Alliance Démocratique des Peuples/Democratic Alliance of Peoples
AFDL	Alliance des Forces Démocratiques pour la Libération du Congo-Zaïre/Alliance of Democratic Forces for the Liberation of Congo-Zaïre
ALiR	Armée pour la Libération du Rwanda/Army for the Liberation of Rwanda
AMISOM	African Union Mission in Somalia
ANC	Armée Nationale Congolaise/Congolese National Army
APL	Armée Populaire de Libération/People's Liberation Army
Asadho	Association Africaine de Défense des Droits de l'Homme/African Association for Defense of Human Rights

AU	African Union
BCK	Compagnie du Chemin de Fer du Bas – Congo au Katanga/ Lower Congo–Katanga Railroad Company
BDK	Bundu dia Kongo/Kingdom of Kongo
CCU	Convention des Congolais Unis/Convention of United Congolese
CEEAC	Communauté Économique des États de l'Afrique Centrale/Economic Community of Central African States
CEPGL	Communauté Économique des Pays des Grands Lacs/Economic Community of the Great Lakes Countries
CIAT	Comité International d'Accompagnement de la Transition/International Committee in Support of the Transition
CIRGL	Conférence Internationale sur la Région des Grands Lacs/International Conference on the Great Lakes Region
CNDD	Conseil National pour la Défense de Démocratie/National Council for the Defense of Democracy
CNL	Conseil National de Libération/National Liberation Council
CNDP	Congrès National pour la Défense du Peuple/ National Congress for the Defense of the People
CNS	Conférence Nationale Souveraine/Sovereign National Conference
COJESKI	Collectif des Organisations des Jeunes Solidaires du Congo-Kinshasa/Collective of Organizations and Youth Associations in Congo-Kinshasa
CONAKAT	Confédération des Associations Tribales du Katanga/Confederation of Katanga Tribal Associations
DOCS	Doctors on Call for Service
DRC	Democratic Republic of Congo

ECOWAS	Economic Community of West African States
EIB	European Investment Bank
EJCSK	Église de Jésus Christ sur la Terre par son Envoyé Spécial Simon Kimbangu/The Church of Christ on Earth by His Special Envoy Simon Kimbangu
FAC	Forces Armées Congolaises/Congolese Armed Forces
FAO	Food and Agriculture Organization of the United Nations
FAR	Forces Armées Rwandaises/Rwandan Armed Forces
FARDC	Forces Armées de la République Démocratique du Congo/Democratic Republic of Congo Armed Forces
FAZ	Forces Armées Zaïroises/Zaïrian Armed Forces
FDLR	Forces Démocratiques du Libération du Rwanda/Democratic Forces for the Liberation of Rwanda
FLEC	Frente para a Libertação do Enclave de Cabinda/Front for the Liberation of the Cabinda Enclave
FLNC	Front de Libération Nationale du Congo/Congo National Liberation Front
FNL	Forces Nationales de Libération/National Forces of Liberation
FNLA	Frente Nacional de Libertação de Angola/National Liberation Front of Angola
GAO	Government Accountability Office
IAC	International Association of Congo
IRC	International Rescue Committee
LRA	Lord's Resistance Army
MIB	Mission d'Immigration des Banyaruanda/Banyarwanda Immigration Mission
MIBA	Minière de Bakwanga/Bakwanga Mining
MLC	Mouvement de Libération du Congo/Congo Liberation Movement

MONUC	United Nations Organization Mission in the Democratic Republic of the Congo
MONUSCO	United Nations Organization Stabilization Mission in the Democratic Republic of the Congo
MPLA	Movimento Popular de Libertação de Angola/ Popular Movement for the Liberation of Angola
MPR	Mouvement Populaire de la Révolution/ Popular Movement of the Revolution
MRC	Mouvement Révolutionnaire Congolais/Congolese Revolutionary Movement
MRLZ	Mouvement Révolutionnaire pour la Libération du Zaïre/Revolutionary Movement for the Liberation of Zaïre
OAU	Organization of African Unity
ONUC	Opération des Nations Unies au Congo/ United Nations Operation in the Congo
PALU	Parti Lumumbiste Unifié/Unified Lumumbist Party
PDSC	Parti Démocrate et Social Chrétien/ Democratic Social-Christian Party
PPRD	People's Party for Reconstruction and Parti du Peuple Pour la Reconstruction et la Démocratie/Democracy
PRP	Parti Révolutionnaire du Peuple/People's Revolutionary Party
PSA	Parti Solidaire Africain/African Solidarity Party
R2P	Responsibility to Protect
RANU	Rwandese Alliance for National Unity
RCD	Rassemblement Congolais pour la Démocratie/Congolese Rally for Democracy
RCD-ML	RCD-Mouvement de Libération/RCD-Liberation Movement
RPA	Rwandan Patriotic Army
RPF	Rwandan Patriotic Front
SADC	Southern African Development Community
SEC	Securities and Exchange Commission

SFVS	Synergie des Femmes pour les Victimes des Violences Sexuelles/Women's Synergy for Victims of Sexual Violence
SMTF	Société Minière de Tenke-Fungurume/ Tenke-Fungurume Mining Company
SOMIGL	Société Minière des Grands Lacs/Great Lakes Mining Company
SPLA	Sudanese People's Liberation Army
UDEMO	Union of Mobutist Democrats
UDPS	Union pour la Démocratie et le Progrès Social/ Union for Democracy and Social Progress
UFERI	Union des Fédéralistes et des Républicains Indépendants/Union of Federalists and Independent Republicans
UMHK	Union Minière du Haut-Katanga/Upper Katanga Mining Union
UNAMIR	United Nations Assistance Mission for Rwanda
UNHCR	United Nations High Commissioner for Refugees (the UN Refugee Agency)
UNITA	União Nacional para a Independência Total de Angola/National Union for the Total Independence of Angola
UNMIS	UN Mission in Sudan
UPDF	Uganda People's Defense Force

Preface

This book is the fruit of decades of study of Congolese politics, from a variety of perspectives. Teaching in Congolese universities, I learned a great deal from my colleagues and from my students. My stints at the University of Nairobi, the University of Tunis-El Manar, and the National University of Rwanda also were very fruitful.

On two occasions, in Zaïre (DRC), and in Rwanda, I experienced a dictatorship establishing its control over the university. In Kenya and in Tunisia, in contrast, the campuses were restive under well-established authoritarian rule. I do not claim to have foreseen the electoral defeat of Kenya's Daniel arap Moi or (even less) the Jasmine Revolution by which the Tunisian people ousted the dictatorship of Zine el Abidine Ben Ali, but the advance signs were visible. I remember riding on a tourist boat operating out of Lamu, flying the Kenyan flag upside down, the universal sign of distress. In Tunis, I attended an evening party at which Tunisian intellectuals excoriated Ben Ali (in French, presumably for my benefit) until one of the wives interjected, "At least he is protecting us from the Islamists." Each of these situations was unique, yet each offered interesting insights into the roles of intellectuals as critics and sometimes as collaborators with authoritarianism. I have tried to draw on these experiences in writing this book.

I would like to thank my professors, my colleagues, and my students, who have taught me so much. I have to begin with Henry Hart, Crawford Young, and Jan Vansina, my professors at the University of Wisconsin. Many of my classmates from Madison have been very helpful over the years; Georges Nzongola, Catharine and David Newbury, Robert Smith, Sandie Turner, and David Henige deserve special thanks.

I would also like to thank Hamadi Redissi of Tunis and Korwa Adar of Nairobi, for their insights into politics in their respective countries. In Rwanda, I learned a great deal from the late Emmanuel Bugingo, Marie-Thérèse Kampire, and Déo Mbonyinkebe.

Other friends and colleagues who have helped me move forward include Augustin Bifuko, Edouard Bustin, John Clark, Charles Gilman, Ruth Kornfield, Allen Roberts, and Herbert Weiss. None of them is responsible for any deficiencies in this text.

In my early research, I tried to balance documentary research in the administrative archives in Congo and Belgium with information and insights from interviews in the field. Over the years, I came to realize the need to broaden the definition of sources. To understand how Congolese remember and interpret their history, in this book I draw on paintings and songs, including Tshibumba's history paintings (several of which are in my collection) and Franco's song "Candidat na biso Mobutu," for insight into Belgian colonial rule and the Mobutu regime, respectively.

This book represents an effort to synthesize what is known about the perennial conflict that has torn apart Congo since the days of Leopold's Congo Free State. The book is not as complete as the two major works of recent years – Filip Reyntjens's *The Great African War* and Gérard Prunier's *Africa's World War* – but it updates the story of the Congo wars and broadens the geographic scope, to deal with politics, minerals, and other topics outside the war zone in the east.

There are several questions that I would like to have answered, but cannot answer at this point. I would like to be able to show at what point the United States government became committed to the Tutsi *reconquista*, carried out by the RPF under the leadership of Paul Kagame. Some of my colleagues – René Lemarchand for one – are convinced that the RPF shot down the plane carrying President Habyarimana, the event that set off the genocide of 1994. I remain agnostic on this point, although the ruthlessness that Kagame has shown since then, particularly in continued support for "rebellions" or "mutinies" of Congolese Tutsi, lends credence to such a claim. I would like to be able to say who exactly gave the order to kill President Laurent Kabila of DRC, in 2001, and to install young Joseph Kabila as his successor, but I cannot.

This book would not have taken the form it has had I not spent more than five years as a Country Specialist on DRC for Amnesty International USA. Amnesty International has an enviable record as an advocate for the cause of human rights over the past half-century. This is particularly the case as regards DRC and the neighboring states of Africa's Great Lakes region. In the late years of the Mobutu dictatorship, Amnesty was a leader in denouncing the violence against democracy protestors and against ethnic minorities, especially Luba-Kasai and speakers of Kinyarwanda (both Hutu and Tutsi). Following the Rwanda genocide, Amnesty pointed out the problems resulting from Hutu soldiers and allied militias (ex-FAR and Interahamwe) operating from Zaïrian territory. Once the Rwandan army and its Ugandan and Congolese allies had crossed the border in 1996, Amnesty was among the first and most consistent critics of Rwandan army abuses committed on Congolese soil, targeting Rwandan and Congolese Hutu and their presumed sympathizers. Ever since, the organization has maintained a consistent record of defense of human rights in the Great Lakes, efforts that are especially important given the efforts of the Rwandan, Congolese, and American governments to rewrite history and obscure their responsibility for these events. I am proud to have played a part in publicizing these abuses, and thank Amnesty for giving me a chance to do so. I was able to refresh my knowledge and understanding of the ongoing crisis in DRC, not least by preparing attestations on behalf of a number of Congolese seeking asylum in the United States.

Finally, I should say that I have learned a great deal about Congo from my wife, Irène Safi Turner, an International Development worker and Ph.D. candidate in conflict analysis and resolution. This book is dedicated to Irène, born in Bukavu, South Kivu, and to our daughter, Benita Olame Turner, born in Harrisonburg, Virginia.

Author's Note ———————————————

This book deals with a state that has been called successively the Congo Free State, the Belgian Congo, the Republic of Congo, the Democratic Republic of Congo, Zaïre, and again the Democratic Republic of Congo.

The name "Congo" derives from the pre-colonial state of Kongo or Congo, which had its capital at Mbanza Kongo (later São Salvador) in northern Angola. The river that flows into the Atlantic through Kongo territory became known as the Congo or Kongo River. The people of the region began to be called Kongo (Bakongo) in the nineteenth century, and their various dialects, Kikongo.

The partition of Central Africa (1885 and thereafter) divided the Congo River basin into three main parts: the Congo Free State, the French colony of Moyen Congo (the present Republic of Congo), and Portuguese Congo. Portuguese Congo comprised two distinct blocs of territory: the northwestern portion of Angola and the tiny exclave of Cabinda, separated from Angola by a narrow neck of DRC.

The Congo River basin, as discussed at the Berlin Conference of 1884–5, extended to the "Crête Congo-Nil" or the Congo–Nile divide. Portions of the present Rwanda were considered to be included in the Congo Free State. Subsequent negotiations between the colonial powers (Congo Free State/Belgium, Britain, and Germany) set the boundaries that continue until today. As in the west, these colonial boundaries cut across political and cultural boundaries.

The following time-line summarizes these changes:

1885–1908   Congo Free State ("Free" in the sense of independent, not belonging to another state). Leopold II, king of the Belgians, was head of state of the Congo Free State in his personal capacity.

1908–60   Belgian Congo (colony of the Kingdom of Belgium).

1960–4   Republic of Congo.

1964–71   Democratic Republic of Congo (name changed under Constitution of Luluabourg).

1971–97   Republic of Zaïre (name changed by President Mobutu, as part of his "Authenticity" campaign).

1997–present Democratic Republic of Congo (reverted to previous name when Laurent Kabila ousted Mobutu).

Map 1 Democratic Republic of Congo

Introduction: Congo, a Perennial Hot Spot

The territory occupied by the Democratic Republic of Congo (DRC) and its historical precursors has been an arena of conflict since King Leopold II of Belgium created the Congo Free State in 1885. The extreme violence of the state, which the king held as his private property, led to a huge international scandal and obliged the Belgian parliament to annex it in 1908. The ill-prepared decolonization of the Belgian Congo in 1960 led to the secession of mineral-rich Katanga province, the ouster a few months later of Prime Minister Patrice Lumumba by Colonel Joseph Mobutu, the murder of Lumumba in Katanga, and a series of Lumumbist rebellions. Congo stayed in the headlines for several years until a second American-sponsored coup by Mobutu in 1965 ushered in over thirty years of dictatorship.

In 1996, Congo became a hot spot yet again, when Rwanda and Uganda invaded eastern Zaïre/Congo (with the participation also of Burundi and Angola). Rwanda put a Congolese face on the invasion by creating a coalition of anti-Mobutu forces, the Alliance des Forces Démocratiques pour la Libération du Congo/Zaïre (Alliance of Democratic Forces for the Liberation of Congo/Zaïre, AFDL). Laurent-Désiré Kabila, a Lumumbist opponent of Mobutu since the 1960s, was spokesman for the AFDL. When the invading forces seized the capital, Kinshasa, and forced Mobutu into exile, Kabila proclaimed himself president and restored the name "Democratic

Republic of Congo" that had been used between 1964 and 1971.

Laurent Kabila soon attempted to distance himself from his foreign backers, thereby provoking the second war, from 1998 to 2003. He was murdered by one of his bodyguards in 2001, with Joseph Kabila taking his place. (On the disputed family relation between Laurent and Joseph Kabila, see Chapter 3, p. 78 below.) International negotiations led to formal peace in 2003 but a welter of Congolese and foreign groups continued to struggle to control eastern Congo and its mineral wealth. The conflict in DRC became known as the deadliest since World War II. DRC supposedly was the rape capital of the world. "Conflict minerals" were said to be financing the armed groups and thus the epidemic of sexual violence, and campaigns were organized to cut the link.[1]

Between these horrendous and highly publicized episodes, Congo largely disappeared from view. Once Leopold's private colony had become the Belgian Congo (1908–60), it became an "empire of silence."[2] Armed resistance to colonial rule – often described as "rebellion" – went on for decades but few outside Congo noticed.

Similarly, during the thirty-two years of dictatorship under Mobutu (1965–97), internal violence attracted little attention. Mobutu was a Cold War ally of the United States and sided with the US during the decolonization of neighboring Angola. In turn, the US, France, and Belgium interpreted threats to his continued rule in Cold War terms and responded accordingly. Zaïre, as Mobutu had renamed DRC in 1971 – he was to rename himself Mobutu Sese Seko the following year as part of the same program of Africanization – attracted considerable attention within academia as a paradigmatic "kleptocracy" but was largely ignored by international media and public opinion.

By 2010, fifty years after Independence Day, DRC had entered a so-called "post-war period." Violence and insecurity remained prominent features of daily life, but cross-border violence had diminished. The United Nations was beginning to withdraw its "peacekeepers." President Joseph

Kabila wished to restore the sovereignty compromised by the presence of the international force, and perhaps to return to the "empire of silence" in which crimes and abuse went largely unreported.

The first problem that this book will address is this pattern of apparent alternation between extreme noise or violence and relative silence. Does the history of Congo really exhibit sharp breaks or are there important continuities? From the perspective of the international community, and the international media, the DRC "hot spot" disappears and reappears. Viewed more closely, violent conflict is perennial, not so much in the sense of "continuing without interruption" as "regularly repeated or renewed."

From a Congolese perspective, violence in DRC is much less episodic than it is for some outsiders. The popular paintings of Tshibumba Kanda Matulu portray continuities in oppression. The artist shows the fifteenth-century Portuguese explorer "Diego Cao" (Diogo Cão) anachronistically dressed in pith helmet and white military uniform meeting the King of Kongo. "Several days later," according to the caption on the painting, Stanley (Henry Morton Stanley) met the Diego/Diogo group, which included Danis (Commandant Francis Dhanis), Bodson (Lt. Omer Bodson), "and the others." The events of the late fifteenth century and those of the late nineteenth century merge in the imagination of this late twentieth-century Congolese nationalist artist.[3]

Opinions differ as to whether the global or regional context has played a greater role in shaping events in Congo. To some observers, the global context is determinant. Congo is a playing field on which extra-continental powers struggle for advantage – a notion that we will examine in the next chapter. There is something to this. The partition of Africa, including the creation of the Congo Free State, took place under the multi-polar balance of power system. The Congo Crisis that erupted in 1960 was a product of Cold War bipolarity, while recent events have taken place under a new multi-polarity, in which the search for minerals and the struggle against Islamist terror both loom large.

The regional context, however, is arguably as important in shaping recent events in Congo as the global context. Some have seen the events in Congo since 1996 as the continuation of Rwanda's Hutu–Tutsi conflict on Congolese soil. Fighting in DRC has both been called genocide and been justified as prevention of genocide. Before we can examine the present crisis further, however, we shall have to review its historical background.

Congo and Its "Free State"

The narrative of Congo as "hot spot" sometimes begins with the arrival of Diogo Cão at the mouth of the Congo River in 1482 (portrayed, as we have seen, by Tshibumba) and the subsequent development of the Atlantic slave trade. Some authors write that evangelization and slavery destroyed the Kongo Kingdom, forgetting that the kingdom (located in western DRC and northern Angola, in modern terms) survived and thrived for centuries. Twentieth-century Kongo-speakers remembered the slave trade that took many thousands of their people across the ocean, never to return in this life, in the form of a story about "the king of the Americans."[4] (We shall return to Kongo ethno-nationalism in Chapter 3.)

Most narratives on the origins of the current crisis begin in the nineteenth century and attempt to establish causal links between the Congo Free State, Mobutu's dictatorship, and DRC's situation early in the twenty-first century. The Belgian monarch Leopold II created a vast personal colony in Central Africa. He was able to see the opportunities opening up in Africa owing to the explorations in the 1870s of David Livingstone and Henry Morton Stanley of Britain and Pierre Savorgnan de Brazza of France. Without setting foot there, Leopold adroitly maneuvered so as to block the efforts of Portugal and France, already present in Central Africa. He concealed his true intentions behind a series of innocuous-sounding front groups. When the German chancellor Otto von Bismarck convoked the Berlin West Africa Conference

(1884–5), Leopold used the occasion to announce the formation of his Free State (free or independent in the sense that it did not belong to another state). The participants, representing fourteen European states and the United States of America, warmly applauded.

To transform the Congo Free State from a claim into a functioning colony, Leopold needed to defeat the rival colonization project of the Arab-Swahili (Tippu Tib and others). He also needed to build infrastructure and to generate profits for his financial backers. However, the means Leopold employed to do this – the campaign to seize ivory and to force villagers to harvest wild rubber – led to millions of deaths and created an international backlash against his private colony. He was obliged to cede possession to the Belgian state in 1908.

Since the nineteenth century, the Congo has been described as the "heart of darkness." This is a favorite cliché of journalists, by which all sorts of atrocities can be attributed to Congo's innate savagery. Most of them seem not to realize that Joseph Conrad had concluded that the ultimate darkness lay in the hearts of white men in their white buildings in Europe, sending their agents to rape and kill in Central Africa.

Just as the second Congo war was beginning in the late 1990s, a book called *King Leopold's Ghost* rose up the bestseller lists. Its author, Adam Hochschild, had begun his research project years before, aiming to establish a parallel between the pillage of Congo by Leopold II and the pillage by Mobutu Sese Seko. Hochschild complained, "Instead of African voices from this time there is largely silence." However, historian Nancy Hunt reminds us that thirteen women testified before the Commission of Inquiry called by King Leopold in 1905–6, in response to the international campaign. Some 170 residents of Equateur province wrote down memories fifty years later, telling of the violence, death, cruelties, and hardships that they had endured during the Free State years.[5]

It is agreed that the Congo Free State was a nightmare, but there is less agreement as to how this nineteenth-century humanitarian catastrophe relates to later disasters. Perhaps the relationship is direct. Journalist Michela Wrong sees Mobutu walking "in the footsteps" of Mr. Kurtz, Conrad's fictional Free State agent. Wrong realized that there was a problem of explaining how Leopold's system was transmitted to Mobutu (who was not even born until 1930). So she consulted experts, asking whether there was "any causal link between Belgium's exploitative regime and the excesses of Mobutu's regime, whether a frighteningly efficient kleptocratic system effectively softened up a community for a repeat performance." Jean Stengers, a leading colonial historian, told her that what was striking was the lack of memories of the Leopold era amongst the local population.

Wrong opined that the memory of the trauma of the Leopold era had been suppressed. The horrors of Leopold's reign were "surely the stuff of family legends passed down from patriarch to grandson." Amnesia, individual or collective, "could sometimes be the only way of dealing with horror, . . . human behaviour could be altered forever without the cause being openly acknowledged."[6]

Mass violence, including the mass violence of the Congo Free State, can be traumatic, but Wrong's diagnosis of amnesia is unconvincing. Congolese tend to consider the Free State era and the Belgian Congo era as one continuous period of humiliation and slavery, which they have kept alive. Lumumba's speech on Independence Day in 1960 was an eloquent appeal to popular memory. Tshibumba's paintings on Congo history convey the same message. The single painting that best represents Belgian colonialism – *Colonie Belge* – portrays a flogging. Middle-class Congolese bought *Colonie Belge* so that their children would remember what colonialism had been like.

Psychoanalyst Vamik Volkan offers a more useful approach to trauma and memory, explaining trans-generational transmission of "chosen trauma" as a key element in large-group identity (including national and ethno-national identity).[7] (This process will be explored in Chapters 3 and 4.)

Pre-colonial political culture, which emphasized personal power and authority, ostentatious displays of wealth, and patron–client relations maintained through the distribution of resources, was another influence on Mobutu and other post-colonial rulers, perhaps more potent than the example of the absent Leopold. The conquest state of Garenganze, which controlled a vast area of Katanga in the nineteenth century, relied heavily on displays of violence. That state gave way to another, equally prone to exhibitions of brutality. In 1891, when the ruler Msiri refused to fly the Congo Free State flag, he was killed by the Belgian officer Omer Bodson, then decapitated, and Free State troops carried away his head. The Free State then used his men, the Yeke, to conquer the region.

The legal transition from the Congo Free State to the Belgian Congo did not mean that colonial conquest had been completed. Primary resistance continued for decades in some parts of the country. Some Nande of northern Kivu and Mongo of northern Kasai were not "pacified" (i.e. obliged to conform to colonial taxes and other impositions) until the 1930s. The argument of Terence Ranger on the links between primary resistance and "modern mass nationalism" is useful in understanding Congo.[8] Any given region of the vast colony may have been under control most of the time. Yet resistance and revolt continued throughout the colonial period, shifting in locus and form in response to the changing Congolese involvement in the colonial political economy.

The nature of the colonial state has been widely debated in recent years. Crawford Young argues that "one consequential factor in the crisis faced by most African states by the late 1970s – and intensifying since – was the singularly difficult legacy bequeathed by the institutions of rule devised to establish and maintain alien hegemony." Young took "Bula Matari," or "crusher of rocks" (an ancient Kongo nickname, applied to Stanley when he used dynamite to clear a path for the railroad), as the condensation symbol not only of the Congolese colonial state but also of the African colonial state in general. Bruce Berman demurs, suggesting that the colonial state was weak. The record supports Berman; once the Belgians openly discussed a timetable for decolonization, their domination began to unravel.[9]

For Mahmood Mamdani, the crucial characteristic of the colonial state was structural: it incorporated Africans as subjects of "native authorities," leading to "decentralized despotism." This ignores the pre-colonial roots of despotism, suggested by the Garenganze case. In any case, Mamdani's argument is too general, leaving one to understand South Africa, Uganda, and perhaps even Senegal and Morocco, as essentially similar.[10] To the contrary, colonial policy differences from Rwanda to Congo, and even from one Congolese local collectivity to another, were crucial in shaping subsequent conflicts.

Most Congolese experienced despotism both on the part of their "chiefs," now incorporated into the colonial bureaucracy, and on the part of the low-level Belgian administrators – territorial administrators and their deputies – who were the bosses of the African chiefs. Jean-Claude Willame has suggested that the Belgian territorial administrator, authoritarian and arbitrary, was a model for Lumumba.[11]

The colonial state in Congo, whether strong or weak, rested on coercion, above all practiced by the colonial army or Force Publique. A common form of mass punishment or intimidation was the *"promenade militaire"* (a rapid march through the villages, designed to intimidate), while recalcitrant individuals received *"la chicotte"* (the lash). Africans of the Force Publique inflicted both forms of repression on their fellow Africans, as seen in Tshibumba's painting *Colonie Belge*. In the speech Prime Minister Lumumba prepared for Independence Day, he denounced "the cells into which the authorities brutally threw those who had escaped the bullets of the soldiers whom the colonialists had made the tool of their domination." (Reading the speech, he prudently omitted the reference to the soldiers.[12])

The military pillar of the colonial regime was less solid than the Belgians professed to believe. Mutinies shook the Leopoldian state, in 1895, 1897, and 1900. Then the Force Publique remained apparently reliable until 1944, when Belgian domination was shaken by another mutiny, this time set off by Western-educated Congolese (the so-called *"évolués"*).

The mutiny that exploded in 1960, five days after independence, resulted from the convergence of two forces: first, the corporate frustration of the men of the Force Publique, who saw *évolués* move ahead while the soldiers were expected to remain as before; and, second, the influence of politicized identity, as political parties linked up with soldiers. In turn, the violence of the mutineers, including reported rape of Belgian women, was used to justify the intervention of Belgian troops, setting off the Congo Crisis of 1960.

The Belgian plan for decolonization was to graft an elected government onto the existing colonial administration. As the first republic slid into chaos, owing to the mutiny, the secession of Katanga, and the Belgian military intervention, the *Loi Fondamentale* (provisional Constitution) was found wanting, notably in the ambiguity of the relationship between the president and the prime minister (king and prime minister, in the Belgian model). When the elected institutions fell away, the Congolese were left with the inherited colonial state.

An alternative line of argument sees the essence of the colonial state not in constitutions and politico-administrative structures but in economic exploitation. Pre-colonial Kongo, Luba, and other states can be seen as political systems based on patron–client relations maintained through the distribution of resources. Leopold's state is rightly identified with the harvesting of "red rubber" and ivory, but it was laying the groundwork for industrial mining on the Katanga Copper Belt and the diamond fields of Kasai. The Compagnie du Chemin de Fer du Bas – Congo au Katanga (BCK, Lower Congo–Katanga Railroad Company) was founded in 1890, but the largest mining company, the Union Minière du Haut-Katanga (UMHK, Upper Katanga Mining Union), did not see the light of day until 1906, on the eve of annexation of the Free State by the Belgian parliament.

The colonial economy rested on forced labor until the end, in 1960. So-called "educational" crops were imposed on unwilling peasants in order to generate cotton, coffee, and other products for export. Where the local labor force was insufficient in number, or judged "unsuitable" (as were some of the peoples of Upper Katanga and of North Kivu), the Belgians brought in outsiders. Two of these recruitment programs – bringing Luba from Kasai to Katanga and bringing

Hutu from Rwanda to Kivu – created problems that are being felt to this day. (This question will be explored in Chapter 3.)

Mobutu initially attempted to legitimate his regime by stealing the clothes of Lumumba and the nationalists. He set up a party-state, similar to that of Ghana or Mali. Rather than perpetuate the colonial trinity of Church, administration, and state-chartered capitalist corporations, he expanded the administration and attacked the Church. Then he veered into cultural nationalism, changing the country's name "Congo" to the supposedly authentic "Zaïre," which was a Portuguese deformation of the Kongo word "*Nzadi,*" meaning river. Mobutu's ideology of "authenticity" had some resonance with the public, but it soon evolved into "Mobutuism," a vacuous cult of the personality, fed by sycophants.

In the economic sphere, Mobutu's measures to give locals a greater share initially were popular. As "Zaïrianization" was succeeded by "radicalization of the revolution," however, it became clear to most people that foreign businesses had been handed over to political cronies and subordinates, who focused on short-term profit and disorganized the economy.

Although Mobutu had come to power through military coups (in September 1960, when he "neutralized" President Joseph Kasa-Vubu and Prime Minister Lumumba, and again in November 1965), he failed to develop a cohesive, professional army capable of defending the country. The army was both the backbone of the regime and its Achilles' heel. Mobutu's regime emerged from a coup but was not a military regime because it never gave priority to the interests of the military. After 1965, Mobutu managed the armed forces by the same methods he used, as chief of staff, to rebuild them after 1960: that is, by tying individual units and officers to him. Rather than a conventional pyramidal organization, the Zaïrian security forces resembled a wheel with Mobutu at the hub. Time and again, when existing units proved to be unreliable, he created new units trained by foreigners. The Forces Armées Zaïroises (Zaïrian Armed Forces, FAZ) remained "an army of mutineers" (in Mobutu's own words), unreliable as a military force and brutal toward civilians.

Mobutu's FAZ seems to have served as a model for the Kabilas' Forces Armées de la République Démocratique du Congo (Democratic Republic of Congo Armed Forces, FARDC). The other military model, represented by the various Mayi-Mayi or Maï-Maï local defense units, derives from the "rebels" who fought Mobutu in 1964–5 in the name of the murdered Lumumba. The Lumumbist Armée Populaire de Libération (People's Liberation Army, APL) captured nearly half the national territory. However, this army owed its initial success and ultimate failure to heavy reliance on magical protection. Its troops, the "Simba" (Lions, in Swahili), were initiated into service, and given both "medicine" to protect them against bullets and a list of commandments they had to follow to preserve the magical protection. In particular, the Simba were to abstain from sexual relations and from steal-ing. Reliance on magic, however, left them vulnerable when meeting resistance from local self-protection forces believed to possess possibly superior magic, or from Europeans.

By the 1980s, Mobutu's party-state had degenerated into a "shadow state" headed by a "warlord," to use William Reno's terminology.[13] The inconclusive struggle for democ-racy at the beginning of the 1990s exposed the weakness of Mobutu's Zaïre. I reject the argument that the invaders of 1996 and 1998 were "sucked in" – that metaphor deprives them of responsibility for the horrors they unleashed – but the weakness of the regime made it possible for the small neighbors of Congo/Zaïre to contemplate an invasion.

The Structure of This Book

In subsequent chapters we will explore in greater depth some questions raised here. In Chapters 1 and 2, the question of the nature of the wars going on in DRC will be dealt with through consideration of the roles of major actors, both extra-continental and African. This will provide an opportu-nity to consider whether extra-continental actors are acting in DRC through proxies: that is, African states or movements that they finance and control. By the same logic, some African governments allegedly intervene in Congo through proxy armies and parties. Neither of these arguments is true by definition; we shall have to examine possible divergence of interests between alleged patrons and their presumed clients. Some interesting problems arise: if Rwanda was a proxy for the United States, and Laurent Kabila's AFDL was a proxy for Rwanda, did Kabila thereby become a proxy for the US? Kabila's efforts to maintain his autonomy became an important thread in the drama that unfolded, from 1996, when the AFDL, the Rwandans, and the Ugandans crossed the border, to 2001, when he was killed by a former child soldier, perhaps under the direction of the Rwandans and/or the Americans.

In Chapter 3, we shall move to consideration of the politics of identity, considering a broader range of identities than those habitually dealt with. In addition to ethnicity and nation, we will consider race, region, language, religion, and class. These ideas tie the individuals of Congo to the state and other social structures. Several myths must be deconstructed, notably the notion that President Yoweri Museveni of Uganda and President Paul Kagame of Rwanda were "new African leaders" (believed in Washington) and that they wanted to incorporate eastern DRC into a state called the "Hima Empire" or "Republic of the Volcanoes" (believed in DRC). Relations between the Kinyarwanda-speaking Tutsi and Hutu of DRC's eastern provinces and those of Rwanda itself are complex. Relations between the Congolese Kinyarwanda-speakers and their Congolese neighbors are complex too. We shall attempt to understand them, with the help of several other case studies of relations between locals (*autochtones*) and outsiders (*allogènes*) in other regions of DRC. There is more to the Congo wars than locals versus outsiders or a transposition of Rwanda's Hutu–Tutsi conflict onto Congo soil, but those are two of the factors involved in Congo's hybrid international–civil war.

The enormous toll of sexual violence in DRC has drawn the attention of international activists, and the resultant activity has mobilized assistance for Congolese women's groups that work to help victims of sexual violence. The problem with such a synecdoche (taking a part for the whole) is that it impedes understanding of the phenomenon. An important part of the sexual violence in DRC results from rape as a weapon. In such cases, women and girls are attacked because of their presumed ethnic or national identity. But there is more to the fighting than sexual violence, and an important part of the sexual violence is not the result of the use of rape as a weapon. We shall attempt to unpack this in Chapter 4, and to untangle the links between identity politics, sexual violence, and conflict minerals.

DRC is enormously rich in terms of minerals, and the illegal exploitation of some of those "conflict minerals" (especially the so-called "3 Ts," i.e. tantalum, tin, and tungsten, plus gold) has been cited as a factor both financing the fighting and, at the same time, giving armed groups a reason to fight. In some cases, campaigners have connected this directly to the epidemic of sexual violence, as in "Does your cell phone cause rape?"[14] The reality is more complex, as we shall see in Chapter 5. In particular, focusing narrowly on the "3 Ts" plus gold means neglecting important conflicts generated by other mineral wealth, including cobalt, diamonds, and petroleum, and even by land and local political office. As such, this chapter will consider regions outside the theatre of war in the eastern provinces, where other minerals, including diamonds and oil, also provoke and finance political conflict.

Rather than a general conclusion, we shall return to the national level and devote Chapter 6 to the question of who is at fault in the multi-faceted Congo catastrophe. Given the extremely high level of mortality and of sexual violence, whose responsibility is it to deal with these problems? In the first instance, it is the responsibility of the state to protect its subjects in exchange for the loyalty they give it. Clearly, the Congolese state is unwilling or unable to provide such protection. In such a situation, the international community (which we shall have to define) is increasingly called upon for humanitarian intervention on behalf of the Congolese population. And, indeed, the international community has moved toward assuming responsibility for prevention of mass violence when the host government is unable or unwilling to exercise that responsibility. The process has been a halting one, however, and often it takes a massive violation of human rights, such as the Rwanda genocide, to nudge it along. Worse yet, as the violations in eastern DRC suggest, "victims becomes killers"[15] and, in so doing, acquire a stake in obstruction of justice. There are no easy answers to these problems, but it is hoped that dispassionate discussion of them will ease the way forward.

1 | Congo as a Playing Field

In October 1996, so-called "Banyamulenge" (Kinyarwanda-speaking Congolese Tutsi) captured the eastern Zaïre cities of Uvira, Bukavu, and Goma. They attacked the UN refugee camps near these cities, sending more than one million Hutu refugees back to Rwanda. Other refugees fled westward, into the Congo forests. Two weeks later, long-time Mobutu opponent Laurent Kabila was presented as the head of a coalition called the AFDL.

Told in this fashion, the story begins in October 1996, and pits various opposition groups against the regime of Marshal Mobutu. In reality, it begins earlier, and was more international than it was made to appear. Many authors trace the war back to the genocide in Rwanda and the seizure of power in Kigali by the Tutsi-dominated Rwandan Patriotic Front (RPF), in 1994. Former US Assistant Secretary of State for Africa Herman Cohen begins the story with the RPF invasion of Rwanda in 1990, an invasion the United States should have stopped, in his opinion.[1] Each of these alternative narratives converts the 1996 war from a civil war into an international war. Strangely, however, the World Bank persisted in classifying the hostilities (including the second war that began in 1998) as a civil war, something that worked greatly to the advantage of Rwanda and Uganda, the principal aggressors in both conflicts.

Those who see mineral wealth as the main motor of conflict in DRC interpret the war of 1996–7 as a resource war much like the war of "partition and pillage" that began in 1998. As the AFDL gained strength, international firms signed deals, effectively treating rebel leader Laurent Kabila as Zaïre's ruler even though he controlled only a small portion of the country.[2]

By 1997, the AFDL forces had rolled across the country and reached Kinshasa. They met little opposition except at Kenge (Bandundu province), where troops from the former Rwandan army and from Jonas Savimbi's UNITA (União Nacional para a Independência Total de Angola/National Union for the Total Independence of Angola) resisted for a time. Successfully overcoming their opponents, Kabila's men entered the capital in May and President Mobutu, who was ailing from prostate cancer, was forced to flee.

Kabila proclaimed himself president of the country and announced a government in which Rwandan citizens and Kinyarwanda-speaking Congolese held a number of key posts. James Kabarebe, a Rwandan army officer, was named chief of staff of the Congolese Armed Forces (Forces Armées Congolaises, FAC).

The pretense that the Congolese had overthrown Mobutu lasted a few more weeks until, in July 1997, Rwandan vice-president Paul Kagame admitted (Georges Nzongola-Ntalaja says he "boasted"[3]) that Rwanda had planned and executed the war, and had assembled the coalition of Kabila's Parti Révolutionnaire du Peuple (People's Revolutionary Party, PRP) and the other groups to give a Congolese face to the invasion.

Kabila performed his job of providing a Congolese face for the Rwanda-led invasion, notably by frustrating the efforts of the United Nations to investigate the massacres of Rwandan Hutu refugees in the Congolese forests. Increasingly, however, the regime was polarized between the Rwandans and their Congolese Tutsi protégés, on the one hand, and Kabila's Luba-Katanga community and Katangans in general, on the other. In July 1998, Kabila pre-empted a rumored coup d'état, transferring Kabarebe from his post as army commander to a powerless position as advisor to the president. A few days later, Kabila announced that he was sending Kabarebe and the other foreign officers home. "Africa's world war" began as a Rwandan attempt to overthrow Kabila. It started with a mutiny at Goma (on the Rwandan border) and an invasion by Rwandan troops. As in 1996, a Congolese cover was provided for a military operation conducted by Rwanda in collaboration with its neighbors Uganda and Burundi. Ten days after the Rwandan troops re-entered DRC, the Rassemblement Congolais pour la Démocratie (Congolese Rally for Democracy, RCD) announced its formation. Rather than moving from town to town as in 1996, the Rwandans hijacked airplanes and flew their troops and Congolese auxiliaries to Kitona military base in Bas Congo province, west of Kinshasa. They freed and recruited a number of men from Mobutu's army being "re-educated" at Kitona. The Rwandans also seized the hydro-electric complex at Inga – cutting off power to millions of civilians, and to the hospitals of the capital – and Congo's major port at Matadi. They were thwarted in their efforts to seize Kinshasa by military intervention by Angola and Zimbabwe. Namibia soon joined its neighbors and fellow Southern African Development Community (SADC) members Angola and Zimbabwe in support of Kabila.

Opposing the pro-Kabila coalition was the same coalition that had invaded in 1996, minus Angola. Rwanda again was the leader, followed by Uganda. Burundi was mostly "minding its back door," as Gérard Prunier puts it,[4] and had no ambitions to impose a friendly regime in Kinshasa. It did, however, seize the chance to strike against Burundian Hutu rebels who had long been based in South Kivu's Uvira and Fizi territories.

The Congolese "rebels" of 1998 were stronger militarily than the Congolese central government, mainly because of their foreign backing. However, that same foreign backing meant that the civilian institutions in the rebel zone were illegitimate in the eyes of the population. Rwanda was unwilling to accept that it was the core of the problem. Instead, the Rwandans ran through a series of RCD presidents, from Arthur Z'ahidi Ngoma, to Prof. Ernest Wamba dia Wamba, to Dr. Émile Ilunga, to Dr. Adolphe Onusumba, to Azarias Ruberwa. The fact that the first four included university lecturers and medical doctors reflects the prestige that comes with academic degrees and titles in Central Africa, rather than the idea that their background might be relevant to the job. Once the possibility of a blitzkrieg victory had passed, a war of "partition and pillage" set in. In the Rwandan occupation zone, administered through the RCD, the combat against the Hutu "*génocidaires*" took a back seat to plunder. The Rwanda/RCD zone comprised a sizable chunk of eastern DRC, from Orientale province in the north to Katanga in the south. The Mouvement de Libération du Congo (Congo Liberation Movement, MLC), a rival movement sponsored by Uganda, controlled a vast swath of northern DRC, principally in Equateur and Orientale provinces. The Kabila government controlled a strip of territory running from southern Katanga through the mineral-rich Kasai provinces, on to Kinshasa, Bas Congo, and the Atlantic Ocean with its offshore oil. Not coincidentally, the entire Congo–Angola border was included in the Kabila zone. The RCD, MLC, and central government zones each housed a complex network by which Congo's minerals and other resources were extracted and sold in international markets.[5]

Efforts to end "Africa's world war" began almost as soon as the war itself. Angola, DRC, Namibia, Rwanda, Uganda, and Zimbabwe signed a cease-fire agreement in Lusaka (Zambia) in 1999, and a UN observer force was approved, but fighting continued. President Laurent Kabila was in no hurry to accept a situation that placed him at a disadvantage. However, with his assassination in 2001 and his replacement by Joseph Kabila, the movement toward peace was facilitated. The following year, a peace agreement was signed in South Africa, leading to the withdrawal of most foreign troops. Nevertheless, several militias continued to fight in eastern Congo, and Congolese civilians continued to suffer.

The formula for moving forward was to create transitional institutions in which each major faction was represented. Joseph Kabila remained president but was surrounded by four vice-presidents, one each from the presidential camp, the

RCD, the MLC, and the unarmed opposition. This government proved very unproductive, prompting a joke among educated Congolese, "1 + 4 = 0."

The various armies were to be integrated but a number of RCD officers refused to accept new posts offered them under the command of Kinshasa. The formula for the transition also involved attributing the provinces and military districts to the various "components" (former government, the RCD, the MLC, etc.) such that no one would control both the civilian and military structures in the same province. South Kivu had been under the military and civilian control of the RCD. The attempt of General Prosper Nabiolwa, a veteran of Mobutu's FAZ, to assume his post in Bukavu set off a mutiny among RCD officers, led by Colonel Jules Mutebutsi, a Munyamulenge Tutsi. Forces led by Tutsi General Laurent Nkunda invaded Bukavu in June 2004 and occupied it for ten days, killing and raping, before Nkunda was persuaded to leave by MONUC (the United Nations Organization Mission in the Democratic Republic of the Congo).

In 2006, Joseph Kabila won the first relatively free and competitive elections since 1965. Jean-Pierre Bemba of the MLC finished second to Kabila in the presidential runoff, necessitated by the failure of any candidate to secure the majority (50 percent plus one) in the first round. The results revealed an east–west split; Kabila carried all the predominantly Swahili-speaking provinces in the east. (These results are analyzed in Chapter 3, on the politics of identity.)

Violence was common, both in the campaign leading up to the vote and afterwards. Locally dominant parties consolidated their position through attacks on their opponents: the Parti du Peuple pour la Reconstruction et la Démocratie (People's Party for Reconstruction and Democracy, PPRD) against the RCD in the Kivus, the MLC against the Union of Mobutist Democrats (UDEMO) in Equateur, and so on. Following the elections, the security forces of the central government clashed with Bemba's bodyguard or personal militia in Kinshasa, leading to numerous casualties.

Although the elections supposedly turned the page, warfare continued. Apart from the clashes in Kinshasa, several other provinces experienced extreme violence. Kinshasa's relations with its former ally Angola deteriorated. Angolan forces apparently occupied several villages in Bandundu, adjacent to the diamond-producing province of Lunda Norte. Angola expelled thousands of Congolese from Lunda Norte and Lunda Sul, and DRC retaliated by expelling Angolans. The expellees in both directions suffered rape and other violence.

Early in 2009, Uganda and Congo launched a joint operation, Lightning Thunder, intended to root out the Ugandan insurrection movement the Lord's Resistance Army (LRA), which had been implanted in Ituri (northeast DRC) for years. The operation was monumentally unsuccessful, scattering the LRA forces but not destroying them, and provoking vicious counter-attacks against Congolese civilians.

In North and South Kivu, a similar agreement had been reached between Rwanda and DRC. "Umoja Wetu" (Our Unity) was designed to destroy the threat posed by the rebel Hutu Forces Démocratiques du Libération du Rwanda (Democratic Forces for the Liberation of Rwanda, FDLR). Perhaps not as spectacularly unsuccessful as Lightning Thunder, it still failed to deal a mortal blow to the FDLR. In fact the operation led some of the Mayi-Mayi to ally with the Rwandan Hutu to fight the FARDC. Following the withdrawal of the Rwandan army, the FARDC launched Operation Kimia II to combat the FDLR with the support of MONUC. Despite these operations, the FDLR survived.

Elections for the presidency and the national assembly were held in 2011. The rules had been changed, requiring a plurality or simple majority rather than an absolute majority, as in 2006. Incumbent Joseph Kabila was declared the winner of the presidential race, with approximately 49 percent of the votes; long-time opposition leader Étienne Tshisekedi of the Union pour la Démocratie et le Progrès Social (Union for Democracy and Social Progress, UDPS) supposedly finished second with 32 percent.

The elections were labeled "seriously flawed" by the US Department of State, which added that it was unclear whether the irregularities had been enough to change the outcome. France and Belgium took similar positions. Kabila apparently would govern the country for (at least) five more years, but the legitimacy of his rule had been diminished.

As summarized here, the Congo conflict involves nation states, international organizations, militias, political parties, and other sorts of actors. The question we need to answer is whether, behind this struggle, with its pillage and backstabbing, the machinations of international, non-African actors are determinant.

Extra-continental Actors

When Rwanda and Uganda invaded DRC in 1996 and again in 1998, many observers assumed that the invasions had been organized by the United States. This made sense, in that Paul Kagame of Rwanda and Yoweri Museveni of Uganda had been called a new generation of African leaders (along with the rulers of Eritrea and Ethiopia) and they were receiving material support from the United States and the United Kingdom. If the US sponsored the invasions, along with the UK, then France supposedly was involved too, in opposition to the "Anglo-Saxons."

The idea of extra-continental powers using Africa as a playing field is very old. By encouraging French competition with Britain in Central Africa in the 1880s, the German Chancellor Bismarck may have hoped to induce the French to forget Alsace-Lorraine. The British apparently supported first Portugal and then Leopold II as a means of blocking French expansion in the Congo Basin. Perhaps in recent years DRC again has been a playing field or a chessboard on which extra-African powers have waged their struggles, using African proxies.

Of the extra-African actors of the 1990s, France most clearly viewed Central Africa as a playing field. The French interpreted the Great Lakes crisis, set off by the invasion of French-speaking Rwanda by English-speaking Rwandan exiles in 1990, in terms of the Fashoda Syndrome: that is, their feeling of having been cheated out of what was rightly theirs by the British, over a century earlier.[6] Moreover, they seem to have believed that Rwanda, where French was the language of administration and instruction, belonged to them in their role as protector of *La Francophonie*, the zone of French language and culture.

The British responded in kind, likewise interpreting the struggle for Rwanda in cultural terms. Britain's New Labour adopted the English-speaking Tutsi leader, Paul Kagame, and indeed Tony Blair, after leaving the British government, served as an unpaid advisor to the Kagame government. Moreover, Rwanda joined the Commonwealth, although it had not been a British colony. The US relationship with Kagame and the RPF was predominantly military in the first instance, but the American embassy in Kigali developed a strong case of clientitis. At any rate, both the United States and the United Kingdom have strong affective bonds to Kagame and the RPF, and the French were right to fear a drastic decline in their influence in this part of Africa.

Is the behavior of the major actors to be explained in terms of the state institutions, the elites that control those institutions, or individual leaders? The reactions of Bill Clinton and Tony Blair, in the aftermath of their failure to prevent genocide in Rwanda, might seem to confirm the individual-level hypothesis. However, leadership change (to George Bush in 2001 and Barack Obama in 2009, and in Britain to Gordon Brown in 2007 and then to David Cameron in 2010) did little to dampen the enthusiasm of the respective governments for Kagame.

Another line of argument also privileges international actors. Leninism and its contemporary variants see the industrial powers competing to acquire overseas territories in order to exploit their natural resources. Many writings on DRC assume such causation, but this needs to be demonstrated.

Proxy or surrogate war – a war that results when two powers use third parties as substitutes for fighting each other directly – has been seen as a prominent feature of African international politics. The Angolan civil war, beginning in 1975, in which the Soviet Union and the United States backed rival Angolan liberation movements, could be seen as an example. Neither of the superpowers put its own troops on the ground in Angola; nor did China, whose anti-Soviet stance had emerged clearly by the mid-1970s. Cuba, South Africa, and Zaïre (DRC) did send troops. The conflict unfolded in an environment of Cold War bipolarity but Cuba was not really a proxy for the Soviet Union. Cuba took the initiative in aiding the Angolan Marxist movement the Movimento Popular de Libertação de Angola (Popular Movement for the Liberation of Angola, MPLA) and the Soviet Union followed the Cuban lead. Eventually, in 1989, the Americans induced the Cubans to withdraw by facilitating the decolonization of Namibia.

A major participant in US foreign policy making, former Assistant Secretary of State Cohen argued that while most wars in Africa have been internal, the ongoing border war between Ethiopia and Eritrea and the successful war of Rwanda and Angola to overthrow President Mobutu of DRC in 1996 have been exceptions. Internal conflicts in Africa could be classified into two categories, civil wars and surrogate wars. Civil wars "respond to a deep set of grievances held by a significant percentage of the population that supports violent action against the regime in place."[7] True civil wars since 1960 occurred in South Africa/Namibia (1966), Ethiopia (1974), Angola (1977), and Sudan (1983), according to Cohen.

Civil wars are to be distinguished from surrogate wars, which are "generated entirely from the outside by neighboring governments that have a variety of reasons for wanting to take advantage of a regime's weakness or fragility." Populations may have grievances but "in most cases reject armed intervention." Cohen's examples of surrogate wars include Rhodesia's and South Africa's intervention in Mozambique (beginning in 1977), the Ugandan-sponsored invasion of Rwanda (1990), and its sequel, the war of Rwanda and others in Zaïre/DRC (1996 onward).

Foreign governments (notably the American government) should base their policy on these distinctions, Cohen suggests. He criticizes both the African Union and the international community for turning away their eyes from the cases of insurgent action organized from abroad:

When the Rwanda Patriotic Army came across the Rwanda border from Uganda on October 1, 1990, with the full complicity and support of the Government of Uganda, there were no complaints filed against Uganda. As the US Assistant Secretary of State at the time, I admit that we made a grievous error in tolerating this action. Instead of threatening sanctions against Uganda, we granted international legitimacy to the insurgents, who had no support within Rwanda. We encouraged negotiations, and at one point, applied heavy pressure on the Ugandan Government in order to force the RPF to enter negotiations with the Rwandan Government. But we continued to provide large amounts of economic aid to Uganda as if nothing had happened. . . .

Cohen fails to explain why the American government chose to support Uganda and the RPF. What interests were involved? Perhaps the US military relationship with Rwanda's Tutsi already had begun. Kagame, then head of military intelligence in Museveni's Ugandan army, was undergoing military training in the United States when the RPF crossed the Uganda–Rwanda border in 1990. Certainly an extensive politico-military alliance between unequal partners emerged after the 1994 genocide and takeover.

The second Congo war also was a "surrogate war," according to Cohen. The armies of Angola and Zimbabwe thwarted the invasion by Rwanda and Uganda, but this short war was followed by "a massive insurgency in the eastern DRC that was organized, financed, and supplied by the governments of Rwanda and Uganda." Despite the fact that this insurgency led to "the unnecessary deaths of millions of Congolese," neither the African Union nor the international community have done anything to hold Rwanda and Uganda "accountable for the death and destruction that their surrogates have perpetrated." In this interpretation, Rwanda and Uganda were acting through their own surrogates. Although Cohen concedes that the United States funded the Ugandan government during the RPF invasion from Uganda and the civil war (1990–4), he does not mention American and British aid to the Rwandan and Ugandan governments, which made it possible for these governments to launch invasions, which later became self-financing and even highly profitable.

Cohen rejects what he calls the "hypothetical and simplistic argument of Jeffrey Herbst, Marina Ottaway, and others, according to which failing states will inevitably be replaced, mainly from the outside." Often, he says, the cure is worse than the disease. In light of the devastating violence in DRC since 1998, it would be hard to disagree.

The French Africanist Gérard Prunier refutes the assumption behind the labels "sponsor" and "proxy" – that powerful interests control Africa through their puppets. He debunks an extreme example of conspiracy theory from the American Wayne Madsen, who wrote:

> With the full backing of the Clinton administration . . . [America Mineral Fields] and its partners stood ready to expand their plans. . . . But something would first have to be done about Zaïre's pro-French leader, Marshal Mobutu Sese Seko. Mobutu continued to favour French, Belgian and South African companies over those from the United States and Canada. A safe platform was needed from which an attack could be launched on Mobutu and his French and Belgian mining benefactors. That platform would be one of the poorest and most densely-populated tinderboxes in Africa: Rwanda.[8]

Every single one of the premises on which Madsen's interpretation rested was false, Prunier writes. Mobutu was "pro-French" mainly in that he realized that his days as America's Cold War ally in Central Africa were over. He was able to convince the French that his continued power in Kinshasa offered the best guarantees for French political and cultural interests in the region. The "French and Belgian mining benefactors" were a French share of the Belgian company Union Minière, which extracted copper and cobalt in Katanga. The French company Empain-Schneider had sold the Société Minière du Kivu (Sominki) to a Cluff Mining–Banro consortium in early 1996. Soon thereafter, Cluff ceased exploration in Congo, given the insecurity. Banro survived, and eventually thrived (see Chapter 5).

Prunier retorts that Kagame "was no more a puppet of the Americans than Mobutu was a puppet of the French." America's game plan was regarded by Kigali as "more of a resource to be tapped than an obligation to be obeyed." Madsen's version of the American game plan has American interests choosing to take over Zaïre with the aid of Jean-Raymond Boulle, "a French-speaking Mauritian British passport holder, freelance diamond prospector, and chance billionaire who never operated in the United States before the mid-1980s." To make sense of the role of Boulle and America Mineral Fields International, Prunier continues, one needs to see them playing a well-known game for smaller independent mining companies:

> Go find a big deal (which you do not have enough money to bring into production), make a lot of publicity, hold on to it for a while, then sell to one of the majors, who will either have the money to exploit it or else enough financial strategic depth to be able to wait for ten or twenty years until the conditions are ripe.[9]

Of course the United States and France were involved in overthrowing the dying Mobutu and in propping him up, respectively. However, their involvement was not primarily aimed at defending stakes in mining. Belgium, in contrast, continued to have important mining interests in DRC (though less than in colonial days), but lacked the means to promote or protect them. It is with Belgium, then, that our sketches of the main external actors will begin.

The Belgian "Uncles"

Absorbed in their struggles to redefine their state as a confederation, or even to split it along linguistic lines, Belgians might seem to have little time to devote to their former dependencies in Africa. Rwanda's genocide, which began in April 1994 with the massacre of ten Belgian soldiers guarding the Rwandan prime minister, soured the Belgian public on Africa.

Yet Belgium and various Belgian groups and interests remain engaged in African affairs; and it is an engagement whose direction is far more controversial than in France or the United States.

The love–hate relationship between Belgium and its former empire can be understood through Hergé's famous comic book *Tintin au Congo*, first published in 1930 but still on sale in Belgian bookstores in the twenty-first century. This book reinforced Belgian views of Congo as a country of jungles and witch doctors.

Congolese read *Tintin* too, as can be seen in the conversations between the European anthropologist Johannes Fabian and the artist/historian Tshibumba Kanda Matulu. Tshibumba was explaining his painting *Simba Bulaya* (Lion of Europe), which portrays Europeans who turned themselves into lions and devoured Africans. Fabian said that he knew about the Aniota or leopard-men, reported in colonial ethnography as dressing up like animals and killing people with metal claws. Tshibumba replied that Fabian's version was like that in *Tintin au Congo*. To him, Simba Bulaya was real and Fabian was like Tintin in denying that reality. The Congolese attitude toward the Belgians is ambivalent: they are outsiders, possibly monsters like Simba Bulaya, and also kin, that is, *banoko* (uncles).[10]

Belgium had been an unenthusiastic participant in the conquest of Africa, but once the country had been pushed into taking over Leopold's disgraced personal colony, it tried to administer the territory in a more creditable fashion. Many administrators were trained and sent out, along with large numbers of Catholic missionaries. Belgian opinion tended to accept the argument of Leopold's apologists that Anglo-Saxon Protestants had unjustly condemned the Free State.

Belgium continually feared that it would lose its colonies. In the late 1930s, its long-time ally Britain allegedly considered the possibility of buying off Hitler by giving him the Belgian Congo. In light of the fate of Czechoslovakia, the Belgian fear was not far-fetched.

During World War II, the "war effort" in the colony was based heavily on forced labor and the Congolese population suffered accordingly. After the war, the administration eased its policies somewhat, and provided more benefits for ordinary Congolese, though the Belgians still moved with glacial slowness in responding to the demands of the *évolués*, or educated Africans, for improved status in the administration, and then for liberal political reforms.

When newly independent Congo plunged into chaos in 1960, that chaos was Belgium's fault, in three main senses. First, Belgium had exported the controversy between Catholics and anti-clericals into its colonies. The formation of a coalition government of socialists and liberals (pro-business, anti-clerical), from which Catholics were excluded, and the naming of the liberal Auguste Buisseret as colonial minister led to the creation of a network of secular schools in the Belgian Congo. The future prime minister Patrice Lumumba met Buisseret and formed the Amicale Libérale of Stanleyville (Kisangani), a pre-political organization of *évolués* who supported the democratic and anti-clerical orientation of Belgium's Liberal Party. This earned him the lasting enmity of the Catholic Church, in Belgium as well as in Congo. Second, the Congo's nascent elite had been given almost no apprenticeship before being asked to direct the country. Third, the Belgians intervened in the affairs of their ex-colony after only a few days of independence. King Baudouin supported the Katanga secession, praising "entire ethnic groups, led by men of honesty and courage, [who] have pledged their friendship and begged us to help them build their independence amid the chaos of what was once the Belgian Congo. It is our duty to respond to all those who loyally ask for our help."[11]

Belgium and the United States apparently worked closely to combat the radical nationalist Patrice Lumumba, but developed separate, parallel programs to eliminate him. In 1990, Belgium accepted "moral responsibility" for the assassination of Lumumba, which is more than the United States has been willing to do. In 1965, Belgian paratroops jumped from American planes to seize Stanleyville (Kisangani), capital of the Lumumbist "People's Republic of the Congo."

Mobutu's brand of nationalism inevitably led to a series of confrontations with Belgium. First "Authenticity," then

"Zaïrianization" and "radicalization of the revolution" attacked the surviving elements of the tripartite colonial power structure, namely the colonial administration, the Catholic Church, and the Belgian state-chartered capitalist corporations. At the same time, the Belgian monarchy constituted a visual model for the Zaïrian (Congolese) dictator, who emulated the Laeken Palace in the presidential residence he built at this ancestral home of Gbadolite.

Because of these entanglements, material and sentimental, relations with Congo remained and remain controversial in Belgium. Mobutu's attempts to persuade the Belgian government to ban *L'ascension de Mobutu* (The Rise of Mobutu), a book published in 1974 by the leftist lawyer Jules Chomé increased doubts about him. (Although efforts to ban the book failed in Belgium, they succeeded in France.) Belgian hesitation to intervene in Shaba I and Shaba II (invasions of Shaba/Katanga by the Angola-based Front de Libération Nationale du Congo, or Congo National Liberation Front in 1977 and 1978) also contrasted with the rapid response of France and was resented by Mobutu.

Relations with Mobutu divided Belgium along ideological, confessional, and linguistic lines. In 1978 an opinion poll revealed that 56 percent of Flemish respondents wanted Belgium to withdraw, while 55 percent of Francophones said "one must do the maximum to preserve Belgian interests in Zaire." Flemish Catholics were much more favorable to Zaïre than were Flemish Socialists. Mobutu played on the divisions in Belgian ranks: at the Francophone summit in Canada in 1987, he praised the "historical contingencies" that had led to the introduction of the French language into his country.

In 1990, when Mobutu's Special Presidential Division reportedly killed dozens of students at the University of Lubumbashi, the reaction in Belgium was sharp. First the United States, then the World Bank, followed the Belgian lead in cutting off aid to Mobutu. Belgian opposition to Mobutu hardened without crystallizing into a clear position in favor of the opposition led by Étienne Tshisekedi. Belgium, France, and the United States formed a "troika" of foreign friends of

Congo, pressurizing Mobutu to reform his regime, without much success. When the Rwandans and Ugandans crossed the Congolese border in 1996, the Belgians took an intermediate position, between the anti-Rwanda French and the anti-Mobutu Americans. Belgium's position as leading export partner for DRC slowly declined during the war years. By 2008, Belgium still was in second place ahead of the United States, but lagged far behind newcomer China. On the imports side, Belgium again was second-leading partner, behind South Africa.

The tense relations between Belgium and Congo were on display on the fiftieth anniversary of Congolese independence in 2010. Baudouin I was dead by then, but his octogenarian brother Albert II visited Kinshasa to take part in the commemoration. A return visit, in which Congolese troops would take part in ceremonies in Belgium, never materialized, in part because of allegations that the Congolese armed forces were guilty of large-scale human rights abuses.

Belgium, administrator of Ruanda-Urundi, had presided over the "social revolution" by which Rwandan Hutu overthrew the Tutsi monarchy, in 1959, on the eve of independence (1962). The former colonial power remained generally supportive both of Rwanda's Hutu president Grégoire Kayibanda (1962–73) and his successor General Juvénal Habyarimana (1973–94). When the Rwandan Patriotic Army (RPA), the armed wing of the RPF, invaded Rwanda in 1990, Habyarimana invited both France and Belgium to send aid. Four years later, when Habyarimana's plane was shot down and Hutu extremists launched the genocide against Tutsi civilians, some of the first casualties were Belgian paratroopers guarding the Hutu prime minister. Soon thereafter, Belgium withdrew its 450 men from the UN force in Rwanda, and the genocide proceeded. In the aftermath of the genocide and its seizure of power, the Tutsi-dominated RPF directed its wrath at the French, seen as the main backers of Habyarimana and the *génocidaires*; Belgium has been relatively untouched. Since Congolese as well as Rwandan Tutsi and Hutu all are well represented in Belgium, the former colonial power has offered a stage for struggles, sometimes violent, over the genocide and its aftermath.

France: "Tenir son rang"

France had been involved in Rwanda, aiding the Hutu regime of Habyarimana, and in Zaïre, aiding Mobutu. To the extent that the Congo wars represent the continuation of the Rwandan civil war and genocide, then of course France was involved. René Lemarchand explains that French backing for the Hutu extremists "must have been a major consideration in the minds of the organizers" of the mass killings:

> Given the extent of French backing – military, logistical, political, and economic – they correctly assumed that the French embassy would look the other way each time it was confronted with irrefutable evidence of massive human rights violations; and they knew, when the circumstances required, how to capitalize upon the close ties of friendship between President Mitterrand's son, Jean-Christophe, and his "buddy," Juvénal Habyarimana.[12]

When the Hutu interim government was driven out of Kigali in 1994, France helped it to regroup in the southwest and then set up shop across the border in Zaïre/Congo.

To understand the French role in Rwanda and in DRC/Zaïre, one can refer to the Berlin Conference or the Fashoda incident (as I did, above), but it may be more illuminating to focus on France's role in the region since the era of independence, circa 1960. "La France doit tenir son rang" (France must conserve its rank), President Jacques Chirac supposedly declared. Only in Africa could France continue to be taken seriously as a great power. From that general stance, more specific policies flowed. France should hang onto its own former colonies, whether or not there were important material interests to be defended, and it should spread the net to include other African states. The former Spanish colony of Equatorial Guinea was incorporated into the CFA franc zone, and the former Portuguese colonies of Angola and Mozambique were wooed. (Mozambique, surrounded by Anglophone states, chose the Commonwealth.) The former Belgian dependencies – DRC, Rwanda, and Burundi – were obvious targets for France, since French had been the language of administration there.

As the French political scientist Daniel Bourmaud has put it, French policy toward Africa has been neo-colonial:

> France can count on the support of African states as long as it refrains from direct involvement in events within the African states. For France, all leaders are acceptable, from Senghor to Bokassa, from the most liberal to the most tyrannical, on condition that they remain faithful to the metropolitan power and to its interests. Every head of state knows that anything will be pardoned as long as they submit to the will of France.[13]

It would be a mistake to assume that France's stubborn backing of Habyarimana had some dark, commercial motivation. Rwanda's coffee, tea, and gorillas hardly constitute commercial magnets equivalent to the oil of Equatorial Guinea. Rwanda mattered because all spots on the map of *Francophonie* matter, however small, and Habyarimana had endorsed *La Francophonie*.

Zaïre was important as the "second largest Francophone state." The French had defended Mobutu during the Shaba I and Shaba II wars (1977–8). In 1977, when the Front de Libération Nationale du Congo (Congo National Liberation Front, FLNC) invaded Shaba (Katanga), France joined Morocco, Belgium, and the United States in providing assistance to repel it. France airlifted 1,500 Moroccan combat troops to Kolwezi, and a combined Zaïrian and Moroccan force counter-attacked. The following year, when the FLNC again seized Kolwezi, France took the opportunity to upstage the Belgians and to endear itself to Mobutu. A battalion of the French Foreign Legion parachuted into Kolwezi under orders to rescue the hostages held by the FLNC and to prepare to evacuate all whites from the war zone. A Belgian paratroop regiment flew to Kamina (more than 200 kilometres north of Kolwezi), and then proceeded by road to Kolwezi. The Belgian commander allegedly had disarmed his men (taking away their bullets) to avoid the possibility that they would fire on Legionnaires committing atrocities. The United States sent C-141 transports to fly logistics missions for both the French and Belgian forces.

After Shaba II, Mobutu again sought foreign assistance to remold his military. In 1980, a French colonel assumed command of the French-trained 31st Airborne Brigade. French officers essentially commanded the brigade down to the company level in peacetime, although they would not deploy with their units to combat. The Belgians trained the 21st Infantry Brigade in Shaba/Katanga and remained as advisors to this unit. The Chinese were invited to train and equip the 41st Commando Brigade in Kisangani, and, after resuming diplomatic relations with Israel in 1982, Zaïre requested and received Israeli military assistance focusing on training the Special Presidential Brigade (later, Division). The FAZ remained largely ineffective, except for the units trained by France and Israel.

From 1990 onward, France worked with Belgium and the United States, pressuring Mobutu to move in the direction of democratic opening. However, France was generally less committed to promotion of democracy, or more tempted to stick by its ties to Mobutu, than were its partners. In 1993, army units mutinied in Kinshasa. The president's attempt to pay soldiers with a new five million Zaïre note, a banknote that had been denounced as worthless by Prime Minister Étienne Tshisekedi, set off conflict between army factions supporting Mobutu and Tshisekedi. An army unit – perhaps pro-Tshisekedi – attacked the French embassy with machine guns, killing the ambassador.

The French stood alone in sharing Mobutu's view that the Rwandan civil war and genocide gave him a last chance to make himself useful in international politics. In 1997, as Laurent Kabila and his Rwandan, Angolan, and Ugandan backers moved toward Kinshasa, Belgium joined the United States in telling Mobutu it was time to go but France failed to join its troika partners.

The replacement of Mobutu by Kabila and the launching of the second war pitting a coalition from the east (Uganda–Rwanda–Burundi) against one from the south (Angola–

Namibia–Zimbabwe) temporarily excluded France from politico-military competition in Congo. The subsequent split between Rwanda and Uganda, however, offered an opening for the French, who prepared a mission to intervene in Ituri as the Ugandans withdrew. President Chirac viewed Ituri as a test case for an operation of the European Union, independent of NATO. The French mission, dubbed "Operation Artémis," was successful but sharply limited, in space (to Bunia and its immediate environs) and in time (June–September 2003, until MONUC could take over).[14]

The European Union dispatched a second, supplementary mission, EUFOR, to DRC, to support MONUC during the period of the 2006 general elections. This time, however, the EU avoided asking a single member to take charge. A German general served as operation commander with a French major general as EU force commander.

Since 2006, the French apparently have been content to cooperate with the other Western powers in managing the politico-military aspects of the Congo crisis. In the economic sphere, however, the French attempted a major move. In 2009, during a visit to Kinshasa, President Nicolas Sarkozy announced with great fanfare that the French nuclear energy firm AREVA (largely state-owned) was acquiring the rights to prospect for uranium in Katanga province. Journalists interpreted this as Congo choosing France over China. (The visit nearly had to be scrubbed, after the French president was quoted as saying that DRC should consider sharing its mineral wealth with Rwanda as a means of ensuring peace in the Great Lakes region.) Two years later, however, AREVA apparently was withdrawing from DRC, concentrating its efforts on Canada and Niger. Similarly, nothing had come of an expression of interest by the French cement company Lafarge in buying into DRC's main cement company. France Telecom has talked about entering the Congolese mobile phone market by acquiring a Chinese company. However, in the new global economy, in which China, India, and other former Less Developed Countries are making major efforts to penetrate resource-rich countries of the global South, France is no longer a major player.

The United States

Belgium had derived much of its international significance from its huge, rich Central African colony, while France's status as a major power was confirmed by its role in Africa. In contrast, the United States' status as a superpower was not dependent on its ties to Africa. Rather, the US chose to defend Zaïre/Congo against the supposed menace posed by the Sino-Soviet bloc. The American conception of defense of the "free world" included maintaining access to strategic resources, but was not reducible to corporate interests.

With the disappearance of the Soviet Union, the United States struggled to redefine its role in Africa, incorporating the struggles against Islamic extremism and for access to oil. American support for the Rwando-Ugandan invasion of Zaïre was motivated by frustration with Mobutu, who was flirting with the Islamist regime in Sudan, and by the opportunity to restructure America's strategic position in Central Africa. Guilt over failure to prevent the Rwandan genocide may have played a part. The mineral wealth of Zaïre/Congo, however, apparently did not figure prominently in American calculations at the time.

American involvement in Central Africa, though episodic, has been long, dating back to the Atlantic slave trade. American newspapers sponsored the explorations of Henry Morton Stanley until Leopold II hired him in 1878. The United States also provided crucial cover to the personal imperialism of Leopold II in the Congo basin. In December 1883, President Chester A. Arthur told Congress that Leopold's work was philanthropic, and the United States could not be "indifferent to this work, nor to the interests of their citizens involved in it." It might become advisable for the US "to cooperate with other commercial powers: protecting the rights of trade and residence in the Kongo [sic] valley free from interference or political control of any one nation."[15] In response to the president, the US Senate voted in favor of recognizing the International Association of Congo (IAC). A few days later the US secretary of state issued a letter recognizing "the flag of the International African Association as the flag of a friendly government." (Confused by Leopold's hocus-pocus, the secretary of state referred to the International African Association when he apparently meant the International Association of Congo.) The IAC mutated into the Congo Free State, with which the United States never established diplomatic relations.

The initial American position in favor of Leopold soon began to shift, thanks to reports from American missionaries describing the atrocities being committed in the Congo. By 1905, the bad reputation of the Free State was cemented when Mark Twain published *King Leopold's Soliloquy*. In addition to mocking the Belgian monarch for his crimes against humanity, he had Leopold say:

> [Miscreants have told how I] hoisted my flag, and "took in" a President of the United States, and got him to be the first to recognize it and salute it. Oh, well, let them blackguard me if they like; it is a deep satisfaction to me to remember that I was a shade too smart for that nation that thinks itself so smart. Yes, I certainly did bunco a Yankee – as those people phrase it. Pirate flag? Let them call it so – perhaps it is. All the same, they were the first to salute it.[16]

Once the Congo Free State became an orthodox colony, most Americans forgot about it. It was not forgotten completely, however. Some Protestant missionaries continued to evangelize in Congo, and the educational charity the Phelps-Stokes Fund sent a team to study education there in 1921–2. Moreover, American capitalists invested in the country's mining enterprises, especially as it became clear that uranium might have military uses. In the 1930s, the American government entered into a contract with the Union Minière du Haut-Katanga, which eventually supplied some of the uranium for the bombs dropped on Japan. After the war, the Atomic Energy Commission maintained close contact with the Belgian government, while developing access to other sources of uranium.

The brusque decolonization of Belgian Africa caught the American government by surprise. The CIA sent its first chief of station, Larry Devlin, to Leopoldville/Kinshasa ten days after independence. By the time he arrived, the Force Publique had mutinied, Katanga had seceded, and Belgium had sent in troops. In this chaos, Devlin seems to have adopted the Cold War as a cognitive framework, if indeed he did not simply defer to the framework prevailing in Washington. In his view and that of his superiors up to President Eisenhower and Allen Dulles (director of Central Intelligence under Eisenhower and Kennedy), Congolese leaders were immature, but that in itself was not a problem. It became a cause for concern only when it led those such as Patrice Lumumba to espouse African nationalism and Pan-Africanism. The immaturity of Moïse Tshombe, Joseph Mobutu, and others willing to cooperate with Belgium's neo-colonial projects did not bother Washington.

After arranging for Lumumba to be ousted by his army chief of staff Mobutu and sent to Katanga to be killed by Katanga secessionists and their Belgian backers, the Americans set about building a "moderate" government in Kinshasa. For several years, they ruled through an informal coalition nicknamed the "Binza Boys" for the luxurious suburb where they lived. Members headed key state organs: Mobutu, armed forces, Justin Bomboko, foreign ministry, Victor Nendaka, state security agency, Albert Ndele, national bank, and Damien Kandolo, interior ministry. President Joseph Kasa-Vubu and Prime Minister Cyrille Adoula lent a veneer of legitimacy to this profoundly illegitimate setup.

Lumumbist insurrections broke out in Kwilu and South Kivu as soon as the protective umbrella of the United Nations was withdrawn in June 1964. The Americans worked with the central government to suppress the rebellions through a substantial infusion of outside assistance, including French- and English-speaking mercenaries, anti-Castro Cubans, and (for the Stanleyville paratroop drop in November 1964) the direct participation of Belgian and American armed forces.

In November 1965, when President Kasa-Vubu seemed to be willing to get rid of the mercenaries before the Lumumbists had been defeated, Mobutu overthrew him and established a new regime.[17] The United States supported Mobutu over the next thirty years, although it cannot have been happy with some of his choices, including the break with Israel in 1973.

When push came to shove, as in the struggle for Angola, Mobutu sided with the Americans. He sent his army across the border, where the Angolans of the MPLA and their Cuban allies defeated it in October 1975. When Angola-based Congolese invaded Katanga in 1977–8 (then known as Shaba), the United States joined with Mobutu's other international "friends" to defeat the invaders.

Mobutu was known as "America's Tyrant" or "Our Man in Kinshasa," and the relationship was described as one of patron to client, despite the important role of France and others in protecting him.[18] In the 1990s, however, the United States found its client had outgrown his usefulness, and Mobutu began to search for alternative patrons with a new urgency.

As Rwanda prepared to invade Zaïre/Congo in 1996, the Americans "actively followed these preparations," according to Colette Braeckman. Top embassy officials attended planning meetings, while Vice-President Kagame's Pentagon friends provided necessary equipment: six rapid patrol boats on Lake Kivu and radio and satellite decryption technology. Later the Americans would provide their allies with satellite photos indicating where the groups of fleeing civilian and military Hutu were located. A composite army was set up, including RPF soldiers (to whom the Americans provided special training), some Ugandans, some Burundians, some Eritreans and Somalis recruited by the Americans, as well as some Congolese opposition figures summoned by Laurent Kabila.[19]

Braeckman's version corroborates what was known at the time. In 1997, Lynne Duke of *The Washington Post* reported, "US involvement with Rwanda's military has been far more extensive than previously disclosed, including psychological operations and tactical Special Forces exercises that occurred a few weeks before [the 1996 invasion]." The ongoing training in Rwanda occurred over three years, presumably beginning right after the RPF/RPA seizure of power in Kigali, and involved hundreds of Rwandan participants. It included "combat, military management, disaster relief, soldier team development, land-mine removal, and military and civilian justice." An official in Washington told the *Post* journalist, "The program has not been as innocuous as it is being made out to be." It reflected American support for the Tutsi-dominated Rwandan army in its campaign against armed Hutu militia groups in Zaïre, a campaign that (in Duke's words) "evolved into a broader offensive that eventually toppled the autocratic Zaïrian president. . . . A high-level Pentagon official acknowledged the possibility that, inadvertently, the United States may have trained some of the fighters who ousted Mobutu."[20] One wonders how inadvertent that could have been.

The Pentagon official told Duke that the United States is always concerned about human rights abuses in countries with which it has relations, but that the training in Rwanda had not been linked to that country's human rights performance. He characterized Rwanda's human rights record as "surprisingly good" in view of the 1994 genocide, which ended when Kagame's Tutsi rebel forces took over the country. American policy in Rwanda was aimed at stabilizing the military. Recent events had demonstrated that "if Rwanda is unstable, that's going to lead to instability throughout Central Africa," the Pentagon official said. But another Washington official involved with Africa policy told the *Post* that the United States was focusing disproportionate military assistance on Rwanda as part of the creation of a "zone of influence" in East Africa, where Rwanda – because of its troubles – emerged as "a target of opportunity."

The US government cannot have failed to know about the abuses committed in eastern Congo by its Rwandan and Ugandan protégés. Over the years, it discouraged official reporting on those abuses, as when restrictions were placed on the circulation of one section of the UN report on illegal exploitation of Congolese resources, a section that named names of governments and companies charged with engaging in such exploitation. The suppressed section was leaked, but the Security Council and its members failed to take action against the exploiters.

The Americans had helped the Rwandans and others to put Laurent Kabila in power in Congo in 1997, but they soon came to question the choice. When the Clinton administration began speaking of African "new leaders" it was clear to Kabila that he was not considered to be one; nor were his SADC backers President Robert Mugabe of Zimbabwe and President Sam Nujoma of Namibia. The second invasion in 1998 and the assassination of Laurent Kabila in 2001 illustrate the problem of "proxies." One can understand each of these events in terms of Rwanda pursuing its struggle against the Hutu *génocidaires* on Congolese soil, and then attempting to get rid of the Congolese who refused to be their proxy or to expel the Hutu. However, Kabila was unsatisfactory from the American perspective as well. He refused to abandon his Marxist ideology, revoked several Western mining company contracts, and turned to China, Cuba, and Venezuela for advice on economic development. A business card from a US military attaché, allegedly found in the pocket of Kabila's assassin, suggests US involvement in the killing, even though the Rwandans may have done most of the work, through their proxies in the RCD.

Joseph Kabila, who succeeded as DRC president, initially was somewhat successful in presenting himself to the Americans and to the international community as a reformer. Many of his policies did not differ greatly from those of Laurent Kabila, but he was willing to pander to the prejudices and preferences of the Americans, Belgians, and others.

If the primary goal of American foreign policy in the Great Lakes region in the mid-1990s was to create an American zone of influence, that goal evolved; since the assassination of Laurent Kabila, the goal has included restoration of cooperative relations between DRC and its neighbors, particularly Rwanda and Uganda. Without accepting responsibility for the murderous consequences of its support for Uganda and Rwanda, the United States assumed a leading role in resolving the conflict. Through the Comité International d'Accompagnement de la Transition (International Committee in Support of the Transition, CIAT), the US was instrumental in guiding DRC through a decade of quasi-trusteeship.

Retired American diplomats served as special representatives of the secretary-general in DRC, and thus as heads of the UN mission (MONUC, MONUSCO),[21] from 2003 to 2007 and from 2010 onward.

The UN played a major part in organizing the elections of 2006, won by Joseph Kabila. In 2011, the Congolese did the organizing (through the National Electoral Commission), although the UN and the European Union paid part of the costs. Kabila was re-elected, despite apparent massive fraud. The United States and other Western governments attempted to distance themselves from both the process and the outcome. A few days before the vote, unspecified "Western embassies" (presumably including the American embassy) told the *New York Times* of their concern that the election of the "firebrand" Tshisekedi might destabilize the country. Once the vote had been held, the US State Department called the elections "seriously flawed" but said it was unclear whether the irregularities were enough to change the outcome. It encouraged the Congolese authorities "to closely review these cited irregularities and proceed with maximum openness and transparency."[22] The Congolese Supreme Court approved the results, and the US government accepted Kabila as president, however "flawed" the process may have been. ("Flawed" has become a standard label used to characterize the 2010 elections in Rwanda and the 2012 elections in Angola.)

In 2012, the contradictions in the American position on the Great Lakes region finally were exposed. The so-called "M23 movement," led by former officers of the Rwandan-backed militia the Congrès National pour la Défense du Peuple (National Congress for the Defense of the People, CNDP) and apparently directed by Rwanda's defense minister, General James Kabarebe, mutinied and seized control of a large area in North Kivu. When the UN Security Council group of experts on the arms embargo confirmed Rwandan involvement, including recruitment of young men and boys in Rwanda itself, the US government finally displayed its impatience with Rwanda. It blocked a small amount of military assistance, as a visible sign of dissatisfaction. The Kagame government denied everything, and launched *ad hominem* attacks on an American member of the expert panel, and on the UN mission MONUC, headed by Ambassador Roger Meece of the United States. Stonewalling by Rwanda and by Uganda (accused of allowing M23 to operate out of Kampala) suggested the weakness of the United States. The Obama administration may have been divided, with the Defense Department continuing to back Kagame and Museveni. Within the State Department it appeared that Susan Rice, US ambassador to the UN, remained supportive of Kagame, while African Affairs Under-Assistant Secretary of State Johnny Carson may have wanted to take a harder line.

Enter China

In recent years, the United States has reacted with pique at what it apparently sees as Chinese intrusion on its turf. The ideological split of the twenty-first century is between two models of capitalism: the state capitalism of China versus the free enterprise capitalism of the US. To a considerable extent, the rivalry turns on the question of access to minerals.

Chinese involvement in DRC dates from the nineteenth century, when Chinese workers helped build the railroad from Matadi to Léopoldville (Kinshasa). However, the Chinese state was not involved until after independence, when Congo was divided between pro-Western forces in Kinshasa, pro-Western secessionists in Katanga and South Kasai, and Lumumbist nationalists based in Kisangani (then known as Stanleyville). Lumumba's minister of education, Pierre Mulele, was sent to Cairo as the external representative of the Stanleyville government. From there he went to China, where he received training in revolutionary guerrilla warfare between April 1962 and July 1963. Mulele returned to Congo and began organizing a revolutionary movement. As Georges Nzongola-Ntalaja relates, "Mulele attempted to systematize the ideas, notions and thoughts of the masses into a coherent analysis of the situation and a programme of action for purposes of changing it radically. His systematization was done through a Marxist-Leninist framework of class analysis together with a Maoist strategy of political education and guerrilla warfare."[23] Chinese influence was evident in Mulele's orders to the fighters to respect the people and not to steal.

China also attempted to aid and guide the less coherent Lumumbist rebellions in the east from its embassy in Bujumbura, Burundi. Guidance, however, proved impossible and aid rather ineffective. Far from following a Maoist strategy of working with the peasants, the "Simba" (Lions) and their leaders traveled from town to town and carried out dramatic public executions. Ethnicity often shaped the choice of targets.

Once Mobutu had consolidated his hold on power, the Chinese government decided to work with him rather than continuing to support the Marxist rebels. Massive Chinese buildings, notably the Palais du Peuple (People's Palace) in Kinshasa, new home of the two houses of parliament, symbolized the new orientation.

When Laurent Kabila was selected by the Rwandans and Ugandans to head the AFDL, he and the Chinese renewed their acquaintance. Joseph Kabila, who had been an officer in the AFDL/Rwandan force that conquered DRC in 1996–7, was sent to get further training at the National Defense University in Beijing. When he returned in 1998, he was given the rank of major general and appointed deputy chief of staff of the Congolese Armed Forces. In 2000, he was promoted to chief of staff of the Land Forces, a post he held until the elder Kabila's assassination in January 2001.

In 2005, Joseph Kabila expressed support for China's anti-secession law. Given the repeated support by American political and academic figures for separation of eastern DRC, as well as American support for Taiwan, territorial integrity was an obvious wedge issue for China to use in its relations with DRC.

China offered DRC a large minerals-for-infrastructure deal in 2008, under which Congo would award China the right to develop copper and cobalt mines in exchange for roads, railways, hostels, and universities built by Chinese state firms. However, the Western-dominated international financial institutions opposed the deal, on the grounds that it would increase Congo's crippling international debt.[24] By 2010, there were also signs that China was becoming discouraged by delays and corruption associated with its Congo construction projects.

By 2011, as Sudan teetered on the edge between separation and renewed war, Beijing strongly sided with Khartoum against the secessionist south of the country, to the consternation of Washington. After the secession, however, China quickly patched up its relations with newly independent South Sudan. It has made efforts to be more cooperative in Africa, expressing support for a coordinated approach to the problem of Somalia and supplying equipment to the African Union's AMISOM mission.

Nowadays, the Sino-American rivalry is driven mainly by the needs of the world's two largest economies for Africa's raw materials. The confrontation of the two in DRC is not greatly different from that in Angola, Nigeria, or other mineral-rich African states. China's preference for parastatal enterprises is shared by Angola and DRC, but many individual firms and businessmen from China also are investing in these and other countries of the region. China's approach is very much economics-based: it does not promote an agenda such as the American insistence on elections and human rights, with its inevitable double standards.

Conclusion

Central Africa can be seen as a playing field on which the United States, China, Belgium, France, and other extra-continental powers compete. The United States is squaring off against China, and it will be interesting to see whether China's emphasis on minerals and infrastructure proves more successful than the American security-oriented approach, for example in Sudan and Chad. Rwanda has come under Anglo-Saxon influence. The United States has maintained its position as the dominant power in the region, and is the dominant external actor from Sudan/South Sudan and Somalia in the northeast to Angola and South Africa in the South. Yet the enumeration of the countries where the United States is the dominant external actor highlights the limitations of American power. American preferences are far from being realized. The United States backs the "transitional government" in Somalia, which controls a small portion of the country. In Sudan, the American plan apparently was to shepherd the country through a pair of referenda, on separation of South Sudan from Sudan and the future of Abyei, which lies along the border between the two Sudans. At the same time, the United States wanted to prevent further mass killing in Darfur and across the region (Uganda–DRC–Central African Republic and even Sudan) carried out by the LRA. It was not evident how these diverse objectives could be reconciled.

In the Great Lakes narrowly defined, the United States disposed of Mobutu, but not until he was at death's door from cancer. By 2010, the US apparently had made considerable progress toward its long-term objective of restoring reasonable relations between DRC, Rwanda, and Uganda. However, the disorder in eastern DRC remained substantial, and the Rwandan and Ugandan regimes, on which the United States counted, were running into difficulties of their own. The "new leaders" of these two countries looked increasingly like Africa's "old leaders," exposing the vacuity of the concept that apparently guided US policy under Clinton. The United States, supposedly the dominant player, was having great difficulty keeping the situation from deteriorating. To see why this was the case requires a closer look at the African proxies through which it worked. This will be the focus of the following chapter.

African Players on the Congo Field

If the United States has been unsuccessful in reaching its objectives in Central Africa, could this be because it is attempting to work through pawns and proxies?

British journalist Nick Young trod a well-worn path in 2010 when he characterized Yoweri Museveni's Uganda as "a pawn in the US's proxy African war on terror." Developing his argument, Young implicitly conceded the limitations of the metaphor. His version of Museveni chooses to be a pawn, serving supposed American interests in the Horn of Africa. The dangers of such a policy were starkly revealed when on July 11 two suicide bombings in Uganda's capital Kampala killed seventy-six people watching the FIFA World Cup Final in popular nightspots. Responsibility for the bombings was claimed by Al-Shabaab, a Sunni Islamist militia believed to have ties to Al-Qaeda, in retaliation for Uganda's support of the African Union's mission in Somalia, AMISOM. Museveni had rushed into Somalia in 2006 because he needed to project Uganda as a "responsible member of the international community" and to deflect criticism of its own army's pillaging (Young writes "alleged pillaging") in DRC:

> More generally, western aid still supplies around a third of
> Uganda's government budget, but donor countries were
> becoming uncomfortable with the corruption that has increas-
> ingly marred Museveni's long rule. Alignment with US-backed

efforts to see Somalia pacified – so as to prevent the incubation and export of terror – serves both to smooth relations and to attract US logistical and training support for the Ugandan army.[1]

If Uganda is a pawn, as Young writes, then it must be stressed that it has chosen to be one. It may be more useful, however, to see the country as an unequal partner of the United States.

The same might be said for Paul Kagame of Rwanda, who has taken one of his few assets, a professional army by regional standards (thanks in part to American aid, described in Chapter 1), and deployed it in Darfur, where his country has no obvious interest at stake. Museveni, Kagame, Kabila, and all of the other Central African heads of state act on behalf of their states, or their own interests passed off as state interests. They compete with one another, much as the French compete with the British, or the Americans with the Chinese.

State actors (in Central Africa as elsewhere) find it useful to exaggerate the influence of international forces. Speaking in Kigali in 2008, DRC's foreign minister Alexis Thambwe Mwamba declared that Rwanda's rebel Hutu FDLR was "a cancer that the international community left us with in Congo without the ability to solve the problem."[2] Thambwe is a survivor, having served under Mobutu, then in "rebel" organizations sponsored by Rwanda and Uganda, and then under President Joseph Kabila. He knew that Mobutu invited the predecessors of the FDLR into Zaïre/Congo (in collaboration with France) and that Laurent Kabila adopted them as surrogates in his struggle against his former patrons, the RPF. Mobutu and then Kabila acted on behalf of the Zaïrian/Congolese state, within the constraints imposed by the international system. The "cancer" was partially self-inflicted. Blaming the international community was convenient for the Kabila government and for Thambwe's hosts, the Kagame government. Kagame, as incredible as it sounds, lectured around the world on the need to reduce aid dependency, even though publicly acknowledged international aid amounted to 45 percent of Rwanda's budget.[3] If one adds in the millions of dollars each year from illegal income derived from trade in Congolese minerals, some of which goes to off-budget military expenditure, then 50 percent of his budget was coming from abroad.

Contrary to Thambwe's claim, the Congo wars can be explained to a great extent in terms of classical realism: that is, the states of the region defending their respective national interests. The 1996 invasion was carried out by a coalition led by Rwanda, and including also Uganda, Burundi, and Angola, along with some anti-Mobutu Congolese. Seven months later, Laurent Kabila had replaced Mobutu. In 1998, Rwanda, Uganda, and Burundi invaded again, because Kabila was not serving their interests; this time Angola, Zimbabwe, and Namibia intervened to save Kabila and a lengthy war ensued. The precise motives varied but there was a common thread in that opposition groups from Rwanda, Uganda, Burundi, and Angola all had been operating in Zaïre/Congo with the support or at least toleration of the Zaïrian authorities. Told this way, the story that opened with the 1996 invasion is simple. The regimes in the four neighboring countries each saw a threat and acted on it, as realist theory would suggest. When the interests that provided the basis for an alliance no longer were shared, then the alliance shifted. Angola switched sides, since it saw that Rwanda was not a reliable partner in its fight against UNITA. Once Kabila was fighting for his life against the Rwandan Tutsi regime in Kigali, of course he would try to use the Rwandan Hutu fighters (the future FDLR) to defend him. Once the initial push to oust Kabila had failed, and Rwanda and Uganda were pillaging minerals in eastern DRC, then it was almost inevitable that they would fight, since they now were rivals. Interests are relatively permanent, from the realist perspective, whereas alliances are contingent. I do not wish to suggest that the United States, France, and other extra-continental players were not involved, only that the so-called "proxies" had their own reasons to behave as they did.

To the west and north of DRC lie the former French colonies, Republic of Congo and the Central African Republic. In the east, DRC shares borders with former British territories (South Sudan, Uganda, Tanzania, and Zambia), as well as Rwanda and Burundi. To the south and west lies the former

Portuguese colony of Angola, with its Cabinda exclave. Since DRC borders on nine other states, conflicts centering on the country tend to become very complex. Nearby, non-contiguous states (e.g. Zimbabwe, Libya, or South Africa) may also choose to participate. Other states (notably Tanzania, Zambia, and South Africa) decided not to intervene militarily in 1996 and thereafter but did influence others to act in line with their own interests and policy preferences.

International organizations can be both playing field and actors, but in Central Africa the regional and sub-regional actors have been weak. As a member of the African Union (AU), DRC is at once a member of the African regional political system and a shared concern or target of action by the AU. The AU remains rather ineffective, but its involvement in resolution of the Congo crisis was consequential at several key moments.

Within the AU and the continental system, sub-regional organizations have assumed a major political–military role: for example, the Economic Community of West African States (ECOWAS) dealt with West Africa's Sierra Leone and Liberia crises of the 1990s, under the leadership of its most important member, Nigeria.

Four regional blocs meet in Central Africa. DRC was the major unit of the former Belgian Africa, along with the much smaller Rwanda and Burundi. DRC, Rwanda, and Burundi are the member states of the Communauté Économique des Pays des Grands Lacs (Economic Community of the Great Lakes Countries, CEPGL), which has accomplished little since coming into existence in 1976. The level of activity of the CEPGL serves as a barometer of relations among the member states.

A potentially more useful regional organization, the Conférence Internationale sur la Région des Grands Lacs (International Conference on the Great Lakes Region, CIRGL) brought together ten countries, from Sudan in the northeast to Angola in the southwest. The initial declaration, signed by ten heads of state and government in 2004, referred specifically to the problem of the Rwandan *génocidaires*. When the Congolese Ntumba Luaba took over as executive secretary in 2011, he mentioned that the CIRGL might focus on "conflict minerals," a useful shift in focus from the viewpoint of the Kabila government. When the CIRGL hosted talks on the M23 mutiny, SADC member Tanzania used this framework to announce its intention to provide troops for a "neutral" force that would combat both M23 and the FDLR. DRC has significant trade and transportation links to all the neighboring countries and blocs, and has chosen which of these to prioritize. President Laurent Kabila chose to join SADC, whose members included the Portuguese-speaking states of Angola and Mozambique and the English-speaking states of southern Africa. SADC had been created in 1992 as the successor to the Front Line States, opposed to the apartheid regime in South Africa. Kabila's choice quickly paid off when three SADC members – Angola, Namibia, and Zimbabwe – came to the aid of DRC as the 1998 war began. South Africa opposed collective action on behalf of Kabila, leading Zimbabwe to initiate an action as chair of SADC's Organ on Politics, Defense, and Security.

A second move, renewing ties with CEEAC, the predominantly French-speaking Communauté Économique des États de l'Afrique Centrale (Economic Community of Central African States), reinforced DRC's diplomatic position. Joseph Kabila (mocked by his opponents for his limited French) was chosen president of CEEAC in 2007. Kabila may have benefited politically, but the weakness of the organization, which has made little progress toward its goals of establishing a customs union and providing for common defense, means that concrete benefits to DRC have been slight. Individual members of CEEAC – Chad, the Central African Republic, and Gabon in particular, have been somewhat active in DRC affairs, providing a counterweight to the Anglophones to the east and south. Rwanda withdrew from CEEAC soon after the beginning of the second war, and became a full member of the East African Community.

Other countries in the region made important contributions to resolving the conflict between DRC and its neighbors. Former President Quett Masire of Botswana served as African Union "facilitator" to promote peace in DRC. Zambia hosted the Lusaka conference of 1999, which led to a ceasefire, while

South Africa hosted the "Inter-Congolese dialogue" at Sun City in 2002, at which the infamous "1 + 4 formula" was agreed (see Chapter 1, p. 19). The neutrality of these neighbors made it possible for them to promote agreement among the belligerents.

Realist analysis becomes more difficult when considering interstate actors. Does the United Nations constitute an actor, pursuing its own interests, or is it only an instrument of its members? Similar questions arise regarding the AU, SADC, and other African international organizations. The question is best treated empirically: for example, SADC was prevented from acting as a unitary actor by strong internal divisions, particularly between Zimbabwe's Robert Mugabe and South Africa's Thabo Mbeki.

The dilapidated Zaïrian state linked two otherwise rather distant conflicts: the civil wars in Sudan and Angola. Mobutu backed the Khartoum government in its civil war (1983–2005) against the southern Sudanese rebels (Sudanese People's Liberation Army, SPLA), who were supported by the United States, Uganda, Ethiopia, and Eritrea. Anti-government rebels from Uganda, Rwanda, Burundi, and Angola operated from Zaïrian territory. As Filip Reyntjens explains, the logic of "the enemy of my enemy" produced two disparate alliances: France, Khartoum, Mobutu's Zaïre, the Hutu rebels (Rwandan and Burundian), and UNITA, versus the United States, Eritrea, Ethiopia, the SPLA, Uganda, Rwanda, Burundi, and the MPLA.[4] The absence of any shared principle beyond opposition to or support for Mobutu was underscored when many of the erstwhile allies – all under so-called "new African leaders" – fought each other soon thereafter: Ethiopia vs. Eritrea (1998–2000) and Rwanda vs. Uganda (1999–2000).

Rwanda and the Congo Wars

Rwanda has been more heavily involved in the Congo wars than any of the other neighboring states. This is due in part to Rwanda's long history of interaction with DRC, although real choices were made in the present.

Some speakers of Kinyarwanda, the main Rwandan language, were included in the Congo when the Belgian colony's borders were set, and many more migrated there during the colonial period. The Rwandan "social revolution" of 1959–62 led to the overthrow of the Tutsi monarchy, the establishment of a Hutu-dominated republic, and the flight of Tutsi refugees into neighboring countries, especially DRC, Burundi, Uganda, and Tanzania. Soon thereafter, Tutsi fighters attacked Rwanda from bases in Burundi and Uganda, but were beaten back.

In 1964, Rwandan Tutsi exiles established an alliance with the "Simba" rebels fighting in eastern Congo. A Congolese army report indicates that the Congolese rebels promised to give them, in "compensation for the services that the Tutsi rebels had already performed and those they would perform, the territories of the Babembe, the Bavira up to Rutshuru." All those territories – necessary to their cattle raising – would be "property of the Tutsi" in case of victory. There were two curious aspects of this agreement. First, the refugees were claiming land in Fizi (territory of the Babembe) and Uvira (territory of the Bavira) even though the local Tutsi of those areas (not yet known as Banyamulenge) were not collaborating with the rebellion. Second, the Lumumbists were willing to give away Congolese land as compensation.[5]

Burundi's "selective genocide"[6] seems to have prompted the Rwandan army under General Juvénal Habyarimana to oust Grégoire Kayibanda, the civilian Hutu president, in 1973. The killing of educated Hutu in Burundi was taken as proof that the Tutsi of either country could not be trusted. Resultant disorder under Kayibanda supposedly was jeopardizing Rwanda's Hutu-dominated regime. Once Habyarimana had stabilized Rwanda, an apparent calm settled over the Great Lakes.

The predominantly Tutsi RPF/RPA used Uganda as launching pad for its invasion of Rwanda in 1990. In Uganda, as in DRC, some Kinyarwanda-speakers had been included in the colony when its borders were drawn. Other Rwandans, especially Hutu farm workers, arrived during the colonial era. Neither of these first two categories have been important in recent political events, although some of them have claimed that they are not "Banyarwanda" so as not to be confused with more recent arrivals.

In 1959, Tutsi fleeing the "social revolution" in their homeland found refuge in Uganda. These refugees faced repression and expulsions, particularly under the rule of President Milton Obote. In response, a minority allied with the Idi Amin regime from 1971 to 1980, and then with Museveni's National Resistance Movement, which overthrew the second Obote presidency in 1985.

The Rwandese Alliance for National Unity (RANU), formed in 1977 by refugees of 1959 and thereafter, initially tried to build a broad movement that could transform the Rwandan state. By 1987, RANU was still trying to find a mass base, claiming that it was "non-political" and merely wanted to unite all Rwandans. It rebranded itself as the Rwandan Patriotic Front and restricted its agenda to eight core aims, including democracy and national unity. But in private the leadership had settled on a military option. By 1988, Rwandan Tutsi members of the Ugandan army were openly preparing to invade Rwanda.

Museveni's example showed the Rwandans that a small, highly disciplined force could take over an African state. One could argue also that Uganda pushed the RPF out of the nest. In a situation that prefigured that of Laurent Kabila in Kinshasa in 1997–8, the presence of so many Rwandans around Museveni became a political liability for the Ugandan leader, who may have encouraged the invasion as a means of getting rid of the troublesome allies.

On October 1, 1990, the Rwandan Patriotic Army, the armed wing of the RPF, deserted its posts in the Ugandan army and invaded northern Rwanda. After initial gains, the offensive was turned back by Zaïrian and French troops sent to reinforce the Habyarimana regime.

During a four-year campaign, the RPA consolidated its position in northern Rwanda. Many hundreds of thousands of Hutu fled southward to the government-controlled zone. The displaced persons' camps later provided many recruits to the Interahamwe and other Hutu militias that took leading roles in the genocide of 1994.

Once the RPF had taken power in Kigali, the extremist Hutu leadership moved out of the country in stages, first into the French-protected Turquoise Zone (Cyangugu–Kibuye–Gikongoro) and then into refugee camps in eastern Zaïre/Congo (near Uvira, Bukavu, and Goma). From these camps, the Hutu military (often called ex-Forces Armées Rwandaises [Rwandan Armed Forces, FAR] and Interahamwe, suggesting their double origins in the former Rwandan army and in a Hutu militia linked to Habyarimana's party) launched attacks on Rwandan territory and on Tutsi in eastern Congo.

Rwanda invaded Zaïre/Congo in association with Uganda and Burundi and a Congolese force subsequently labeled the AFDL. The AFDL comprised four components. Two were small Lumumbist opposition groups: Laurent Kabila's PRP and André Kisase Ngandu's CNDP. Two others represented Rwandophones and other Kivu ethnic groups: the Mouvement Révolutionnaire pour la Libération du Zaïre (Revolutionary Movement for the Liberation of Zaïre, MRLZ) of Anselme Masasu Nindaga and the Alliance Démocratique des Peuples (Democratic Alliance of Peoples, ADP) of Déogratias Bugera. Kabila was spokesman for the AFDL and Kisase Ngandu its military commander, but the AFDL was not so much an autonomous actor as a collection of four small groups, offering an alibi for the Rwandan-led invasion.

The contradictions between Rwanda's interests and motivations and those of the AFDL and its components soon came to the fore. Kisase Ngandu was murdered in January 1997, allegedly because of his strong opposition to Rwanda's role in DRC. Masasu Nindaga was arrested by the Kabila regime in November 1997, and kept in prison until a general amnesty in 2000. He was re-arrested in November 2000 and killed soon thereafter. Laurent Kabila was assassinated in January 2001. The circumstances of these murders remain unclear. Laurent Kabila has been accused of eliminating rivals. Rwanda has been accused of killing Kisase Ngandu and Kabila, men who resisted Rwandan control.

The second war was the direct result of Laurent Kabila's expulsion of his Rwandan handlers, notably General James Kabarebe, who had been imposed as his commander in chief of the armed forces. As in 1996, Rwanda launched the war before announcing the formation of a Congolese organization that supposedly was rebelling against Kabila. The RCD brought together a hodgepodge including leftist intellectuals, veterans of the Mobutu dictatorship, and Rwandophone Congolese. The RCD-Goma[7] could win a seat at the table by force of arms, but had no hope of winning an election.

The "mapping report" prepared by the UN High Commissioner for Human Rights and released in 2010 drew considerable attention for its assertion that the attacks by the Rwandan army and the AFDL against Rwandan and Congolese Hutu in 1996–7 might have amounted to genocide. However, as Belgian journalist Colette Braeckman points out, the report is as interesting for what it leaves out as for what it says.[8] The "abominable tragedy" that unfolded in eastern DRC cannot be understood without reference to the genocide in Rwanda in 1994, and to the roles of France and the United States in facilitating the transfer of the Tutsi–Hutu struggle to Congolese soil. That tragedy was the direct consequence of the genocide and of the exodus toward Congo of more than one and a half million Hutu refugees. The authorities of the overthrown Hutu regime brought into exile not only the funds of the national bank but also a supply of arms. In the camps on Congolese soil, along the border with Rwanda, troops and militiamen were not disarmed. The authorities of the former regime maintained their hold over the civilians, dissuading them from returning to Rwanda because they wished to use this mass of people to negotiate an eventual return to power. In the meantime, they launched armed attacks on Rwanda from the camps.

The refugee camps were encircled, bombarded, and a million civilians, caught in a pincer movement, were practically obliged to flee in the direction of Rwanda, where they were sent on to their hills (residential units, Rwandan equivalent of villages).

While the Canadian general Maurice Baril (former head of the military division of UN peacekeeping operations) assured that the deployment of an international force was not necessary since all the refugees had returned to Rwanda, and the

American ambassador to Kigali estimated that only 20,000 Rwandan Hutu were still in Congo, in reality half a million civilians, who had been crammed into the Mugunga camp and then bombarded, left in other directions, pushing into the Congo forest, still in the charge of armed men. Civilians, including women and children, were used as a human shield, protecting the dignitaries and the soldiers.

This race across the forest, in the direction of Kisangani, represents one of the most atrocious and least known pages of Congolese history, according to Braeckman.[9] While the mixed troops of the AFDL continued their progress and Kabila, kept in the rear, was led into the cities only after they fell, another war was waged by the Congolese Tutsi trained in Rwanda (between 5,000 and 10,000 men) and the Rwandan special units.

The mission of these teams of killers, who operated autonomously within the rebel troops, was to liquidate the *génocidaires* and their allies, according to Braeckman. These men had been given advanced communications equipment and had infiltrated "facilitators" into the teams of the UN Refugee Agency, the UNHCR, and the humanitarian organizations. While the latter tried to find the refugees in order to provide them with aid, the "facilitators" communicated to the soldiers the exact location of the fugitives.

In these groups, women and children in the front line received and transported the humanitarian aid, which was recuperated afterwards by the fighters who were hiding in the forest. When the AFDL soldiers arrived, the civilians were the first victims. Many Congolese who had fled with the Rwandan Hutu also were massacred. The operation verged on genocide since in North and South Kivu, many Hutu with Congolese nationality or from other groups that had sympathized with or collaborated with the refugees were likewise massacred; summoned to meetings in open air, they were killed without distinction and thrown into mass graves.

Rwandan intervention in DRC strains the realist model with its postulate of rational pursuit of national interest. Rwandan intervention reflected "complex reasons," according to Timothy Longman.[10] "Humanitarian interests and ethnic solidarity" – responding to attacks on Tutsi on Congolese soil – could be seen as a genuine motivation or a smokescreen. To the extent that it was genuine, it would have motivated Rwanda's Tutsi leadership more than "Rwanda" as a whole. The same can be said for Longman's second reason, "security threats from the Congo." Other Rwandans, associated with the Hutu regime overthrown in 1994, were posing the threat, and many Hutu apparently sympathized with the rebels.

Longman's third reason, "domestic security concerns," likewise is paradoxical. An assertive foreign policy is a well-known means of promoting national unity, but such a policy ran the risk of importing foreign disorder into the newly pacified Rwanda. Both Rwanda's new Tutsi leaders and the exiled Hutu leadership understood that the genocide in Rwanda and the victory of the RPF, in 1994, represented the end of a stage in the struggle for dominance in Rwanda but not the end of the struggle. Keenly aware of its origins in exile in Uganda in the years after 1959, the RPF was determined not to allow the Hutu to constitute a similar long-term threat from a base in DRC.

There was no reason to assume that those who returned to Rwanda were innocent of participation in the genocide of 1994; nor was there any reason to assume that all the Hutu who fled westward were *génocidaires*. Some of those who returned to Rwanda intended to continue killing Tutsi. When the Kigali authorities realized that they were re-importing genocide, they cut off the returns to Rwanda and stepped up the killing in Congo. The RPF/RPA apparently did not intend to kill as many Hutu as possible but to destroy Hutu communities under the control of the former Rwandan authorities.

The war in northwest Rwanda waged by the ex-FAR and Interahamwe (by now known as ALiR, or Armée pour la Libération du Rwanda/Army for the Liberation of Rwanda) between 1996 and 1998 represented another stage in the ongoing war between the RPF and its Hutu opponents. The Hutu forces concentrated their attacks on the northwest quadrant of Rwanda, not only because of its proximity to DRC, but also because it was the home area of the late

President Habyarimana and other key figures in the former regime. US military personnel accompanied the Rwandan army on missions in the northwest, and reported back on the level of armament and the evolution of the tactics of the Hutu infiltrators.

"Economic interests," Longman's fourth reason for intervention in DRC, is in fact a cluster of reasons. The presence of Rwandans (and Congolese of Rwandan culture, sometimes with dual citizenship) meant that the invasion of eastern DRC led to a reversal of fortune notably in the "*petit nord*" or the southern portion of North Kivu province. Banyarwanda, especially Tutsi, took advantage of the occupation to recover property they had lost in recent years, and to acquire new property. Congolese Tutsi constituted one of the major blocs in the ruling coalition in Kigali, which meant that local interests in North Kivu were linked to national politics in Rwanda and to Rwanda–DRC relations. During the second Congo war, the pillage of Congolese natural resources became so important in financing the war effort that the fight against the Hutu exiles took a back seat. Even when the war had largely ended, Kigali's struggle against the Hutu was episodic.

Longman adds a fifth factor, which he calls "political triumphalism." RPF successes in the civil war had reinforced the feeling that their efforts had an inevitability to them. Their role in stopping the genocide of Rwandan Tutsi imparted "a sense of moral rectitude." The violence against Congolese Tutsi convinced the RPF that no one else was willing to defend the Tutsi people.[11]

Kabila, Rwanda's former front man, was killed in 2001 by a member of his bodyguard, Rachidi Kasereka, a former child soldier from North Kivu. Colonel Edy Kapend, one of Kabila's closest military advisors, apparently killed Rachidi. Joseph Kabila, supposedly a son of Laurent Kabila, emerged as successor to the murdered president. After a "shambolic" trial, Colonel Kapend, General Yav Nawej (FARDC commander of the city-province of Kinshasa), and dozens of bodyguards were found guilty of murder and sentenced to death. Numerous rumors have circulated as to the responsibility of Rwanda, Angola, the United States, and other actors for the death of

Kabila. In 2011, a film called *Murder in Kinshasa* summarized the case and the trial and strongly suggested an assassination plot carried out by Rwanda and its allies of the RCD, with (at least) the approval of the United States.[12]

A decade after the death of Laurent Kabila, the question of relations with Rwanda remains a central issue in Congo politics. The Kagame government made two gestures in 2011, in an apparent effort to turn the page. A large quantity of minerals was impounded in Rwanda and turned over to the Congolese authorities. Four high military officers, including the former head of the "Congo Office" in the Rwandan presidency, were arrested on charges of conducting private business with "civilians" in DRC. Each of these gestures seemed to acknowledge that Rwanda had in fact engaged in officially sanctioned pillage in eastern Congo, although nothing of the sort was said. Much of the rest of the story of Rwanda's involvement in DRC will be told in two subsequent chapters, which correspond to two of the motives identified by Longman, namely the politics of identity and "conflict minerals."

Uganda's Role in Congo

Uganda intervened in DRC twice, first against Mobutu and second against Laurent Kabila, because its protégé Rwanda had done so. So says John Clark, who proceeds by a process of elimination. Clark notes that Uganda in this context means President Yoweri Museveni, or Museveni plus a few close military advisors.[13]

The first explanation to be examined and discarded is the notion, popular among Congolese, that Uganda and Rwanda were acting to build a "Tutsi–Hima" empire in the Great Lakes region. Kagame and other Rwandans served in Uganda's army under Museveni, who then supported their invasion of Rwanda in 1990. But this was an arrangement of convenience or opportunism rather than a manifestation of "primordial ethnic fealty." Museveni's base of support in Uganda is far broader than the Hima or the Banyankole as a whole, "and it is unlikely that he would jeopardize this support in such a misguided course."[14]

Clark likewise dismisses the notion of an "Anglo-Saxon" conspiracy. There is no reason to think that Museveni wanted to make Rwanda into an English-speaking country.

Clark then considers four more serious explanations for Uganda's re-entry into Congo in 1998. First is "the official argument that Uganda intervened in Congo because of serious threats to its security emanating from the border regions." Although the Allied Democratic Forces (ADF)[15] were operating in eastern DRC, and occasionally carried out bloody raids on Ugandan territory, the logical action on Museveni's part would have been to occupy and "pacify" the immediate border region. Instead, he sent the Ugandan army far to the west, and in so doing spared the ADF.[16]

A second possible motive is ideological. Museveni is supposed by some to have acted to export his own style of governance. To suppose that Museveni was ideologically opposed first to Mobutu, then to Kabila, means that one takes seriously the argument that Museveni represents a new breed of African leader. While Museveni may have disapproved of the style of governance of Mobutu, he found a *modus vivendi* with him between 1986 and 1996. Had Museveni really wanted to promote democracy and development in Zaïre/Congo, would he have supported Laurent Kabila, whose shortcomings were well known?[17]

Having disposed of the alternative explanations, Clark reaches "the most plausible explanation" for Uganda's participation in the second Congo war by putting the alliance with Rwanda at the center of the argument. Kagame did not consult Uganda in planning his airborne attack on Kinshasa, and once he had been stymied by the intervention of Angola and Zimbabwe, "the Rwandan leader's regime was left in a highly vulnerable position."[18] The collapse of Kagame's regime would have been costly to Museveni in terms of prestige and the burden imposed by the likely return of large numbers of Tutsi to Uganda.

Clark notes also the economic dimension of Uganda's involvement in Congo. Gold from Congo had a major impact on the Ugandan economy, accounting for 12 percent of all export revenues in 1997.

The uneasy partnership between Museveni and Kagame did not survive very long. A recently declassified document provides a revealing (and entertaining) look into the relationship as of 1999, when Rwanda and Uganda were collaborating with the RCD, then still headed by Professor Ernest Wamba dia Wamba.

In October 1998, following allegations and counterallegations about misconduct in the operations in DRC, Museveni hosted a meeting with the Rwandans.[19] The two sides agreed to set up a joint committee with four tasks: (1) to inform the RCD that "the RPA and UPDF [Uganda People's Defense Force] were not allowed to engage in or carry out any form of economic activity or interfere with civil administration"; (2) to examine civil–military relations in areas of operation in DRC; (3) to draft a code of conduct to govern the RCD, Rwandan, and Ugandan forces operating in Congo; and (4) to suggest ways of making joint command and control more effective.

Following armed clashes between the Rwandan and Ugandan armies at Kisangani, the "Joint Uganda–Rwanda Probe Committee on the Ongoing Operations in the Democratic Republic of the Congo" met in the city. Museveni had directed that the death of ex-minister Seth Sendashonga be discussed, along with the fate of "people allegedly arrested in joint RPA–UPDF operations." Sendashonga, a Hutu and former interior minister in Rwanda's post-genocide government, had been killed in Nairobi after he had complained about human rights abuses by RPA troops. The joint committee also was to discuss with the RCD leadership "ways of achieving a vibrant political mobilization programme." These additions to the committee mandate reflect Museveni's concern that the Rwandans relied excessively on violence. The Rwandan government members on the committee agreed to look into the matter of suspects arrested during joint operations. The Sendashonga murder (a more sensitive topic) would be "referred to the top leadership of the governments of Rwanda and Uganda."

On October 17, 1998 the probe committee visited Goma and held a meeting chaired by Wamba. The aim of the meeting was to make the RCD leadership aware of the need for "political mobilization in the liberated areas" and for "economic activities in the liberated areas in order to sustain military operations and ameliorate the suffering of the population in these areas," in "close and efficient liaison with officials of Rwanda and Uganda." Wamba "highlighted the need to do more political mobilization and diplomatic work." He claimed that the RCD's economic performance was being hampered by several problems, including "lack of investors" (owing to Laurent Kabila's failure to honor mining concessions awarded during the 1996 war), inadequate transportation, communication, and banking. It suffered from lack of experts in trade and tax management, and from high debts and expenditures. Wamba wished to discuss "the reported differences between his allies," Rwanda and Uganda.

The two committee leaders informed the RCD leadership that economic management was a Congolese responsibility "in order to support the liberation struggle and no member of either the UPDF or RPA was to engage in any business activities." The RCD had to take full charge of civil administration in the liberated areas, but Rwanda and Uganda could provide technical assistance in the areas of banking and taxes. The political situation would be discussed later.

In Kisangani the joint committee met with Rwandan, Ugandan, and Congolese military leaders, the governor, the mayor, religious leaders, and the provincial representative of the RCD. Despite the committee's commitment to tell the RCD that "no member of either the UPDF or RPA was to engage in any business activities," the committee could not meet with Brigadier James Kazini of the UPDF – identified by the UN as a leader of pillage of Congo resources – "who was out of station for the two days the committee sat in Kisangani." All participants presumably were well aware that both Rwandan and Ugandan officers were engaged in "business activities."

The RCD, unable to fulfill its obligations to its international backers, soon split. Dr. Émile Ilunga became head of what became known as RCD-Goma, while Wamba refused to quit and instead became head of the RCD-Kisangani. The RCD-Kisangani moved to Bunia and split again, with Mbusa Nyamwisi heading the RCD-Mouvement de Libération (RCD-ML). Uganda also sponsored the MLC, led by Jean-Pierre Bemba. Ugandan efforts to merge the MLC and the RCD-ML failed.

The Ugandans attempted to reorganize DRC's Ituri district, which lay just west of the Uganda's West Nile subregion. In so doing they aggravated a pre-existing conflict, contributing to tens of thousands of deaths and hundreds of thousands of displacements. Conflict over land between the Hema and the Lendu ethnic communities had long plagued Ituri. In 1999, Uganda began arming the Hema. Ugandan general James Kazini made Ituri (until then a district of Orientale province) into a separate province and imposed a Hema governor; these actions helped ignite a new ethnic war. The decisive contribution of Ugandan interference was made clear when Wamba of the RCD-Goma fired the Hema governor Mme Adèle Lotsove and replaced her with an Alur from northern Ituri. Hema–Lendu violence subsided.

Uganda's relationship with Ituri militias continued at least until 2006. UN investigators believe that Ugandan border officials turned a blind eye to weapons shipments into Congo. Uganda allowed illicit flights from Entebbe airport to bush airstrips in DRC. In return for supplying arms, Uganda was plundering the area controlled by its favored rebels, becoming a major exporter of Congolese gold.

A UN investigation in 2004 concluded that Congolese militias benefited from unchecked imports from Uganda, which could contain arms, ammunition, or other military supplies. Uganda's failure to stop this "could be construed as wilful neglect, which facilitates the execution of illicit operations or violations of the embargo." After gunmen killed nine Bangladeshi peacekeeping troops, Museveni, fourth largest recipient of British aid in Africa, came under intense international pressure to stop backing the Mouvement Révolutionnaire Congolais (Congolese Revolutionary Movement, MRC). In April 2006, Museveni's government arrested ten senior MRC figures in Kampala. Until then, Uganda had denied that there were any MRC fighters in the country.

The Uganda insurrection movement, the Lord's Resistance Army, has devastated northeastern DRC. The Ugandan army, which had driven the LRA out of Uganda, sent several missions into DRC after the LRA but failed in its efforts to kill or capture Joseph Kony or other top leaders. In December 2008, the US military provided intelligence and financial support to the Ugandan-led Operation Lightning Thunder, which flushed LRA fighters from their main hideout in Congo, Garamba National Park. But rebel leaders including Kony escaped the ground and air assault and immediately embarked on a series of massacres in remote villages. The Uganda army and their regional allies appeared (to Human Rights Watch) to lack the capability, will, or expertise to apprehend the top leaders.

In May 2010, President Obama signed into law the LRA Disarmament and Northern Uganda Recovery Act, which renewed US commitments to deal with the LRA threat. Six months later, the strategy document said the United States had spent more than $23 million on support for the Ugandan military since Operation Lightning Thunder, but added that more money was needed. The new US strategy supposedly had four main objectives: to increase protection for civilians, encourage rebel defections, improve humanitarian access, and "apprehend or remove from the battlefield Joseph Kony and senior commanders." The Americans said little about the second half of the supposed task, namely to promote recovery in North Uganda, and in particular Acholiland, home area of Kony.

Ending the LRA insurgency had proved beyond the Ugandan military when the LRA operated in northern Uganda for twenty years, and the rebel fighters have proved equally able to survive in DRC and other countries to the west. The Enough Project warned that the LRA's propensity for violence remains undiminished, even though its fighting force had been reduced to just 400. Obama's plan signaled a more hands-on approach by the US military in regional counterinsurgency operation, according to Enough. However, Chris Bain, head of UK aid agency Cafod, warned that the military approach is a "dangerous one if it doesn't ensure the protection of innocent civilians." He argued, "A negotiated solution is the only long-term solution."[20]

American involvement was necessitated by the abject failure of the United Nations to deal with the LRA and its civilian victims (see also Chapter 6 on "responsibility to protect"). The UN had missions in three areas affected by the LRA – DRC, the Central African Republic, and South Sudan – but they lacked a cross-border mandate that would allow them to address the full scope of the LRA problem, and they were not focused on addressing LRA violence. The UN peace-keeping force in Congo, MONUSCO, was the largest in the region, with nearly 18,000 troops, but only 850 UN peace-keeping troops were deployed in the LRA-affected areas. No peacekeepers were based in Bas Uele district, on the border with the Central African Republic, despite repeated LRA attacks and abductions in the area. The UN had no peace-keepers in LRA-affected areas in the Central African Republic, and only a handful of humanitarian staff. The United Nations mission in Sudan (UNMIS) was present in Western Equatoria but had also proven ineffective at protecting civilians from LRA attacks. Late in 2011, US troops arrived in Uganda, and from there began moving into the neighboring countries, accompanying the Ugandans.

In 2010–11, the Allied Democratic Forces (whose activity had justified Uganda's intervention in DRC in 1996 and 1998) were again active. The FARDC launched attacks against ADF fighters in 2010, killing a number of them. In 2011, the ADF attacked the prison in Beni, apparently hoping to free the prisoners. As in the case of the LRA, the Ugandan government apparently was content to address the problem militarily, rather than dealing with the grievances of ADF activists.

DRC's relations with Uganda were tense also because of attempts to exploit petroleum deposits in the "Albertine Graben" (rift or depression around Lake Albert). These will be discussed in Chapter 5, on conflict minerals.

Burundi and Its Back Door

Burundi was a junior partner in the invasions of the DRC in 1996 and 1998. It limited its incursion to South Kivu, and more especially to Uvira-Fizi, which Prunier labels its "back door."[21]

Since the 1960s, western Burundi had served as a base for Congolese insurgents opposed to the Kinshasa government. The Chinese embassy in Burundi channeled aid to "progressive" forces in Congo, including the Conseil National de Libération (National Liberation Council, CNL), based in Brazzaville and comprising Lumumbists and others opposed to the American-backed regime in Léopoldville/Kinshasa.

During the rebellion of 1964–5, Antoine Marandura and Louis Bidalira established a bridgehead in the Uvira area, from which rebel forces moved south to Kalemie (Katanga), and west to Kindu (Maniema), and Stanleyville (Orientale). After the collapse of the Lumumbist insurgency and the consolidation of power in Kinshasa by Mobutu, some of the Lumumbists of South Kivu (including members of the Bembe community) took up residence in western Burundi and Tanzania. Others fled from South Kivu to escape the exactions of Kabila's PRP and the Mobutu forces sent to combat them.

Burundians also fled to neighboring countries, especially in the aftermath of the genocide of Hutu at the hands of the Tutsi-led army. Tanzania and DRC both hosted many thousands of Burundians. Most were women and children and wanted nothing more than shelter and a chance to return home once calm had been restored. However, Tanzania and DRC also served as rear bases for Hutu rebel groups fighting against the Tutsi-dominated government in Bujumbura.[22]

Under pressure from the international community and from the Hutu majority, the Tutsi-dominated government of Burundi agreed to hold elections, which led to the victory of Melchior Ndadaye's Frodebu and the installation of a pro-Hutu government in 1993. A few months later, Tutsi soldiers assassinated Ndadaye. In revenge, some Frodebu members massacred Tutsi, and the army responded with violence against Hutu. Burundi was plunged into an ethnic conflict that claimed perhaps 300,000 lives. As René Lemarchand suggests, this episode hardened ethnic lines in Rwanda, and contributed indirectly to the genocide.[23]

Despite this setback, Burundi did continue its transition to majority rule, through a combination of electoral politics and guerrilla warfare, with the international community pushing the process along. In November 1995, the presidents of Burundi, Rwanda, Uganda, and Zaïre (DRC) announced a regional initiative for a negotiated peace in Burundi facilitated by former Tanzanian president Julius Nyerere. In July 1996, former Burundian president Pierre Buyoya (defeated at the polls by Ndadaye in 1993) returned to power in a bloodless coup. He declared himself president of a transitional republic, even as he suspended the National Assembly, banned opposition groups, and imposed a nationwide curfew. Widespread condemnation of the coup ensued, and regional countries imposed economic sanctions pending a return to a constitutional government. Buyoya agreed in 1996 to liberalize politics, but fighting between the army and Hutu militias continued. In June 1998, Buyoya promulgated a transitional constitution and announced a partnership between the government and the opposition-led National Assembly.

Burundi joined the Rwanda–Uganda invasion of DRC soon after the Buyoya coup. The army apparently killed a number of wounded Hutu fighters being treated at the Protestant hospital at Lemera, and then destroyed the hospital itself.

In the aftermath of the occupation of South Kivu by Rwanda and Burundi, a *de facto* alliance was formed between the FDLR or ex-FAR/Interahamwe (Rwandan Hutu), the two main Burundian Hutu armed groups (CNDD and FNL), and various Congolese Mayi-Mayi or local resistance groups. This alliance continued to shape events in the area. At Gatumba (western Burundi, a few miles from the Congolese border), 156 Banyamulenge (Congolese Tutsi) refugees were massacred in 2004, allegedly by Rwandan and Burundian Hutu and Congolese Mayi-Mayi fighters.[24]

Burundi's transition to majority rule continued. Pierre Nkurunziza of the predominantly Hutu CNDD was elected president, and re-elected in 2010 in an election boycotted by opposition parties. However, the FNL faction headed by another Hutu insurrectionist, Agathon Rwasa, apparently was returning to the *maquis* to fight, using Burundi's backyard of Uvira-Fizi as a base. Nkurunziza is from Bujumbura while Rwasa is from the far north, near Rwanda. This reminds us that regional splits are as important in some contexts as the better-known Tutsi–Hutu split. Moreover, Burundi's backyard in southern South Kivu promised to remain a local "hot spot" even if relations between the national governments of the two countries had stabilized.

Angola

The Angolan war of independence and ensuing civil war had been among Central Africa's bloodiest conflicts of the 1970s and 1980s. Angola's MPLA government took part in both Congo wars (1996–7 and 1998–2003) for the same reason: to defend itself against its long-time adversary, Jonas Savimbi's UNITA. Sympathy for Laurent Kabila was at best a secondary motivation, and in 2001 Angola perhaps aided, or at least welcomed, his assassination.

In the first Congo war, Angola contributed decisively to the overthrow of Mobutu by Kabila. The intervention of Angola and Zimbabwe was decisive in preventing the second war from ending in a rapid overthrow of Kabila. Since then, DRC has paid a heavy price for its debt to the Angolan regime.

Since its rescue of Laurent Kabila in 1998, Angola maintained a small military presence in DRC, mainly in oil-rich Bas Congo. In the aftermath of the defeat of Kabila's forces, including Zimbabweans at Pweto (Katanga), it was reported that Angola had sent troops to participate in a counter-attack.

Intervention in DRC was fairly successful as a second front in the war against UNITA; the rebel movement was weakened. However, the Angolan government was dissatisfied with Laurent Kabila on at least two counts. First, he was incapable of winning the war despite considerable aid from his allies. Indeed, as Pweto suggested, he was capable of losing the war to a pro-UNITA coalition. Second, Kabila was obstructive as regards a negotiated end to the war, a position the Angolans came to favor.

The long border both separates and links Angola and DRC. Angola comprises two blocs of territory on the Atlantic coast. By far the larger lies south of the Congo River and DRC. The so-called "Cabinda Enclave" (not really enclaved since it borders on DRC, the Republic of Congo, and the Atlantic Ocean) lies north of the Congo River.

The Congo–Angola border divides several shared mineral fields. These include onshore and offshore petroleum deposits, running from Cabinda to DRC to Angola proper, and diamond fields (in Angola's Lunda provinces as well as DRC's Kasai provinces).

The border has defined several transnational communities. The first important Angolan nationalist, Holden Roberto, was of Kongo ethnicity. He allegedly was born in São Salvador (Mbanza Kongo) in 1925 but moved with his family to then Belgian Congo as a two year old. He launched his political party, the Frente Nacional de Libertação de Angola (National Liberation Front of Angola, FNLA) in 1962 and gained considerable support from the Kongo people of northern Angola. Farther east, the Lunda have played a major role in Angola–Congo relations. The "Katanga gendarmes" (many of them Lunda) have figured prominently in the recent Congo wars. When the Katanga secession was crushed in 1963, the secessionist leader Moïse Tshombe (a Lunda) sent a major portion of his gendarmerie across the border into Portuguese-ruled Angola. When Tshombe became Congo prime minister in 1964, he used these fighters to suppress the Lumumbist insurgency. When Katangans mutinied in 1966 and 1967 in support of their exiled leader, Mobutu had many of them killed. Others regrouped in Angola, where they fought first on behalf of the colonial government, then on behalf of the MPLA against Holden Roberto's FNLA and Mobutu's FAZ. In 1977 and 1978, Katangan Tigers from Angola, calling themselves the FLNC, invaded their home province. The independence of Angola in 1975 led to "mutual encirclement" between Angola and Zaïre/Congo, as I. William Zartman has pointed out.[25] That is, Mobutu saw Zaïre as encircled by leftist regimes (Congo-Brazzaville, Tanzania, and Angola) whereas the MPLA of Angola saw itself encircled by Zaïre, Zambia, Namibia, and ultimately South Africa.

Following Angolan independence, Roberto's FNLA was quickly defeated on the battlefield. The civil war continued, pitting the MPLA (which controlled the capital Luanda and the oilfields) against UNITA (which controlled the diamond fields). The United States supported elections as a means of disengaging from Angola. When the MPLA won the elections in 1992 and UNITA refused to accept the result, the US withdrew support from UNITA, which, however, survived until the death of Savimbi in 2002. According to some conspiracy-theory narratives on Central Africa, the United States provided GPS data on the whereabouts of Savimbi, in exchange for Angola's role in eliminating Laurent Kabila a year earlier.

In return for its support of Laurent Kabila in 1996–8, Angola received Congolese support in its campaign against the Cabinda separatists of the Frente para a Libertação do Enclave de Cabinda (Front for the Liberation of the Cabinda Enclave, FLEC). Angola was granted the right to carry out anti-FLEC activities on Congolese soil, including an operations center in the Congolese town of Tshela, near the Cabinda border. FLEC offices were closed, and many of its militants arrested, tortured, and, in some cases, deported to Angola.

After the formal end of the war in 2003, the divergent interests of Angola and DRC came to the fore. These focused on minerals – oil and diamonds in particular – and will be discussed in Chapter 5. What matters here is the disparity between formal equality of two neighboring states and the inability of DRC to deal with Angola as equal to equal. When Angola deported thousands of Congolese from the diamond areas of Lunda Norte and Lunda Sur, DRC responded by deporting thousands of Angolan nationals, many of whom had been in DRC for decades and presumably had no connection to minerals. When Angolan troops occupied a cluster of villages in southern Bandundu (in an area through which Angolan diamonds apparently transited), Congolese could only grumble. Similar incidents apparently have taken place in Bas Congo. The two chiefs of state have met, without resolving the problems.

Realism in Central Africa

Libya, Chad, and Sudan took part in the Congo wars, at least briefly. Others decided not to intervene (Zambia and South Africa, for example), and this decision impacted the outcome. Some of the states apparently responded to short-term contingencies, making the best choice among the available options. Others, like Rwanda under Kagame, for example, clearly had a long-term goal in mind, of restoring and preserving Tutsi hegemony in Rwanda, and pursued that goal whenever they saw an opening. Julius Nyerere of Tanzania was another long-term thinker, wanting Mobutu ousted because of his sabotage of the front-line states, and recognizing that Rwanda and Burundi would continue to be dangerous to the region if they were not anchored to East Africa. (A comprehensive review of interstate relations along DRC borders would deal with Zambia, the Central African Republic, and Congo-Brazzaville.)

One of the limitations of realist analysis of events and processes in Central Africa lies in the area of presidential decision-making and national interest. For more than twenty years, Uganda has equaled Museveni, for better or for worse. Kagame was the leader in Rwanda, even while he still was vice-president and minister of defense. The ouster of President Pasteur Bizimungu, a Hutu RPF member, amounted to dropping the veil. However, one should avoid the error of assuming that the interests of Museveni and Kagame and their households coincide with the interests of the state they head.

In a very general sense, the "international community" imposed the FDLR on Congo (as Thambwe Mwamba maintained) and the United States, United Kingdom, and France in particular should not be allowed to say that this is none of their business. Nor should Kabila and Kagame be allowed to escape their own responsibility for the continued existence and crimes of the FDLR, AFDL, and RCD, committed on Congolese soil (and, in the case of some of the FDLR men, committed on Rwandan soil in 1994). Rather than engage in polemical discussion about puppets, one should focus instead on the policies adopted and the decisions made by the politicians in the Central African arena and beyond.

Each of the Central African states is weak, vulnerable, and poor. They are all vastly unequal to those seen as the "movers and shakers" within the international system. While contemporary neorealist thinkers discuss interdependence, the Central African states are dependent on the more powerful states that attempt to advance their own global and regional agendas.

The Central African states (which in most contexts means each of the chiefs of state) each have their own team, some more talented than others. Some managers also use the team to better advantage than others. Quality of play determines outcomes on the field. Such is the logic of "subaltern realism."[26] However, the field of play metaphor may be misleading, in that quality of play includes not only competition with one's neighbors but also successful management of pressures emanating from the international system. Today's small and weak states are "faced with severe problems related to the operation of international norms and the recent changes that have occurred in that normative environment, largely at the behest of the developed states of the global North."[27]

Subordinate realism is a useful perspective in that it recognizes that the security dilemma in Central Africa is primarily a domestic rather than an interstate phenomenon. The question is not whether the Congo war has been an international war or a civil war, but how these two aspects of the conflict are intertwined. As Séverine Autesserre has suggested, insufficient attention to the local dimension of the war in the eastern DRC has handicapped efforts to end the fighting.[28]

In the meantime, DRC remains a hell on earth. One aspect of that hellish situation is identity-based conflict, both within DRC and between DRC and its troublesome neighbors. Groups compete in elections, of course, but also use more drastic means, including arson, sexual violence, and all-out war. We shall explore this in Chapter 3.

3 | Identity as a Driver of Conflict

In this chapter we shall explain the predominance of ethno-nationalist language in the politics of DRC and the Great Lakes region, and the near absence of the language of class. Indeed, national and ethnic identities, in particular, structure the political conflict in this region, a situation that journalists often misconstrue, in the mistaken belief that ethnicity (often called "tribalism") and nationality are mutually exclusive.

Other important identities link individuals to sub-national territories (provinces, districts, territories, towns, and quarters), or to religion: Catholicism and Kimbanguism,[1] for example, prove significant in some political contexts. Region – eastern Congo versus the west – emerged as a crucial cleavage with the Rwando-Ugandan invasion, fronted by the easterner Laurent Kabila, although sometimes this division was recast in linguistic terms: Swahili as language of the east versus Lingala as language of the west. Party-political identity proved important in the 2006 and 2011 DRC elections, particularly in the strong showing by the Parti Lumumbiste Unifié (Unified Lumumbist Party, PALU) and the UDPS and their respective elderly leaders Antoine Gizenga and Étienne Tshisekedi. Of all the identities, however, none are quite as strange as the quasi-linguistic, virtually racist identities of "Nilotics and Bantus," which we shall consider below.

As Kevin Dunn has shown, Congo itself was a creation of the Western state of mind. Western discourses have been the wellspring for the violent interventions into Congolese territory, and have been prominent in shaping the internal contests over local identity.[2]

Identities are multiple, fluid and situational. The situations to which individuals and groups respond are geopolitical, and the same person or small group can respond in terms of a different identity, depending on the situation. At the systemic level, the Congolese (like the rest of the global population) have moved in the past two decades from the supposedly bipolar world of the Cold War to a rather different situation in which the United States is the leading power but not hegemonic (as suggested by its labors to restore a modicum of order to Iraq and Afghanistan).

With the rise of China, a Sino-American bipolar system may be emerging. Indeed, the Congolese recognize that in the context of this great power rivalry there are certain advantages to dealing with the Chinese. However, that does not mean that they identify with the Chinese, as fellow members of the global South or the third world. Rather, some Congolese apparently classify the Chinese, like Europeans and Americans, as "white," in contrast to which they (the Congolese) are "black."

Often, the people of the Great Lakes region describe their unity and diversity in terms of a taxonomy that derives from nineteenth-century European raciology. Autochthons or sons of the soil of eastern Congo think of themselves as "Bantu," taking "Bantu" and "Nilotic" to be quasi-racial terms, describing people's physical as well as cultural characteristics. Since Congo is a Bantu country, so the argument goes, Nilotics such as the Tutsi must be foreigners. The Tutsi in Rwanda, Burundi, and eastern Congo speak Bantu languages (Kinyarwanda or Kirundi), so the term "Nilotic" refers to their "morphology" and supposed origin in the Nile Valley or beyond.[3]

For decades, Congolese learned in their schools (largely run by missionaries) that there were four kinds of people in their country: Bantus, Sudanese, Nilotics, and Pygmies. These people were characterized by their language, their physical appearance or "morphology," and their way of life (agriculturalist, pastoralist, hunter-gatherer). From there to the identification of Congo as a "Bantu" country, where Sudanese and Nilotics are outsiders, is a short step. This perspective is widely shared among the various groups in Central Africa. The only apparent exception is Rwanda under the RPF, where all references to ethnicity are banned. Behind the façade, however, Rwandan Tutsi and Hutu think in much the same terms as their neighbors. American journalist Josh Kron has told of being approached in Rwanda by many Tutsi who apparently consider that, as a Jew, he is their brother.[4]

Many Congolese, especially in the east, draw on this same set of ideas to explain the Rwandan invasions and their response to them. The Mayi-Mayi fighters, in particular those led by General Joseph Padiri Bulenda, explain their fight against the invaders by invoking the supposed plan to incorporate eastern DRC into a "Tutsi–Hima Empire."[5] The Mayi-Mayi (or Maï-Maï) illustrate one of the paradoxes of identity politics in contemporary DRC. There is not one unified Mayi-Mayi movement, but a cloud of autonomous groups, each drawing most of its members from a single ethnic group or subgroup; yet they unite through this shared myth and through the concept of "resistance," responding to a shared international challenge.

The language of identity in Congo, as elsewhere, is primordialist, presenting the various categories of local people, neighbors, and foreigners from far away as unchanging. In reality, the identities and categories typically represent an amalgam of local elements and imported frameworks. One such framework is the Western-style state system, with its linear boundaries; the ethnic maps dear to colonial administrators and ethnographers, represent another such framework, attributing each portion of the colonial/national territory to a particular ethnic group. Yet another framework is the nineteenth-century raciology according to which the world population was divided into red, yellow, black, and white races. In Central Africa, Tutsi and other pastoralists of east-central Africa became black Europeans, born to rule.

The weak Congolese state proclaims its existence notably through adoption of laws defining Congolese nationality. The Congolese Constitution has been revised on numerous occasions in order to include or exclude various categories of people from Congolese nationality. The Constitution of 2006 specifies that Congolese nationality is "one and indivisible" (there is no dual nationality) and attributes Congolese nationality to "all persons belonging to the ethnic groups whose peoples and territories constituted what became Congo at Independence." Although the Constitution is written in general terms, it is understood that the problem particularly concerns people of Rwandan origin or culture. The nationality question was muted during the years of the Mobutu dictatorship, but the move toward multiparty competition after 1990 heated up the question of who is Congolese. The Sovereign National Conference (Conférence Nationale Souveraine, CNS) of 1991–2 offered local "autochthonous" leaders from North and South Kivu an opportunity to seize the advantage over their Rwandophone rivals by barring them from participation.[6]

The constitutional provision is regularly invoked in the ongoing war of words with Rwanda. The only Rwandophone Tutsi elected to the Congolese national assembly in 2006 (to my knowledge) was Baudouin Dunia of Masisi territory, a candidate of Jean-Pierre Bemba's MLC. In September 2009, Dunia was arrested in Rwanda, where he had a bank account (since the banks did not function on the Congolese side of the border). Kinshasa newspapers made much of the fact that a Rwandan court allegedly found him to be of Rwandan nationality. It is unclear whether Dunia was guilty of the charges against him, relating to failure to repay a loan. What is interesting here is that despite having revised the nationality law on numerous occasions, and adopting a revision in 2006 that grants Congolese nationality to many speakers of Kinyarwanda, the question keeps coming back.

The nationality question often sinks to the level of slurring one's political rivals by questioning their claim to be Congolese, much as "birthers" in the United States persist in believing that Barack Obama is not a native-born US citizen. Even after the death of Mobutu, some people assured me that the late dictator was not Congolese by birth. According to one informant, Mobutu's alleged mother, Marie-Madeleine Yemo, had been a *femme libre* (prostitute), crossing back and forth across the river, between northern DRC and the Central African Republic. Baby Mobutu was born to another prostitute, herself a Central African, and then adopted by her friend Mama Yemo. Various versions of this story began to circulate on the Internet as soon as this came into being in the 1990s.

According to a similar story (also propagated by political rivals), Joseph Kabila is not the son of Laurent Kabila. Rather, he is the son of a Rwandan Tutsi woman who was one of Laurent Kabila's many concubines. Preparing the election campaign of 2006, Joseph Kabila's camp put forward another Kabila wife, this one from Maniema, as his "real" mother. The notion that Joseph Kabila is not really Congolese was very useful to the rival candidate, Jean-Pierre Bemba of the MLC, who presented himself as a son of the soil. If Joseph Kabila is not merely a foreigner, but a Rwandan Tutsi, so much the better for all those who wish him ill.[7]

Mobutu and Kabila are not the only victims of such arguments. Fighting in North Kivu reopened the question of the nationality of rebel General Laurent Nkunda. He claims to have been born in Rutshuru Zone, North Kivu, but Congolese almost universally call him "Rwandan." Some refer to him as "Nkundabatware," a long version of his name (meaning "loves the chiefs") that makes him sound foreign to non-speakers of Kinyarwanda. During the presidential campaign of 2011, moreover, opposition candidate Vital Kamerhe (a Shi from Bukavu) had to face allegations that he was in fact from Cyangugu, the city in Rwanda located a few miles from Bukavu. He found himself insulted as a Rwandan at public gatherings and on the Internet.

Locals and Strangers

The conflict between self-styled *autochtones* (locals) and *allogènes* (non-natives) in North and South Kivu is reminiscent of conflicts that occurred in all regions of Congo just before independence. They were set off by the introduction of electoral competition in the towns. It often was argued that the Belgians had brought in the *allogènes*, or strangers, and that as the Belgians were leaving, so should their protégés. Shortly after independence, the creation of new provinces (the so-called *provincettes*) triggered a new round of ethnic conflicts, often splitting hitherto united communities. The "rebellions" of 1964 set off yet another spate of communal conflicts, even though these Lumumbist insurrections ostensibly were directed against the "new class" that profited from independence.

The Mobutu dictatorship, which took shape following the coup of November 1965, was able largely to eliminate such conflicts between locals and strangers by rendering elections meaningless and suppressing insurrections. By 1990, however, as the dictatorship fell into an advanced state of decay, conflicts between *autochtones* and *allogènes* resurged. Mobutu himself fanned the flames in some cases, as when he supported anti-Rwandophone politicians Anzuluni Bembe of South Kivu and Nyamwisi Mavungi of North Kivu, who were struggling against people they saw as foreigners.

Language and Politics

Karl Deutsch argued that nation building does not happen in a vacuum. Integration and mobilization potentially conflict with one another. Social mobilization is the process whereby people become uprooted from their traditions and thus amenable to new patterns of communication and behavior. Deutsch demonstrated that this process increased the likelihood of political integration among peoples who already shared the same language, traditions, and social institutions, while it accelerated the forces toward disintegration of states whose peoples did not share such traits.[8] Viewing DRC from a Deutschian perspective, it is astonishing that the state has not disintegrated. There must be some countervailing forces working to promote integration.

Language is, of course, the basis of social communication. There are some 200 languages in DRC, each supposedly the mother tongue of one community or another, although distinguishing languages from dialects and ethnic communities from subgroups (sometimes called "tribes") is difficult and controversial. The Belgians introduced French as the administrative language, back in the days when French was the dominant language in Belgium as well. French remains the "official language" of DRC, spoken mainly by those who have completed secondary school. It is a factor of national integration and also stands for achievement (it is a sort of class marker), but since the 1980s, with the pauperization of the educated, one often hears the mocking question from other Congolese: "Can you eat your French?"

More pertinent, in Deutsch's terms, are the four "national" or vehicular languages, used in elementary education and in radio and television broadcasting. Each is dominant in a relatively well-defined region: Kiswahili in the east, Lingala in the north, Tshiluba in the south-central region (East and West Kasai provinces), and Kikongo in the southwest. Congolese census data are not useful for a comprehensive Deutsch-style analysis but it is possible (for example) to show from figures on language use that Sankuru district occupies an intermediate position between Equateur province (home of Lingala), southern Kasai (home of Tshiluba), and Maniema (where Kiswahili prevails). Lumumba, a son of Sankuru who spoke all three of these vehicular languages, was well prepared for a position as Congo's leading nationalist.

The complexity of the linguistic situation in Congo and the directions of change are not easily represented on a map. The cartographers of Ethnologue show mixed zones along the border between Kiswahili and Lingala in Orientale province, between Kiswahili and Tshiluba in East Kasai, and between Lingala and Kikongo in Bandundu (see Map 2).

Many Congolese recognize the importance of language as a factor of integration. During the Sovereign National Conference of 1991–2, there was a proposal that elementary school children should begin learning a second national language, beyond the one in which they were being taught.

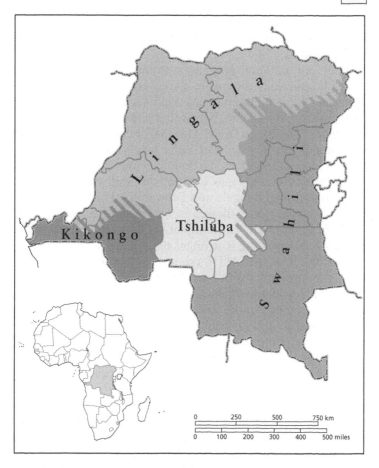

Map 2 Distribution of national languages
(Based on: M. Paul Lewis, ed., *Ethnologue: Languages of the World*, 16th edition (Dallas: SIL International, 2009). Online version, 2009: *http://www.ethnologue.com/.*)

Of the four "national languages," Lingala most nearly deserves this title. There are people who speak it in all corners of DRC, especially in the towns and around the military bases.[9] It is also the language in which most of Congo's famous Rumba music is sung, and through which ideas concerning love, sorcery, and politics are transmitted to all corners of the country where at least some young people understand it.

The four national languages define and stand for four broad quasi-ethnic groups. In a song composed for the 1970 elections, Franco (Luambo Makiadi) sang, "Mokongo no, Mongala no, Moluba no, Moswahili no; we are all brothers." The terms "Mokongo" and "Moluba" include not only people who accept the Kongo and Luba labels as primary ethnic identity, but others from the regions where Kongo and Luba are the vehicular languages. ("Mongala" and "Moswahili" are singular forms of Bangala and Baswahili.) This regional solidarity is strong, even though in other contexts such people might be bitter rivals. The sentiment of national unity to which Franco was appealing is stronger than many people realize.

In 1996, when the AFDL crossed the border together with the Ugandans and Rwandans, Mobutu's fleeing troops justified their scandalous behavior by suggesting that this was an affair among "those people": that is, easterners. When Laurent Kabila and his backers set up shop in Kinshasa, they were widely perceived as foreigners by the Lingala-speakers of the capital. This reaction was understandable. As journalists noted, tall gentlemen who did not speak French surrounded Kabila. The first banknotes distributed by the AFDL government used English and Swahili on the verso: for example, the numeric value 200F was translated as "two hundred" and "mia mbili." Whether or not this was intended as a provocation of speakers of French and Lingala, it succeeded in provoking.

During the second war, which began in 1998, the two main "rebel" movements opposing Kabila enjoyed contrasting responses from the Congolese population of the occupation zones. The Rwandan-sponsored RCD, which occupied much of the Swahili-speaking zone in the east, was despised. In contrast, the Ugandan-sponsored MLC of Jean-Pierre Bemba, whose occupation zone was mainly Lingalaphone, earned a degree of acceptance since he was seen (as he put it) as "100 percent Congolese." (Some Congolese found this ironic, since one of Bemba's four grandparents was European.)

When elections finally were held, in 2006, the results reflected a political and socio-linguistic fracture (see Map 3). Joseph Kabila won the eastern, Swahili-speaking provinces of Orientale, Maniema, North Kivu, South Kivu, and Katanga. Bemba took Lingala-speaking Equateur and Kinshasa, and Kongo-speaking Lower Congo. He also carried the Tshiluba-speaking Kasai provinces, although vote totals were very low,

Map 3   Presidential election, 2006, first round, results by province

thanks in part to a boycott called by the UDPS, presumably the most popular party among the Luba-Kasai. Gizenga of PALU carried his home province of Bandundu, where the main vehicular language is State Kikongo (Kikongo ya Leta).[10] The east–west split has deepened since, and one hears westerners say, "Baswahili are Rwandans."

It is difficult to compare the results of the 2011 elections to those of 2006, given an apparent high level of cheating (both suppression of the opposition vote and stuffing the ballot box on behalf of the incumbent Kabila). It appears that Tshisekedi carried Bas-Congo, Equateur, Kasai Occidental, Kasai Oriental, and Kinshasa. Kabila supposedly carried Bandundu (fief of PALU), and all of the eastern or Swahili-speaking provinces, from Oriental in the north to Katanga in the south. His reported vote totals for North and South Kivu were greatly reduced as compared to 2006; Kamerhe did quite well in both Kivus. Kabila's reported totals and percentages in some of the eastern provinces, Maniema and Katanga in particular, were suspiciously high.

Opposition candidates were able to exploit ethno-regional discontent with the Kabila regime. In Bandundu province, the people of Bandundu City apparently felt that Kabila had lavished too much attention on the City of Kikwit. As a consequence, the Bandundu people (predominantly Yansi) voted massively for Tshisekedi. In North Kivu, Kamerhe won the support of Hunde and other *autochtones* who resented Kabila's alliance with Rwanda and the Tutsi.[11]

The elections of 2011 set off violence that appeared to reprise the inter-ethnic violence of 1959–62. Luba-Kasai were attacked and forced to flee Katanga, as in 1959–60 (and in 1993). At Lodja, local "people of the forest" attacked Tetela of the savanna, as in 1962–4. However, a closer look revealed important differences. In Katanga, Luba-Katanga took the lead in driving out their Kasaian homonyms, whereas in 1959–60 Lunda and other southern Katangans had led the campaign. At Lodja, the fighting pitted forces loyal to Lambert Mende, Kabila's minister of information and head of the Convention des Congolais Unis (Convention of United Congolese, CCU), against people associated with Dr. Adolphe

Onusumba, former head of the RCD-Goma. In 2011, radio stations controlled by Mende and several other Tetela politicians had exchanged verbal attacks, preparing the way for open violence. The dominant theme of 1960–2, according to which the savanna people were *"arabisés"* ("arabized")[12] had disappeared, or at least had been augmented by references to corruption under Kabila.

These cases, and presumably others as well, confirm that rival leaders often incite ethnic violence in conformity with their own agendas.

Ethnic Consciousness in Congo

The predominance of ethnonationalism in DRC is due in part to the fact that the movement for decolonization first acquired momentum in Léopoldville (now Kinshasa) in the mid-1950s and that the pace was set by the Kongo (Bakongo) people, whose ethnic identity was more ideologized than those of most other Congolese. In Deutsch's terms, they were more mobilized and less integrated than other peoples.

A central element in Kongo sub-nationalism is the belief that all the Kongo-speaking people descend from the inhabitants of the Kingdom of Kongo, which had been divided by the French, Belgians, and Portuguese. This belief is a myth. The Kingdom included six provinces, three of which lay in what is now DRC. The remainder, including the capital São Salvador (aka Mbanza Kongo), lay in Angola. North of the Congo River, in what are now DRC, Cabinda, and Congo-Brazzaville, were a number of other kingdoms, culturally related to the Kingdom of Kongo, but politically independent.

The Kingdom of Kongo ceased to exist on a large scale by the eighteenth century. By the twentieth century, the French sociologist Georges Balandier could write that there was no one in the remotest village of the Kongo country who could not recite the tale of São Salvador, where all Kongo came from and still had relatives to receive them.[13] The spread of this myth seems due in part to migrations from the capital, but also to early European visitors picking up the claims of the Kings of Kongo that neighboring kings were their vassals; the missionaries fed the resultant myth back to the Kongo through their schools. The Kongo political party ABAKO of the 1960s (see below) and the present-day politico-religious movement Bundu dia Kongo both claim that Kongo live in Angola, Congo-Kinshasa, Congo-Brazzaville, and Gabon. However, Kikongo-speakers in Congo-Brazzaville and Cabinda do not share this attachment to the former Kingdom. No one in Gabon seems to identify as Kongo. The colonial town of Léopoldville was founded just upriver from the Kongo area (the local people were Hum and Teke). From the early days, the Kongo constituted a major part of the town's population and they came to consider it "their" town.

The major "ethnic group" competing with the Kongo in Léopoldville was the "Bangala," almost entirely a product of colonial ethnogenesis. Henry Morton Stanley reported encountering the Ngala, "the Ashanti of the Congo . . . unquestionably a very superior tribe." These people with their vast (fictional) state were among the early recruits to the colonial army or Force Publique. A lingua franca spoken along the Congo River, Lingala, was adopted as the language of this army.[14]

Large numbers of upriver people settled at Léopoldville, where Lingala began to be used increasingly not only as a language of administration but also as a language of instruction, to the detriment of Kikongo. This led Kongo intellectuals in 1950 to found the Association des Bakongo pour l'Unification, la Conservation et l'Expansion de la Langue Kikongo (Association for the Maintenance, the Unity, and the Expansion of the Kikongo Language), known by the acronym ABAKO and later becoming a political party under the name Association des Bakongo (Bakongo Association). The Belgians recognized ABAKO as a cultural association, and it spread as such from Léopoldville, Matadi, and Thysville (Mbanza-Ngungu) to rural areas. ABAKO was on the ground, ready for the transition to anti-colonial, electoral politics.

In 1956, a Belgian professor, A. A. A. J. van Bilsen published a proposal for decolonizing the Congo over the next thirty years (a radical idea at the time) and the Kongo and Ngala elites immediately took up the idea. A group of *évolués*, mainly "Bangala" in a broad sense and associated with the Catholic journal *Conscience Africaine*, issued a manifesto defending the right of Congolese to be consulted on their future and in favor of Congolese unity. ABAKO responded with its own manifesto, calling for immediate independence. On unity, ABAKO maintained, the "historically, ethnically and linguistically united or related groups" should form their own political parties.

ABAKO won a sweeping victory in December 1957. Many voters from Kwango and Kwilu districts (where Kikongo ya Leta, State Kikongo, was the language of administration and instruction) chose ABAKO. The explosion of popular anger against the colonial administration in January 1959, and the administration's attempt to scapegoat the ABAKO leadership, made the Kongo leaders martyrs in the eyes of many.

In 1959–60, ABAKO's main rival in Léopoldville province was the Parti Solidaire Africain (African Solidarity Party, PSA), in aspiration a national, Congo-wide party. In practice, the PSA largely represented people of Kwilu district, living in the city of Léopoldville and in Kwilu itself. In the 1960 elections, ABAKO swept the Kongo areas, but took only thirty-three seats in the provincial assembly, to thirty-five for the PSA. In response, ABAKO's autonomist tendency came to the surface. Its leaders announced the formation of the province of Kongo Central, with Léopoldville as its capital. "Central" referred to the province's position between the Kongo of Angola and those of Congo-Brazzaville. The centre of Kongo country is the former capital, in northern Angola.

A party using the acronym ABAKO and called the Alliance des Bâtisseurs du Kongo (Alliance of Builders of Kongo) won three National Assembly seats in the 2006 general election. By 2011, this ABAKO had split and two "wings" attempted to register candidates under that label. There does not seem to have been much organizational continuity with the historical ABAKO, but the label remains potent.

ABAKO's province of Kongo Central has proven an enduring feature of the map of Congo. Under Mobutu it existed as "Bas Zaïre." In 2006, the new Constitution recognized Kongo Central as one of twenty-two new provinces. The other great historic demand of the Kongo elite of the 1950s, the defense of their language, is much further from realization. Kinshasa has become a predominantly Lingala-speaking city of 8–10 million people.

In West Kasai, a similar drama played out, with the Lulua playing the role of *autochtones* and the Luba-Kasai that of *allogènes*. The European penetration of Kasai led to crystallization of several distinct ethnic identities among the Luba-speakers of the province. The Europeans initially saw the people who became known as Bena Lulua (Lulua people) as a superior group, and looked down on those who became known as Baluba or Luba-Kasai. After the Lulua had revolted against the Congo Free State, the Luba became precious auxiliaries of the Europeans and dominated the provincial capital, Luluabourg. The groundwork had been set for the drama. In 1944 the Force Publique mutinied, under the influence of Luba *évolués*. Soon thereafter, the Lulua elite organized an ethnic association called Lulua-Frères (Lulua Brothers), which benefited from Belgian support against the Luba, more numerous in the Congolese elite. Large-scale violence broke out, and a million Luba were forced to flee from Luluabourg and environs to the Luba home area around Bakwanga (later, Mbuji-Mayi).[15]

Similar conflict between so-called "locals" and "foreigners" occurred in other areas as well in 1960, directed against Luba-Kasai in the Copper Belt cities of Katanga, against "Kusu" or Maniema people in Bukavu, and so on. The formation of the new *provincettes* in 1962 brought new or previously unnoticed cleavages to the fore, including forest people vs. savanna people among the Tetela, and up-stream people vs. down-stream people among the Luba-Kasai. These cases from the 1950s and 1960s and more recent cases of violence, notably during and after the elections of 2011, offer support to the generalization of Peter Geschiere and Stephen Jackson:

Dangerously flexible in its politics, nervous and paranoid in its language, unmoored from geographic or ethnocultural specificity, borrowing energy both from present conflicts and deep-seated mythologies of the past, the idea of autochthony has permitted comparatively localized instances of violence in the DRC to inscribe themselves upward into regional, and even continental logics, with dangerous implications for the future.[16]

The Kongo and Luba-Kasai communities remain strongly represented in the Congolese elite. Their advantage over other ethnic groups, which began under colonial rule, has continued. Yet neither community has been strongly represented in ruling circles in recent decades. The disparity between educational level and professional attainment, on the one hand, and political power and influence, on the other, is a major source of tension in the Congolese political system.

The Kongo community suffers from fragmented leadership. In the 2006 presidential elections, there were at least six Kongo among the thirty-three presidential candidates. Three of the candidates were women, including the daughter of the first president, Justine Kasa-Vubu, and two sisters, Wivine Nlandu (widow of former premier Nguz Karl-I-Bond) and Marie-Thérèse N'Landu Mpolo Nene (former *chef de cabinet* of the same Nguz). None of the six Kongo candidates passed the bar of 1 percent of the votes cast.

Bundu dia Kongo (Kingdom of Kongo, BDK), an ethno-nationalist and separatist movement, presented candidates in the 2006 parliamentary elections and its leader Ne Muanda Nsemi was elected to the National Assembly. Bundu dia Kongo supported Jean-Pierre Bemba in the second round of the presidential elections. On Daily Motion, YouTube, and other websites, one can follow a fascinating episode in which Ne Muanda Nsemi exposes the ideas of his movement, only to be attacked by another Kongo deputy, Yves Kisombe. The latter argued that the ethnic separatism of Bundu was in sharp contradiction with the line taken by Congo's first president, Joseph Kasa-Vubu. Kisombe was expelled from the MLC on the grounds that he had deviated from party policy in attacking Ne Muanda. This parliamentary exchange followed in the wake of violent repression of Bundu dia Kongo by Congo's national police force.[17] Another prominent Kongo political figure of the past decade is Professor Ernest Wamba dia Wamba. Wamba agreed to become a figurehead for the Rwanda–Uganda invading force in 1998, as president of the RCD. His criticisms of Laurent Kabila were pertinent but his method of action was questionable. Perhaps the most important aspect of Wamba's initiative was the demonstration that some Kongo intellectuals were strongly committed to the Congolese national project. This can be seen also in the major role played by Eugène Diomi Ndongala, a Kongo and head of Démocratie Chrétienne (Christian Democracy), supporting the presidential campaign of the Luba Étienne Tshisekedi in 2011.

The Luba-Kasai, for their part, remain equally as disaffected as the Kongo. Tshisekedi and his UDPS remain the most popular Luba leader and party. However, Tshisekedi persisted in maintaining that he was the legally elected prime minister and consequently called for a boycott of voter registration in 2006. In 2011, in contrast, he attempted to oust Kabila by the ballot box. He clearly defeated the president in Kinshasa and in East and West Kasai. Had he established an electoral alliance with other important candidates, notably Kamerhe of South Kivu, he might have been able to win the support of a majority of voters. During the election campaign, and especially after the vote, UDPS members and ethnic Luba-Kasai were targets of regime violence.

T. K. Biaya wrote in 1999 that many Luba-Kasai had withdrawn into a self-governing ethnically defined community, within but opposed to the modern state.[18] This is exaggerated, in that many Luba-Kasai remain active not only in politics but in business, education, religion and other fields.

Ethnicity and Autochthony in the Kivus

The Luba-Kasai and Kongo are two of the leading ethnic communities in the national elite, and each has suffered from the resentment of neighboring groups. Much the same thing occurred in the former Kivu province (now divided into North Kivu, South Kivu, and Maniema). In South Kivu, the Shi were the leading ethnic group and at the same time the leaders of the *autochtones*. The main Rwandophone group, the Banyamulenge, lagged far behind.

In North Kivu, the "Banyarwanda" (and especially the Tutsi among them) were a leading group like the Luba-Kasai, resented by other groups. There was the crucial difference, of course, that the Banyarwanda or Rwandophones included people whose ancestors had been in Congo for centuries, and others who had come very recently. I will discuss South Kivu first, and then come back to talk about North Kivu.

The Banyamulenge and Their Neighbors in South Kivu

The Banyamulenge of South Kivu, in whose name Rwanda invaded Zaïre/Congo in 1996, are the product of recent ethnogenesis. They are the strangers, the *allogènes*, as opposed to the self-proclaimed locals, especially the Bembe, Lega, Furiiru (or Fulero), Vira, and Lega of Fizi, Mwenga, and Uvira territories. They are the people of Mulenge (a village in the Chefferie des Bafulero) as opposed to other Rwandan Tutsi, including those who fled the "Social Revolution" in 1959 and thereafter, some of whom joined the Simba Rebellion (Lumumbist insurrection of 1964–5).

Although many consider the Banyamulenge to be foreigners, some of their forebears almost certainly arrived in South Kivu before the founding of the Congo Free State in 1885. One should not assume that all the ancestors of the Banyamulenge left the same point of origin, traveled together, and reached their destination at the same time. Although the Belgians referred to the future Banyamulenge as "Ruanda" and the majority of the Banyamulenge themselves claim Rwandan origins, some Banyamulenge families claim to be of Rundi descent.

Under colonial rule and since, having one's own administrative subdivision has symbolized identity, in addition to instrumental advantages. The Belgian administration tended to ignore the presence of the Tutsi pastoralists in South Kivu or to consider them to be foreigners. Some time after World War II, it recognized a *groupement*[19] of "Ruanda" within the Chefferie des Bavira, even placing people of other ethnic origins under the authority of the chief of this *groupement*. In 1952, however, it dissolved it. The Banyamulenge resisted taxes and the census. They supposedly posed a danger of dominating "the Congolese people," according to the geographer Georges Weis, and because of their uncooperative attitude, they faced "severe discrimination."[20]

The questions of chieftaincy and administrative structure have continued to perturb relations between the Banyamulenge and their neighbors. In 1961, the territorial council of Uvira territory refused a request for formation of a separate *groupement* for Banyamulenge within the Chefferie des Bavira. Not until the second Congo war, when the RCD was running South Kivu on behalf of Rwanda, were the Banyamulenge of Fizi, Uvira, and Mwenga united in a single territory of Minembwe. Once DRC had been reunited, Minembwe territory and other creations of the RCD administration (Bunyakiri territory, Chefferie de Buzi, Collectivité Urbano-Rurale de Kashi) disappeared from the map.

The Banyamulenge pastoralists had remained largely detached from national politics in 1960, but were forcibly brought into the broader political arena in 1964, when Uvira-Fizi became the launching pad of the eastern front of the Lumumbist rebellion. Once they had been defeated in the Ruzizi Plain and at Uvira, many rebels of Fulero, Bembe, and Vira origin retreated to the high plateau. The rebels taxed the Banyamulenge or raided their cattle. In response, the Banyamulenge sided with the Armée Nationale Congolaise (Congolese National Army, ANC). This transformed the rebellion against the Kinshasa government into an ethnic war between Bembe, Vira, and Fulero on the one hand, and Banyamulenge, on the other. Young Banyamulenge, armed and trained by the ANC, pushed back the rebels, enabling civilians to return to the high plateau. As compensation, the Congolese government offered "full access to education, social services and employment opportunities. The result was the formation of a new politico-military Banyamulenge elite and a socio-political emancipation of the entire Banyamulenge society that became well aware of its own identity and its delicate position within Congolese society."[21] To differentiate themselves from the Tutsi refugees of 1959 who had supported the Lumumbist rebellion, the Banyarwanda Tutsi of the high plateau adopted the ethnic label Banyamulenge. From the late 1960s onward, the Banyamulenge struggled on several levels. Locally, they continued to seek their own collectivity. They also sought to represent Uvira in the national legislature. Gisaro Muhoza, a university administrator, was elected deputy in 1977, with support especially from Protestants. Gisaro, who died in the early 1980s, was the last Munyamulenge legislator until Rwanda occupied South Kivu. Banyamulenge candidates were barred in 1982 and 1987.

The Banyamulenge (and the Banyarwanda of North Kivu) also struggled to establish their Congolese nationality. The law of January 5, 1972 granted Zaïrian identity to "all persons of whom one of the ascendants is or was a member of one of the tribes established on the territory of the Republic of Zaïre in its limits of 15 November 1908." People from Ruanda-Urundi living in the province of Kivu before January 1, 1960, and having continued to live in Zaïre, acquired Zaïrian nationality on June 30, 1960. The first clause would appear to recognize as Congolese all true "Banyamulenge," whereas the second would grant recognition also to later immigrants to South Kivu, including some of the Tutsi refugees fleeing the "Social Revolution" in Rwanda. Gisaro was elected during the time when this liberal law was in effect.

In 1981, a more restrictive law replaced the law of 1972. Now one had to demonstrate majority descent from a member of one of the tribes living in Congo before August 1885 (the supposed date of creation of the Congo Free State). This gave rise to a far-fetched argument that since the Free State had army bases in what is now western Rwanda, people from that region should also be able to claim Congolese nationality.

The effects of the 1981 law were more political than legal. The law was not enforced, and identity cards of

Kinyarwanda-speakers were not revoked. However, politicians who feared the number of votes represented by Kinyarwanda-speakers in proposed elections stirred up feelings against them among members of neighboring ethnic groups. In 1989, a special census was conducted to identify Congolese and non-Congolese. It clearly was aimed at "Rwandans" since it was conducted only in North and South Kivu and in two territories of northeast Katanga, just south of the South Kivu border. In some sites, the census was completed without difficulty, but there were accusations of bribery by persons wishing to be certified as Congolese. In several locations, census-takers were chased away by stone-throwing youths.

At the Sovereign National Conference in 1991, Anzuluni Bembe, from the Bembe ethnic community of South Kivu, moved to exclude the Banyamulenge, claiming they were Rwandans. Banyarwanda from North Kivu were similarly excluded from the Conference. After this, leaders of other ethnic groups increasingly challenged the right of Banyamulenge and other Kinyarwanda-speakers to citizenship.

Events in Burundi and Rwanda severely impacted the already bad relations of the Banyamulenge with their neighbors. When the Hutu president of Burundi was assassinated in 1993, many Burundians fled to South Kivu. Banyamulenge were stoned in the streets of Uvira where thousands of Burundians had sought refuge. In 1994, the transitional parliament responded to the flight of hundreds of thousands of Rwandan Hutu to North and South Kivu by creating the "Vangu Commission" to investigate the situation of "foreigners" in the east. The Commission's conclusions reflected a spirit of "ethnic cleansing," according to UN rapporteur Roberto Garretón. It alleged that Rwanda had been attempting to acquire Congolese territory and to supplant its indigenous inhabitants for years and that the Tutsi now were preparing to create a "Hamitic Kingdom," to be known as the United States of Central Africa or the Republic of the Volcanoes.[22]

Feeling increasingly threatened by harassment and arrests and talk of expulsion, many young Banyamulenge men went to Rwanda to join or be trained by the RPA (the army of the new Tutsi-dominated government in Rwanda), which also supplied them with weapons. Others organized their own militia in South Kivu.

In September–October 1996, the conflict between the Banyamulenge and their neighbors became entangled with a conflict between Rwanda and Congo. There were demonstrations against Banyamulenge and further attacks on them by civilians in Uvira. More than thirty-five Banyamulenge allegedly were "extra-judicially executed" and others "disappeared." The Kinshasa government accused Rwanda of having enrolled 3,000 Banyamulenge in its army and of training and infiltrating them to destabilize eastern Zaïre, and Burundi of providing them with rear bases. Banyamulenge who had been officers in the Congo army but had gone to Rwanda after the RPF victory in July 1994 allegedly were commanding the infiltrators. Mortar fire was exchanged across the Rwanda–Congo border. A cease-fire was agreed and promptly broken.

Violent combat was reported in Uvira on October 18–20. So-called "Banyamulenge" attacked the Uvira refugee camp. It seems likely that many of the attackers were in fact regular troops from Burundi and Rwanda, passing themselves off as Banyamulenge. Several hundred thousand refugees were displaced, mainly Rwandan and Burundian Hutu. Some fled south into Tanzania, others north to Bukavu.

On October 25, a week after the first attack on the Uvira camp, the "rebels" announced the creation of the AFDL. This supposedly was an alliance of four Congolese resistance groups, including one of Banyamulenge and other ethnic groups from South Kivu. The AFDL could not have launched the first attacks at Uvira, since it did not exist at the time.

The seizure of power first in South Kivu, then in Kinshasa, left the Banyamulenge in a paradoxical position. The war had been waged first in their name, then in that of the AFDL. Even before Laurent Kabila's forces reached Kinshasa, however, the rebel movement was disintegrating. Kabila and other Congolese "rebels" were asserting their independence vis-à-vis Angola, Rwanda, and Uganda. "Tutsi" and "Katangans" exchanged gunfire at Goma and at Lubumbashi.

The Banyarwanda and Their Neighbors in North Kivu

Politics in North Kivu has been dominated by the Rwando-phone question. It is particularly difficult to understand who is who in this province. In part, this is because the historical record is vague on key points. To a large extent, however, it is because North Kivu is peripheral to Rwanda, the history of which is so heavily ideologized. Rwandan history, particularly as synthesized by Abbé (Father) Kagame, was center-focused and teleological. It tended to confuse the zone of Rwandan culture with the zone of state control. It may be useful to think comparatively, comparing pre-colonial Rwanda to pre-colonial Luba, with a monarchy at the core and various populations at the periphery, speaking similar languages and considering themselves Rwanda or Luba in some contexts.

The largest population of Kinyarwanda-speakers of pre-colonial North Kivu was the Banyabwisha (people of Bwisha), mostly Hutu. There were some Tutsi pastoralists, who (like the future Banyamulenge, to the south) had fled beyond the control of the Rwandan state. Other Tutsi seem to have been sent out by the Rwandan court during times of military expansion as a way of claiming this Kinyarwanda-speaking area for itself. Royal control over Bwisha was never reliable. As in Bugoyi (western Rwanda, east of Bwisha), this was an area that never really responded to the call of the court, although it was not overtly resistant, as were the Kiga populations (in what is now northern Rwanda and Uganda).

Some descriptions of the Bwisha/Rutshuru area mention the transmission of taxes to the court in central Rwanda; others stress that the local rulers (the *mwami* or *muhinza* of each microstate) did not accept orders from anyone and continued an independent life. Both descriptions are partly valid, in that the area was marginally and episodically linked to the Rwandan court.

Apart from the Banyabwisha, there were Kinyarwanda-speaking Tutsi pastoralists in the present North Kivu. Like the Banyamulenge of South Kivu, these people came in very small independent groups. They sought open land and good grazing. Far from representing the extension of Rwandan state power, they were refugees from it. Dr. Richard Kandt, the German Resident (colonial administrator) at the Rwandan court in the 1890s, met some of them near the Mokoto Lakes, in what is now Masisi territory. He wrote that "several Watussi" visited him. He found them to be "likable and simple" but "not so handsome and elegant" as the Tutsi of Burundi and Rwanda, because these men had to work. They were not the "sovereigns of the country" but lived in small villages, alongside the farmers who were the first inhabitants of the region. This was near Kischari (i.e. Gishari), where a Rwandophone *chefferie* would be created under Belgian rule.[23]

The Belgians were of two minds as to the Kinyarwanda-speakers of the Congo. Colonial ethnography, intended to guide administrative activity, sometimes refers to Banyarwanda and mentions Tutsi, Hutu, and Twa subcategories. Other documents refer to the Hutu of Rutshuru and the minorities of Tutsi and Twa disappear.

The Belgians tended to move toward what Vlassenroot calls the "territorialization of ethnicity."[24] They created two predominantly Nande territories, Beni and Lubero. Rutshuru was a Hutu (Rwandophone) territory, although there were some Tutsi and some Hunde living there. Masisi included one *chefferie* each for the Hunde, Nyanga, and Kano. It also included a separate *chefferie* of Gishari for transplanted Rwandans. In the aftermath of a revolt in 1944 sparked by the Kitawala millenarian movement, the Belgians transformed these *chefferies* (with hereditary rulers) into sectors with appointed chiefs to facilitate tighter administrative control.

Rutshuru was divided into two territories in 1953. The new Rutshuru territory corresponded to the *chefferie* of Bwisha while the Bukumu *chefferie* became the territory of Goma. In the same year, Masisi was cut in two; the new Masisi included the Bahunde and Gishari *chefferies*, while Walikale included the Nyanga and Kano sectors.

The final changes of administrative structure came in 1957. Gishari *chefferie* was eliminated and its Banyarwanda population absorbed into the Bahunde *chefferie*. Goma and

Butembo, the two most important towns of North Kivu, became *centres extra-coutumiers* (i.e. towns not governed by customary law).

Belgian manipulation of Congolese populations and administrative boundaries exacerbated the problems of local Congolese. Rutshuru was densely populated when the Belgians arrived, yet they moved people around in ways that increased pressure on the land. They moved Hutu out to clear space for European coffee planters. They created the Virunga National Park, which took up half of Rutshuru territory, and cut the Bwisha *chefferie* in two.

In contrast, Masisi territory was sparsely populated, mainly by Hunde. The Belgians decided to "develop" it, by bringing in Hutu from Rwanda to work on European plantations. They needed "suitable," willing workers, and the Hunde supposedly were less "suitable" and less willing to work for Belgian planters. Another motivation was to ease population pressure in famine-prone Rwanda.

In 1937, the Belgian authorities in Rwanda and Kivu and the parastatal Comité National du Kivu signed an agreement to create a new body called the Mission d'Immigration des Banyaruanda (Banyarwanda Immigration Mission, MIB). The MIB was charged with managing immigration of Rwandans to Masisi, including their political organization and the salaries to be paid to the plantation workers.

The Belgians had recently fused many tiny Hunde chiefdoms and placed the resultant Chefferie des Bahunde under a single neo-traditional *mwami*, André Kalinda. They then persuaded the new *mwami* to sell a piece of Hunde land to the newcomers.

The Belgians next asked the Rwandan authorities to supply a number of their subjects as emigrants. They promised Rwanda's Mwami Rudahigwa the emigrants would preserve close political ties with Rwanda. The Belgians were aware that this arrangement might lead to problems. Under international law, the mandated territory of Ruanda-Urundi and the Colony of Belgian Congo were absolutely distinct. Belgium could not permit a conflict over the rights of the Rwandan *mwami* to lead to a call for annexation of part of Kivu to

Rwanda. That would draw unwelcome attention from the League of Nations, or later the United Nations.

About this time, Abbé Kagame published an account of Rwandan history according to which Rwanda had conquered vast portions of the present eastern Congo as early as the fifteenth century. Implicitly, in buying Gishari from the Hunde, Rwanda was merely reasserting its control over its own rightful property. This point of view is endorsed in contemporary Rwanda, which nonetheless maintains that it respects the boundaries of its DRC neighbor.

Over 80,000 Rwandans were settled in Masisi between 1937 and 1955. Initially the Rwandan monarch attempted to send a majority of Tutsi. Once the Belgian administration discovered that this was happening, it reversed the trend and the majority of those transplanted were Hutu, deemed more "useful" (i.e. useful to the Belgian colonizers).

Given Belgium's policy of territorialized ethnicity, it was important to the transplanted Rwandans that they have their own collectivity. The Belgians initially recognized a Chefferie de Gishari, on an equal footing with the Chefferie des Bahunde from which the land had been detached. Conflict continued, now in the form of efforts by the Rwandophones to enlarge their circumscription at the expense of their Hunde neighbors. In 1957, the Belgians abolished the Gishari unit, but transplantation had proceeded to the point that the reunified Chefferie des Bahunde had a Rwandophone majority. Other Rwandophone majority circumscriptions in North Kivu included the Centre Extra-Coutumier de Goma, and the Bwisha, Bwito, and Bukumu chefferies.

The predominantly Hutu Banyabwisha and the scattered Tutsi pastoralists constitute a first category of Rwandophones in North Kivu, populations of pre-colonial origin. A second category includes migrants of the colonial period. This migration generally was coercive. In addition to the migration organized by the MIB (mainly but not only to Masisi), this included significant recruitment to Katanga's mines. Many of these people stayed and became permanent residents of Congo. Some signed up as a way of avoiding the demands of the chiefs in Rwanda, but their migration was highly regulated. A third subcategory of colonial migrants comprised Rwandans who fled west individually to evade the exactions of the chiefs. Such people often sought to include themselves in the structures of Congo, to obscure their origins, and they often became long-term workers on plantations, and so on, sometimes in fairly high positions.

The "Social Revolution" in Rwanda, when Hutu overthrew the Tutsi monarchy and killed or chased out many of their Tutsi neighbors, led to a third wave of migration to Congo (and to other neighboring countries: Uganda, Tanganyika, and Burundi). Many of the 59ers, and those who came in 1963 in response to renewed anti-Tutsi violence, were from very high-status families. They often were wealthy, and quickly blended into Congolese society, as professionals and bureaucrats. Some settled on Ijwi Island (briefly annexed by Rwanda late in the nineteenth century), where they gave cows to the local authorities, who in turn gave them land and guaranteed their security. The presence of a large Rwandophone community in Congo made it easy for the refugees of 1959 and 1963 to melt in, especially since Hutu–Tutsi tensions in Congo were not as great as they would become later on.

The "locals" tended to react to the influx of *allogènes* in the light of previous experience. Around Ihula (Walikale territory), land was available and relations between the Tutsi refugees and the local Nyanga apparently were good. In Masisi territory, by contrast, the refugees were settled despite fierce opposition from the locals. Under pressure from the UNHCR, Hunde notables granted provisional permission for the refugees to settle at Bibwe, but insisted that the land on which they settled remained Hunde property.

In 1963, tensions between Rwandophones and their Hunde neighbors boiled over in Masisi owing to a mutual sentiment of injustice. The Rwandophones paid Hunde chiefs for access to land. Politically the Rwandophones were dependent on the Hunde, and economically the Hunde were dependent on the Rwandophones. The Rwandophones felt they already owned the land they were farming and did not see why they should continue to pay "customary" rent to the chief. The Hunde saw the Rwandophones as trying to escape from their obligations. Hunde had replaced the Hutu administrators put in place by the Belgians. As a consequence, Banyarwanda started losing land, houses, shops, cattle, and plantations. They tried to fight back to reclaim their rights. The result was the two-year war called "Kanyarwanda," after a mythical ancestor of all Rwandans.[25]

The Banyarwanda or Rwandophones of North Kivu constituted one of two main ethnic elites in North Kivu, the other being the Nande of Beni-Lubero ("*le grand nord*" in local parlance). The "*grand nord*," evangelized by the Assumptionist Fathers, had a relatively dense network of primary and post-primary schools, resulting in a sizable Nande elite.

The southern portion of North Kivu (where most of Congo's Banyarwanda lived) was part of the Apostolic Vicariate of Bukavu until 1959, when a separate Vicariate of Goma was created. Because the network of primary and post-primary schools was relatively less developed in the Goma area, pupils from Goma, Rutshuru, Masisi, and Walikale had to go south to Bukavu to pursue their studies. Within the southern portion of North Kivu, missions and schools were set up almost exclusively among the Banyarwanda. The Hunde and especially the Nyanga were neglected.

These disparities show up in the political sphere, and constitute a potent source of conflict at both elite and mass levels. Two Banyarwanda and one Nyanga of North Kivu served as minister under Lumumba in 1960. The governments of Cyrille Adoula (1961–4) included two Banyarwanda, one Nande, and one Nyanga. The imbalance in the Catholic Church hierarchy was even more striking, as Yves Musoni Musana shows.[26]

Shortly after independence, Congolese politicians decided to divide the six colonial provinces into smaller *provincettes*, in part as a means of incorporating ABAKO's "Kongo Central" into Congo's constitutional structures. In Kivu, there was considerable controversy around maintaining Kivu unity versus dividing it to create the *provincette* of North Kivu. The Banyarwanda tended to favor Kivu unity since they were dominant in Goma but also had important interests in

Bukavu. The Nande tended to favor a North Kivu from which the Rwandophones would be excluded.

The Simba or Lumumbist rebels never entered Masisi, their path having taken them from Uvira west to Maniema and on to Kisangani. However, the Hunde and others accused the Banyarwanda of rebellion. On that basis they obtained the aid of Mobutu's army to crush their enemies.

After taking power in 1965, Mobutu reunified most of the provinces, while stripping them of their autonomous governments. In 1988, he redivided Kivu and re-established North Kivu (as the first step in a plan to divide most provinces). Also under Mobutu, the colonial system of land control and alienation was transformed. The Bakajika Law of 1973 made all land in Zaïre/Congo state property. This set off a series of land conflicts that has yet to subside, not least in North Kivu.

The Congo wars of 1996 and 1998 came to a North Kivu already in flames. The two wars interacted with the ongoing war in the province. Losers in one round of fighting became winners in the next. Failure to understand this helps to explain the failure of efforts to bring peace to the province.

As Stanislas Bucyalimwe Mararo argues, North Kivu was "the only province in the DRC that suffered from an uninterrupted war in the last nine years (1993–2002). The war itself is the result and/or the expression of 'multilayered conflicts' although some outdo others in historical depth, scale and consequences. The actors are always the same." During the years of warfare – two decades and counting – what has changed "is only the stakes involved and the strategies set up to cope with them."[27]

The effort of the Rwandan Patriotic Front to seize power in Rwanda had a direct impact on North Kivu. The RPF war began with an invasion from Uganda in 1990, but Bucyalimwe claims that the RPF was active in North Kivu starting in 1987 or 1988, recruiting and training fighters and building up a rear base for its upcoming military campaign. These activities could not fail to have consequences in a North Kivu region already characterized by tense relations among the various communities and their respective elites.

Between 1990 and 1992, localized clashes were recorded in several areas of North Kivu: these included widespread incidents over the population census called "identification des nationaux" within Masisi; Hunde against Hutu in Bukumbiriri (Masisi); and Tutsi against Hutu in Jomba (Bwisha, Rutshuru) and Kihondo (Bwito, Rutshuru).[28]

Starting in 1992, inter-ethnic violence increased, and was often carried out with the complicity of Zaïrian (Congolese) provincial and national leaders and security forces. By 1993, there was a real war, as the entire territory of Masisi and some parts of Walikale and Rutshuru were driven into bloody violence.

The conflict originally pitted the Hutu and Tutsi ethnic groups, collectively known as the "Banyarwanda," who constituted half of the population of North Kivu but had been largely excluded from regional political office and administrative posts, against the Hunde, Nyanga, and Nande ethnic groups, who consider themselves native to the region and have sought to protect their political power. Some of the locals expressed the fear that the Banyarwanda had designs to take over North Kivu.

It is often said that the Mayi-Mayi were created in response to the 1996 Rwanda–Uganda invasion. In reality, starting in March 1993, Hunde, Nyanga, and Nande militia groups called Mayi-Mayi or Bangilima, which apparently had the support of local political officials, began to attack the Banyarwanda in several territories of North Kivu. In response, the Hutu, who were the main targets of the attacks, formed their own militia. Attacks and counter-attacks by rival ethnic militias continued for nearly six months, leaving approximately 6,000 dead and displacing an estimated 250,000. Through the action of local nongovernmental organizations, churches, and the central government, which deployed elite troops in Masisi, a tenuous peace was restored to the region in July 1993, and most people were able to return to their home communities. However, none of the underlying political issues were resolved, thus setting the stage for the resumption of violence.

The genocide in neighboring Rwanda in 1994 and the subsequent flight of mostly Hutu Rwandan refugees into

North Kivu fanned inter-ethnic tensions in the province. Some of the Rwandan refugees arrived well armed, and they worked to politicize and organize the local Hutu population, joining Congolese Hutu to form joint Interahamwe militia groups. The massive inflow of refugees augmented significantly the numerical advantage of the Banyarwanda, increasing tensions between them and other groups. At the same time, ethnic conflict and genocide in Rwanda led to a divide within the Banyarwanda community in Zaïre/Congo between Hutu and Tutsi, and thousands of Tutsi crossed over to Rwanda and Uganda in the months following the end of the genocide.

In late 1995, the level of violence in North Kivu intensified sharply, following several confrontations in Masisi between government soldiers and various militia groups. Attacks by rival Interahamwe and Mayi-Mayi/Bangilima militias quickly spread throughout Masisi and Rutshuru Zones. In contrast to the 1993 conflict, Hutu had the upper hand in these clashes, owing to their abundant armaments and extensive militia organization, but Mayi-Mayi also succeeded in pushing Hutu out of certain areas, particularly in Walikale, Lubero, and Rutshuru. Both Interahamwe and Mayi-Mayi attacked the Tutsi, and thousands were forced to flee into Rwanda.

Zaïrian (Congolese) authorities showed little interest in ending the violence, according to Human Rights Watch.[29] On the contrary, witnesses reported that local officials and soldiers participated in militia attacks against Tutsi, and there was evidence of official involvement in attacks by Hutu and Hunde militias since the beginning of the conflict in 1993. National and regional politicians apparently were unwilling to take steps that might halt the attacks, including publicly denouncing the abuses and supporting a disciplined military presence in the region to protect civilians. The few soldiers and police stationed in the area themselves frequently profited from the situation, looting from the various sides and essentially selling their services to the highest bidder, which contributed to the climate of impunity. The provincial governor fueled the conflict in 1993 when he suggested that security forces would assist efforts by Nyanga and Hunde to "exterminate" the Banyarwanda.

The international community responded to the growing conflict in North Kivu with silence and indifference, Human Rights Watch writes.[30] The poor handling of the refugee crisis exacerbated the simmering conflict, with predictable consequences. Efforts by local and international NGOs to alert the international community about the potential for renewed violence were ignored. In April 1996, as killings were taking place on a daily basis in North Kivu, France announced a resumption of bilateral aid to the Mobutu government, which had been cut off in late 1991.

Rwanda and Zaïre each accused the other of manipulating the refugee situation in their respective countries and both sides denied citizenship to the Tutsi refugees. The Zaïrian government went so far as to deny that Kinyarwanda was spoken in Zaïre. The Rwanda government contended that the refugees were Zaïrian citizens fleeing violence, and established a refugee camp in Gisenyi, about a kilometer away from the border. Despite appeals by the UNHCR that the camp be moved away from the border, the government refused.

The theme of ethnic conflict was prominent throughout the first and second wars, and has been in the so-called "postwar period" since 2003. However, the conflict was never as simple as one ethnic group struggling against another, even though the media tended to propagate such simplifications, and of course to focus on individuals to the neglect of constituencies and coalitions associated with them. Thus it was that the conflict in North and South Kivu was presented to a large extent in terms of Tutsi versus Hutu or even the fight of Tutsi General Laurent Nkunda against the Kabilas in Kinshasa.

After the formal end of the second war in 2003, extreme violence continued. Various ethnically defined forces – including but not limited to Tutsi and Hutu – struggled to control the mineral-rich provinces of North and South Kivu. Rwanda also continued to support Tutsi forces in DRC. (Plunder of minerals will be discussed in greater detail in Chapter 5.)

Under the terms of the peace accords, the "rebel" armies were to be merged into the national army. Nkunda, a

Kinyarwanda-speaking Tutsi from North Kivu, had joined the RPA during its fight against the Habyarimana government. He served in the army of the Rwanda-sponsored RCD-Goma during the second Congo war (1998–2002), and directed the brutal suppression of an anti-Rwandan (or anti-Tutsi) mutiny at Kisangani; 160 people were killed.

In 2003, with the official end of the war, Nkunda joined the new integrated national army as a colonel and was promoted to general in 2004. However, he soon rejected the authority of the Kinshasa government and retreated with some of the RCD-Goma troops to the forests of Masisi territory, North Kivu.

In May 2004, Nkunda's forces occupied Bukavu (South Kivu), where they were accused of committing war crimes. Nkunda claimed he was attempting to prevent genocide against the Banyamulenge (Tutsi of South Kivu), a claim that was rejected by the United Nations mission (MONUC). Following UN negotiations, Nkunda and his men withdrew to North Kivu. Banyamulenge troops under Colonel Jules Mutebutsi left for Rwanda.

In 2005, Nkunda called for the overthrow of the Kinshasa government owing to its corruption; increasing numbers of former RCD-Goma soldiers deserted the DRC army to join his forces. In January and August 2006, his troops clashed with DRC army forces. MONUC refused to act on the international warrant that was issued for Nkunda's arrest, stating (incredibly): "Mr. Laurent Nkunda does not present a threat to the local population, thus we cannot justify any action against him."

During both the first and second rounds of the violent 2006 general election, Nkunda had said he would respect the results. On November 25, however, shortly before the Supreme Court ruled that Joseph Kabila had won the second round, Nkunda's forces undertook an offensive at Sake (near Goma) against the DRC army, clashing also with MONUC peacekeepers. The UN called on the DRC government to negotiate with Nkunda, and the government sent the interior minister, General Denis Kalume, to eastern DRC to begin talks.

In December 2006, ex-RCD-Goma troops attacked DRC army positions in North Kivu. With military assistance from MONUC, the DRC army reportedly regained its positions, with about 150 RCD-Goma men having been killed. At the end of 2006, Nkunda and his men announced that they were fighting on behalf of the CNDP.

In early 2007, the Kinshasa government attempted to reduce the Nkunda threat by trying to integrate his troops further into the FARDC, using so-called "*mixage*." In DRC military French, *brassage* is the process whereby ex-combatants are retrained, integrated into the FARDC, and deployed far away from their former operational area. *Mixage*, a neologism, supposedly was preparatory to *brassage*. As carried out in North Kivu, it involved creating mixed brigades by putting battalions loyal to Nkunda and to the central command under the same commanding officers. It had the effect of expanding Nkunda's influence beyond his base in Rutshuru territory. From January to August 2007, Nkunda controlled five brigades of troops rather than two.

Faced with continued fighting, the United Nations changed its public stance on Nkunda. In July 2007, the UN peacekeeping head, Jean-Marie Guéhenno, stated, "Mr. Nkunda's forces are the single most serious threat to stability in the DR Congo." In early September, Nkunda's forces had a smaller DRC force under siege in Masisi, and MONUC helicopters were ferrying government soldiers to relieve the town. Scores of men were reported killed. On September 5, 2007, after the government forces claimed they had used a Mi-24 helicopter gunship to kill eighty of Nkunda's rebels, Nkunda called on the government to return to a peace process. "It's the government side who have broken the peace process," he said. "We are asking the government to get back on the peace process, because it is the real way to resolve the Congolese problem." Also in September, Nkunda's men reportedly raided ten secondary schools and four primary schools, where they took the children by force. Girls were taken as sex slaves and boys were used as fighters, in violation of international law.

The government set a October 15, 2007 deadline for Nkunda's troops to begin disarming. This deadline passed without action and on October 17 President Kabila ordered the military to prepare to disarm Nkunda's forces forcibly. Government forces advanced on the Nkunda stronghold of Kichanga. There were separate reports of government troops engaging units under Nkunda around Bunagana. Fighting in the "*petit nord*" was estimated to have displaced over 370,000 since the beginning of the year.

In early November 2007, Nkunda's troops captured the town of Nyanzala, 100 kilometers (62 miles) north of Goma. A government counter-offensive in early December resulted in seizure of the town of Mushake, overlooking a key road. This followed a statement by MONUC that it would be willing to offer artillery support to the government offensive. In a regional conference, the United States, Burundi, Rwanda, and Uganda pledged to support the Congolese government and not support "negative forces" (an expression habitually used for the FDLR, but which could refer to Nkunda's men in the current context).

Early in 2008, a peace deal was signed, including provisions for an immediate ceasefire, the phased withdrawal of all rebel forces in North Kivu province, the resettlement of thousands of villagers, and immunity for Nkunda's forces. Neither the FDLR nor the Rwandan government took part in the talks. The agreement encouraged the FARDC and the United Nations to remove FDLR forces from Kivu. Dissatisfaction with progress and lack of resettlement of refugees caused the CNDP to declare war on the FDLR and hostilities to resume, including atrocities against civilians.

On October 26, 2008 Nkunda seized a major military camp, along with Virunga National Park. The park was taken owing to its strategic location on a main road leading to the city of Goma. On October 27, civilians pelted the United Nations building in Goma with rocks and threw firebombs, claiming that the UN forces had done nothing to prevent the rebel advance. The Congolese national army also retreated under pressure from the rebel army. MONUC peacekeepers used helicopter gunships and armored vehicles to halt the advance of the rebels, who claimed to be within 7 miles (11 kilometers) of Goma. MONUC head Alan Doss explained the necessity of engaging the rebels, stating that "[the UN] can't allow population centers to be threatened."

On October 28, rebels and combined government–MONUC troops battled between the Kibumba refugee camp and Rutshuru. Rebel forces later captured the town. Civilians rioted, at some points pelting retreating Congolese troops with rocks. On October 29, the rebels declared a unilateral ceasefire as they approached Goma, though they still intended to take the city. That same day several countries refused a French request for a EU reinforcement of 1,500 troops. Throughout the day the streets of Goma were filled with refugees and fleeing troops, including their tanks and other military vehicles. The UN Security Council unanimously condemned the recent rebel advance and demanded it be halted. On October 31, Nkunda declared that he would create a "humanitarian aid corridor" to allow displaced persons to return to their homes. On November 6, however, CNDP rebels broke the ceasefire and took control of the town of Nyanzale.

At the end of 2008, having failed to defeat Nkunda, Kabila was forced to reach a "secret" agreement with Kagame. The Rwandan army entered North Kivu for joint operations against the FDLR. In exchange, the Rwandans lured Nkunda into the open for a meeting, and then arrested him. The Kinshasa government began dealing with an alternative CNDP leadership under General Bosco Ntaganda. "The Terminator," as Ntaganda was known, was another Kinyarwanda-speaking Tutsi from North Kivu. Embarrassingly for MONUC (which had pledged to support the FARDC in its efforts to eliminate the FDLR), he had been indicted for war crimes committed in Ituri when he was fighting on behalf of the Rwanda-supported, predominantly Hema movement, the UPC. The imprisoned Nkunda retained considerable support in the CNDP and the Congolese Tutsi community in general, despite a campaign of assassination of pro-Nkunda elements, carried out by Ntaganda or his Rwandan backers.[31]

Among the Tutsi of North Kivu, Nkunda was known as a Munyanduga: that is, a Tutsi from the core area of the Rwandan monarchy, established in North Kivu for generations. Ntaganda, born near Ruhengeri (northwest Rwanda), was a Mugogwe, from a Tutsi group autonomous vis-à-vis the monarchy and seen as an outsider imposed on North Kivu by Kigali.

By 2011, two years after the secret deal between Kagame and Kabila, it was clear that the attempt to resolve the deadly conflict in eastern Congo by military force was failing and would have to be modified fundamentally by the Kinshasa government and the international community. Government soldiers still were battling militias for control of land and mines. Neither side had the strength to win, but both had the resources to prolong the fighting. Civilians continued to suffer extreme violence, and the humanitarian situation was deteriorating. Ethnic tensions had worsened in anticipation of the repatriation of tens of thousands of Congolese refugees who fled to Rwanda during the 1990s. The UN Security Council had watched the deterioration of security in eastern Congo without opposing the decisions of Kagame and Kabila. But as the International Crisis Group pointed out, "A strategy based on secret presidential commitments, however, will not bring peace to the Kivu[s]: the present approach must be re-evaluated and broadened in order to engage all local communities and prepare the future of the region in a transparent dialogue that also involves neighbouring countries."[32] That would mean that the Tutsi-dominated government in Kigali would have to engage in negotiation with the FDLR, perhaps through intermediaries. It continued to refuse to do so, and instead carried out assassinations of FDLR leaders.

In 2010, the role of Rwanda in the Congo conflict had attained greater visibility (or audibility, for those who prefer the metaphor of "silence"). The Mapping Report of the United Nations High Commissioner for Human Rights made it clear that all parties to the conflicts had committed serious abuses in the period 1993–2003, and that the Rwandans and their Congolese allies may have committed genocide against Rwandan and Congolese Hutu. About the same time, it became known that about 500 Congolese women, men, girls, and boys had been raped in Walikale territory. The perpetrators apparently included FDLR fighters (predominantly

Rwandan Hutu), but also the Mayi-Mayi Cheka (a local force) and a Tutsi-led group under Emmanuel Nsengiyumva, which had defected from the FARDC. The various groups were somewhat defined by their ethnicity, yet the attacks cannot easily be defined as "ethnic conflict": what ethnic groups were fighting one another? There presumably is a link to Walikale's tin mine, but it is not clear how the "conflict minerals" argument explains these mass rapes. "Rape as a weapon" may be a more useful label.

Neither the mass atrocities in Walikale nor the overall situation in eastern DRC since 1993 offers evidence to support the idea that the Tutsi of DRC and Rwanda and their supposed ethnic brothers (Tutsi of Burundi, Hema of Uganda and Ituri, etc.) have been attempting to create a "Tutsi–Hima Empire" in the Great Lakes region. The vicious fighting between the Rwandan and Ugandan armies at Kisangani, Rwanda's attacks on Munyamulenge general Pacifique Masunzu of the FARDC (who responded by allying himself with Hutu of the FDLR and Burundi's FNL), Kagame's betrayal of Nkunda and apparent support for his successor Ntaganda – all these and many other examples suggest that ethnic solidarity is too fickle to have much explanatory value. Despite this, many Congolese, especially in the east, draw on this set of ideas to explain the Rwandan invasions and their response to it. The Mayi-Mayi fighters of General Padiri explain their fight against the invaders by invoking the supposed plan for a "Tutsi–Hima Empire" and ignore all of the contradictory evidence. The Tutsi–Hima Empire theme provides a vehicle for uniting against the outsiders and their presumed fifth column. This theme also is useful in avoiding a discussion of class, including the roles of intellectuals, businessmen, and military officers in prolonging and profiting from the conflict.

During the days of the RCD "rebellion," the Rwandans and their Congolese allies attempted to set up a miniature Rwandan regime in North Kivu, in which the Tutsi minority would dominate the Hutu, and the Banyarwanda (Tutsi plus Hutu) would dominate the other half of the population of the province. This effort was doomed to fail, on at least two counts. First, despite the efforts of General Nkunda and other Tutsi leaders to impose Rwanda-style Tutsi hegemony (condemning their Hutu opponents on grounds of "ethnic hatred" and "divisionism"), the Congolese Hutu had potential allies in Kinshasa, as the 2006 elections made clear. Second, other ethnic communities, including the Hunde and Nyanga of the *"petit nord"* and the Nande of the *"grand nord,"* understandably resisted and continue to resist such a project.

Ethnicity, Province, and Nation in Katanga

North Kivu shares a number of difficulties with other provinces, including problematic relations with the central government and management of revenues deriving from substantial mineral resources. Rather than attempting a series of comparisons, I will examine the complex interaction of ethnic, provincial, and national identities in Katanga province, which has caused so much trouble to the central authorities since independence in 1960. During the election campaign of 2011, a trial was held in the provincial capital, Lubumbashi, of alleged plotters for Katanga independence. The prosecution alleged that these plotters had direct links to the "Katanga gendarmes" of 1960–3. Anti-Kabila forces suggested on the Internet that the trial was a masquerade, organized for electoral purposes by people close to the president, to show him and his provincial allies defending national unity. Certainly, the timing lent itself to such an interpretation.

In February 2012, one of Kabila's closest advisors, the former governor of Katanga Augustin Katumba Mwanke (nicknamed "AK47"), was killed when the private jet in which he was flying crash-landed at Bukavu airport, in South Kivu. The American pilots also were killed. Other passengers, seriously wounded, included the minister of finance Augustin Matata Ponyo, the governor of South Kivu province, and a roving ambassador. Two civilians on the ground were crushed under the plane. Rumors immediately swirled, according to which the mission was to involve a trip to Ijwi Island, in Lake

Kivu. Supposedly Katumba and Matata had been carrying large sums of cash. The story of development of a tourist site on the island supposedly was a cover for a secret meeting with Rwandan officials. The full details may never be known. Whether or not the plots of 2011 and 2012 were real, there has been a struggle for ethno-regional dominance within Katanga since the days of the secession. The four administrative districts of Katanga, which were supposed to have become separate provinces in 2009 under the Constitution of 2006, correspond to four bundles of ethnic and material interests. Haut Lomami district/province, corresponding to the Luba-Katanga homeland, has no international border. In contrast, Lualaba, Haut Katanga, and Tanganyika each have a separate set of problems arising from ethnic, economic, and other ties to neighboring states of Angola, Zambia, and Tanzania.

The Lunda of southwestern Katanga (from whom many of the so-called "gendarmes" of 1960–3 and thereafter have been recruited) have been unenthusiastic about Joseph Kabila, particularly since the conviction of Colonel Edy Kapend and General Yav Nawej (both Lunda) for the murder of Laurent Kabila. The Lunda may also be frustrated by Kabila's failure to create Lualaba province, in southwest Katanga, which they would dominate. Laurent Kabila was a Luba-Katanga by his father and a Lunda by his mother. Since the Lunda practice bilateral descent, Laurent Kabila was a Lunda as well as a Luba. The younger Kabila apparently does not maintain ties with his putative Lunda relatives. (Of course, if Joseph was a Rwandan Tutsi adopted by Laurent Kabila, as critics of Joseph maintain, then all this discussion of Luba and Lunda is moot.)

The Luba-Katanga (or "Balubakat," as they are known, to distinguish them from the Luba-Kasai) constitute the majority of the population in northern Katanga. Joseph Kabila's supposed ethnic family, the Luba of Katanga, has tended to support him and he has reciprocated, using Luba-Katanga in key posts. General John Numbi, commander of the Congolese national police, is a Luba-Katanga and key Kinshasa ally of the president. Another Luba-Katanga, Pastor Ngoy Mulunda, chair of the National Electoral Commission in

2011, had been a close associate of Kabila for years. The president of the Katanga provincial assembly, Gabriel Kyungu, is also a Luba-Katanga. Kabila cannot afford to have Kyungu oppose him (as he threatened to do prior to the 2006 elections); yet neither can he appear to be too close to him if he is to continue to promote national unity, since the ethnic chauvinist Kyungu instigated the anti-Kasaian violence of the 1990s.

Kabila has attempted to balance his Balubakat base by connections to the east of Katanga. Professor Guillaume Samba Kaputo, his national security advisor, until his untimely death, was a Tabwa, born in Moba (Tanganyika district) and raised in Bukavu (South Kivu). Katumba Mwanke of Pweto (Tanganyika district), killed in the plane crash of 2012, was one of Kabila's closest associates and business partners. Moïse Katumbi, wealthy businessman elected governor of the province in 2007, supported Kabila for years but appeared to lose patience with the central government in mid-2011 when the electricity failed in Lubumbashi and Kabila sold assets of the mining company Gécamines to Israeli Dan Gertler. Katumbi and his older brother Katebe Katoto are sons of a Sephardic Jewish businessman named Nissim Soriano, a fact that has furnished grist to the mill of conspiracy theorists. Both brothers were born to Bemba mothers in southeast Katanga's Luapula Valley (Haut Katanga) and became rich in marketing fish. (For more on Katumbi and Gertler, see Chapter 5, pp. 153–4 and 174.) Katumbi was asked to consider being a candidate for president in 2011 but his reply always was that he supported Kabila. By 2011, when the lights went out in Katanga owing to the failures of the national electric company SNEL, Katumbi complained about Katanga being the milkcow of the Congo; this is a traditional Katanga argument, first heard from the Europeans of Katanga under colonial rule.

Perhaps the biggest difference between Katanga and the Kivus is simply that the main problem of autochthony pits "authentic" Katangans against other Congolese, the Luba-Kasai, whereas the equivalent problem in the Kivus concerns the Kinyarwanda-speakers. Following from that, there is no equivalent effort on the part of Angolans or Zambians to persistently intervene in Katangan affairs, as Rwanda does in the Kivus, and especially in North Kivu.

Ethnicity is everywhere in the Great Lakes region, as an idiom of conflict (or occasionally as an idiom of cooperation). In Ituri, conflict supposedly pits Hema against Lendu. On closer inspection, some Hema speak Kihema (a Bantu language, similar to the language of the Toro and Nyoro of Uganda) while others speak the non-Bantu language of the Lendu. The label Lendu may also include the Ngiti, depending on context. There are fourteen ethnic groups in Ituri, according to some accounts, and members of many if not all of these groups have been involved in recent conflict in the Ituri area, as have members of other Congolese ethnic groups (notably the Nande of North Kivu) and of foreign groups (especially from Uganda and Rwanda). Conflicts inevitably are oversimplified, not least by making them "ethnic" when this is only partly the case.

Ethnic groups are not actors. Unlike states, which have designated leaders and decision-makers, they are incapable of taking and executing decisions, even though some political figures may claim to be acting on behalf of the community and other community members may acquiesce for a time.

States and the borders that separate them are everywhere too, even in a part of the world characterized by weak states. The passport control and customs posts on the Uganda–DRC border or on the Rwanda–DRC border attest to the importance of states, even when they are evaded. People who cross borders are recognized first and foremost as citizens of the state they left. A young Congolese of Nande ethnicity said he had been living in Uganda since the age of six. He believed he could pass for a Konjo from Kasese in other parts of the country. However, James said he would still assert his Congolese citizenship: "Actually, your motherland, it is difficult to deny it. For us Nande, we say there is a tree that is planted for your grandfather. If you deny that place, you won't be good in life." For James, Nande were Congolese, despite their historic link to the Konjo in Uganda, and even though the political border between Uganda and DRC is a more recent phenomenon.[33] Many journalists err in discussing ethnicity or "tribalism" without taking into account the most important identity in Central Africa, which is national identity. It is, however, to another significant source of identity, religion, that we finally turn.

Religious Identity in DRC

Religious identity is very important in DRC, as we were reminded once again during the election campaign of 2011 and its immediate aftermath. Congo has become a very Christian country since the nineteenth century, and the communities and identities associated with it are very active in politics.

At the time of the founding of the Congolese state in the 1880s, most Congolese practiced indigenous religions. There were some Christians, mainly among the Kongo people along the Atlantic coast. New missions had been arriving, beginning in the 1860s. The traders from Zanzibar brought in Islam about the same time. Congolese began forming their own Christian or semi-Christian movements, the most important of which are Kimbanguism and Kitawala. By the twenty-first century, roughly 50 percent of the population were estimated to be Roman Catholic; Protestants were about 20 percent; Kimbanguists and Muslims 10 percent each. These faiths constitute identity communities, cross-cutting ethnic and administrative maps.

The Catholic Church had been a pillar of the colonial regime, and was heavily involved in the demonizing of Lumumba in 1959–60. After Mobutu had consolidated his control of the state, he launched attacks on the surviving pillars of the colonial regime, namely the state enterprises, such as the Union Minière du Haut Katanga, and the Catholic Church. The church fought back against Mobutu's "authenticity campaign," under which Christian names were banned. The ensuing struggle was dubbed "the war of the two Josephs" (Cardinal Joseph Malula and Joseph-Désiré Mobutu).

The Catholic Church was strongly involved in the struggle to defeat Mobutu once he had conceded the end of the one-party monopoly. The opposition coalition called itself the Union Sacrée de l'Opposition Radicale et Alliés (Sacred Union of the Radical Opposition and Allies). One of the major members of the coalition was the Parti Démocrate et Social Chrétien (Democratic Social-Christian Party, PDSC), which mobilized many Christians (including some Protestants). Many other Christians supported Tshisekedi's UDPS. The massive "march of the Christians" in Kinshasa in February 1992 signaled the end of Mobutu's hegemony, although (with hindsight) the label "birth of democracy" seems premature.

Monsignor Laurent Monsengwo, cardinal of Kinshasa and *de facto* primate of Congo, played a major role during the struggle for democracy. The Sovereign National Conference appointed him as president because of his reputation for integrity. However, when Mobutu defied the decision of the Sovereign National Conference (CNS) naming Tshisekedi prime minister, he also ordered Monsengwo to shut down the CNS, which he did. When Mobutu created his own parliament, parallel to the parliament emerging from the CNS, Monsengwo aligned himself with the Western powers calling for negotiations between the two blocs. And when the two rival parliaments were merged, he accepted a position as president or speaker of the combined body. Some say the archbishop was too concerned with finding a compromise position to push decisively for democracy, while others go further and suggest that he was trying to advance his own political career.

The Catholic Church has continued to oscillate between two roles in the democratic process, that of facilitator and that of critic. For the first elections under Joseph Kabila, a Catholic priest, Father (Monsieur l'Abbé) Apollinaire Malu Malu, chaired the Independent Electoral Commission. Apart from his own administrative capabilities, he lent the Commission a degree of legitimacy by being a clergyman. In 2011, he handed over the chairmanship of what was now the National Independent Electoral Commission to a Protestant clergyman, Pastor Ngoy Mulunda. When it became clear that the 2011 elections had been a débâcle, the Catholic Church again showed two faces. Archbishop Monsengwo said flatly that Tshisekedi had received more votes than Kabila. Djomo Lola, bishop of Tshumbe and president of the Conférence Episcopale (Conference of Bishops) said that it was not the job of the Catholic Church to count ballots. Supporters of Tshisekedi criticized Djomo for implicitly siding with Kabila. Soon thereafter, the Conférence Episcopale called for the members of the National Independent Electoral Commission to resign. In the meantime, Tshisekedi had declared himself elected and named his own ministers. The whole scenario resembled 1992–4.

Throughout the Kabila years, the other major religious communities have attempted to benefit from the gulf between the presidency and the Catholic Church. Apart from the role of Ngoy Mulunda as chairman of the National Electoral Commission, there were other signs of tension: a Kimbanguist pastor was beaten to death in Kinshasa in December 2011, supposedly because of his support for Kabila. This incident confirms that religious affiliation is a distinct category of identity. The pastor probably was a Kongo, but he was attacked not on that basis but because of his Church affiliation. Similarly, Eugène Diomi Ndongala of Démocratie Chrétienne finds it easy to ally himself with Tshisekedi of the UDPS because both are Catholics and their common adversary Joseph Kabila is a Protestant.

The Absence of Class

Conspicuously absent from the torrent of words surrounding recent events in DRC is any significant attempt to explain what is going on, and to articulate a program for the future, cast in terms of class. This is all the more striking given the dominant position of Marxist ideas in Congolese intellectual circles. Many of those intellectuals, however, seemed to throw their Marxist vocabulary overboard when recruited into Mobutu's single-party regime, or into Wamba's RCD. In both cases, using a lexicon that implied a radical analysis of society would only have exposed the opportunism of the individual using it.

Laurent Kabila, supposedly a Marxist, was not a man of ideas. As French journalists put it, his career linked combat and business. The Belgian leftist Ludo Martens took Kabila seriously, the Congolese scholar Georges Nzongola-Ntalaja less so.[34] As for Joseph Kabila, he has attempted to appeal to the legacies of Lumumba and Mulele, and of course of Laurent Kabila. However, his public utterances and policies are incoherent: notably he gave a speech before the Belgian Senate in 2004 that praised Leopold II and Belgian colonialism.[35]

It does seem that a dose of Marxian analysis and consciousness-raising might do Congo some good. For example, people might describe a conflict in the Minova area, near the border between North and South Kivu, in ethnic terms, as pitting "autochthonous" or "indigenous" people (Havu or Hunde) against Banyarwanda. To the extent that the so-called indigenous people are coffee growers, and the Banyarwanda are cattle raisers, the poor prices paid for coffee and the much better prices paid for milk and beef might mean that the living standards of the indigenous coffee growers fell far below those of the cattle raisers; in turn, that gap in living standards may have encouraged young men to join local militias. But a closer look might reveal that most Kinyarwanda-speakers in the area were not big cattle raisers. On the other side, the coffee growers were not the poorest people by a long shot. The poorest were landless itinerant agricultural laborers, who might work for cattle raisers or coffee growers. One could take the analysis one step further and ask who has an interest in obscuring the question of the ownership or control of the means of production. To promote the idea that "the Banyarwanda" or "the Tutsi" or for that matter "the *autochtones*" do this or that might be a good way of avoiding some awkward questions.

I turn next to an identity that cross-cuts all classes, all regions, all ethnic categories, and that is women.

4 | Congo's War Against Women

The Democratic Republic of Congo may be "the worst place" in the world to be a woman or a child, as many aid workers claim, or it may have lost ground to Niger or Afghanistan in that dubious contest. Whether or not DRC is the worst, it is a terrible place to be a woman or a girl. First of all, warfare has resulted in millions of deaths since 1996. (These are "extra" deaths, beyond those to be expected in a country with DRC's level of development.) Many women have died, and those who have survived have often lost a husband, a child, or other close relative. Second, there has been mass – and frequently multiple – rape of women and girls. (Some men and boys have been raped too, an aspect I will discuss below.) A large number of these rapes have resulted in pregnancies; in many cases, rape victims have been infected with HIV and then been victimized again when their husbands or families have repudiated them.

All sides in the Congo wars have been guilty of rape and other sexual violence. Typically, however, various belligerents put forward partial and partisan accounts in which their own offenses are omitted and those of the opposing forces are highlighted. Even the United Nations force (MONUC, later MONUSCO), supposedly charged with protecting civilians, conforms to this pattern.[1]

The linked topics of mass deaths and mass rapes have generated international controversies, pitting researchers and humanitarian activists against one another. Some of the disputes have followed disciplinary lines, setting demographers in opposition to epidemiologists. Reports on each topic raise similar problems of how to generalize from limited data, both across regions and across time. Are the limited number of individual informants and households, usually in the former combat zone of the east, typical of the entire combat zone and/or the entire DRC? What is the baseline against which change can be measured, and how can "snapshots" at a point in time be interpreted so as to indicate the direction and magnitude of change?

These battles among specialists, amplified and simplified by journalists and human rights activists, blanket the globe, giving the lie to the oft-repeated call to end the silence. Rather than a silence, there is a cacophony concerning DRC. One must sort out what has happened and is happening before sensible decisions can be made as to how to curb the massive sexual and other violence afflicting Congolese, especially women and girls.

Killing and Raping: The Numbers Game

The level of violence in DRC has been very high; just how high is the subject of noisy disputes. The International Rescue Committee (IRC) estimated, on the basis of a series of surveys, that more than 5 million deaths from 1998 to 2008 could be attributed to the war. The majority of those people were not killed in combat but died from hunger or disease, often after having been forced to flee from their homes. Nearly half of the "extra" deaths were of children under five years old. These died especially of fever/malaria (34.2 percent in the east, 35 percent in the west), neonatal death (15.5 percent in the east, 12.9 percent in the west), measles (9.9 percent in the east, 4.8 percent in the west), and diarrhea (9.7 percent in the east, 12.8 percent in the west).[2]

Deaths due directly to violence were most common among males five years and older, as one might expect. This cohort provided most of the fighters, and was disproportionately targeted when armies and militias attacked civilian villagers. As a result, many villages in the war zone include vast numbers of widows. The disproportion is so great as to justify use of the term "gendercide"[3] The deaths of women and girls, both in the east and in the west, were attributed to fever/malaria, tuberculosis, and "maternal" causes.

The excess mortality revealed by the IRC occurred across the country, from the eastern war zone along the border with Uganda, Rwanda, and Burundi to the Atlantic coast in the west. Three of the hardest-hit areas were Kunda, in southern Maniema province, Ankoro, in northern Katanga province, and Ngandajika, south of Mbuji-Mayi in East Kasai. Kunda and Ankoro were in the "east," as defined by the IRC – that is, the zone controlled by Rwanda and Uganda and their allies or proxies in 2002 – whereas Ngandajika (often spelled Gandajika) was in the "west," nominally under control of the Kinshasa government. In reality, Kunda, Ankoro, and Ngandajika represent areas with almost no social services whatsoever. Ankoro is deep in North Katanga, an anarchic area where Mayi-Mayi militias battled government forces and one another for several years.

In contrast to these abandoned areas, the war zones of North and South Kivu provinces had received significant international assistance, both from governmental and nongovernmental sources, during the war years. This may explain why the mortality figures for these provinces were less atrocious than for areas such as Kunda, Ankoro, or Ngandajika.

The IRC studies are seriously flawed, but the figures have been widely accepted, by Amnesty International and the US State Department among others. The IRC assumed that the number of people dying each year in DRC in peacetime would be similar to rates elsewhere in other parts of sub-Saharan Africa, and used an average of these rates as a baseline. It then analyzed how many people had died from 1998 to 2008 and attributed the difference in the two figures to the conflict. However, this approach is unrealistic. Researchers from the Human Security Report Project at Simon Fraser University point out that large numbers of Congolese would have died without the conflict, simply because basic living conditions in DRC were so tough and health services almost non-existent. When the researchers used their higher base rate to recalculate the figures, they found the number due to the conflict dropped below 3 million.[4]

Two Belgian demographers – André Lambert and Louis Lohlé-Tart – entered the fray in 2008 with a paper entitled "Excess Mortality in Congo (DRC) during the Troubles of 1998–2004: An Estimation of the Extra Deaths Scientifically Established by Means of Methods of Demography." Their estimate was 200,000. The paper eventually reached the Congolese, some of who reacted violently. A Kinshasa journalist, Benjamin Litsani, denounced what it called the "cynicism or sadism" of the Belgian demographers or people claiming to be such. He accused them of "spitting on the memory" of the Congolese victims and of insulting Secretary of State Hillary Clinton (who had adopted the IRC figures). Litsani claimed to be particularly offended by the suggestion that the higher estimates were "profitable lies," as though no international organization had any material interest in exaggerating the suffering of the Congolese.[5]

War zone statistics are inevitably political. When a methodology similar to that of the IRC led to the conclusion that over 390,000 and perhaps as many as 940,000 Iraqis died in the three years following the US invasion, these results were used to denounce Bush's Iraq war. On the right, the results themselves were denounced as biased or intolerably vague. Whether Congo's death toll was over 5 million or less than half that many, however, it is unacceptable.

The Rape Toll

The question of mass rape generated a controversy similar to that concerning the death toll, but it was more intense due to the involvement of women's rights advocates. The questions to be answered were: how many rapes have occurred; where; and who is being raped? In May 2011, headlines in print and electronic media proclaimed that forty-eight Congolese women were being raped per hour. The study that set off the flurry of new articles appeared in the *American Journal of Public Health* and was based on a survey of health problems in the Congolese population, including AIDS and other sexually transmitted diseases, in 2006.[6] In this context, it was entirely appropriate to ask about sexual activity, including non-consensual sexual activity. However, it is worth reflecting on the possible influence of the context upon data gathered: for example, the respondents may have offered information in the hope of obtaining treatment.

Journalist Jina Moore pointed out that since the data on which the study was based were five years old, they might not accurately represent current reality. *Foreign Policy* blogger Elizabeth Dickinson asked pertinently, "What if rape has actually become systemic – not a brutal act of conquest so much as a systemic, even rational occurrence in a system that has been built upon violence?" Political Scientist Charli Carpenter pointed out the problem with focusing only on women as victims and noted the need for more studies of the rapists.[7] I agree, and will make some suggestions, below.

Two themes emerged from this recent round of reporting and discussion: first, the level of sexual violence in DRC is very high (even if forty-eight rapes per hour implies that we know more about the phenomenon than we do); and, second, that far from being mainly produced by men in uniforms, rape is often and perhaps increasingly the work of civilians, including women. Spousal rape and rape by other household members are important problems but should not be lumped in with war-related rapes, as remedial measures necessarily will be different.

HIV/AIDS and Congolese Women

One particular vector of mortality – the HIV virus – has been highly politicized. Many Congolese are convinced that the very high incidence of AIDS in their country is directly attributable to Ugandan and Rwandan policy. A rumor circulated that Uganda and/or Rwanda had recruited 2,000 HIV-positive rebels and sent them into DRC for the specific purpose of spreading AIDS among Congolese.

Intentional transmission of HIV was included in a list of alleged human rights violations committed by Uganda and Rwanda (and to a lesser extent Burundi) that was submitted by the Congolese government to the African Commission on Human and Peoples' Rights in 1999. After interminable delays, the Commission found in favor of the complainant, and against the three neighboring countries, in 2003. In 2006, the summary of the original complaint and the lengthy process that ensued was made public. The story of DRC's complaint and the African Commission's very slow response is summarized here, as a demonstration not only of the role of a dysfunctional intergovernmental organization, but of the low priority given to the rights of women, both in the Great Lakes region and elsewhere.

In March 1999 – eight months after the start of the second war – the Congolese government wrote to the African Commission on Human and Peoples' Rights, charging Burundi, Rwanda, and Uganda with grave and massive violations of rights committed by their armed forces.[8] Sexual violence was one theme among many. Congo began by charging the invaders with massacres of disarmed officers and men of the Congolese armed forces at Kavumu airport, outside Bukavu. The letter went on to cite the burial of more than fifty corpses, mostly of civilians, in Bukavu itself. The Rwandans and Ugandans were charged with disrupting the lives of millions of civilians by seizing the Inga hydroelectric dam outside Kinshasa, and with killing many patients in the hospitals by cutting off the electricity to incubators and operating rooms.

Sexual violence was invoked in connection with massacres of more than 850 people in Kasika and Mwenga, including many women and children. "The women had been raped before being killed by their murderer, who slashed them open from the vagina up to the abdomen and cut them up with daggers." Other massacres were cited, in Luberizi, Bwegera, Luvingi, and Makobola, also in South Kivu.

The DRC next claimed that the Rwandan and Ugandan forces intentionally spread sexually transmitted diseases. The DRC complaint, as summarized by the Commission, was vague as to which offenses had been committed by Uganda and which by Rwanda. Allegedly, about two thousand AIDS-suffering or HIV-positive Ugandan soldiers were sent to the front in the eastern provinces of Congo "with the mission of raping girls and women so as to propagate an AIDS pandemic among the local population and, thereby, decimate it." The document went on to list instances of rape committed by the Ugandans and Rwandans. Allegedly, Uganda (but not Rwanda) had used HIV-positive soldiers, with the specific purpose of ethnic cleansing.

Both Rwanda and Uganda allegedly had massacred Congolese and had deported other Congolese to "concentration camps" on Rwandan territory. The goal of these operations was to make the indigenous people disappear and thus to establish "Tutsiland" on Congolese territory.

Finally, the Congolese government charged Rwanda and Uganda (and to a lesser extent Burundi) with systematic looting of gold, coffee, wood, and cash. This set of accusations was similar to that made by the UN experts panels (discussed in Chapter 5).

The three accused governments managed to string out the process of dealing with the DRC complaint. In 2000, the Commission ruled that the communication was "admissible" and "requested parties to furnish it with arguments on the merits of the case." Rwanda objected on procedural grounds. The DRC communication supposedly was inadmissible because other competent bodies (Organization of African Unity: OAU; UN Security Council) were dealing with the substance of the complaint; Rwanda also "refuted allegations of human rights violations made against it by the Democratic Republic of Congo and justified the presence of its troops in this country on grounds of security, while accusing the Democratic Republic of Congo of hosting groups hostile to Rwanda." Similarly, Uganda said its troops were in DRC to prevent Ugandan rebels from attacking Ugandan territory. It characterized the charges relating to HIV/AIDS as "the most ridiculous allegation" and denied involvement in the illegal exploitation of Congolese natural resources.

The African Commission deferred consideration of the DRC complaint in 2001 on the grounds that Burundi still had not responded to the charges against it. In 2002, the Commission did not consider the matter because the OAU had not responded to the DRC request for an extraordinary session on its charges against its neighbors.

In 2003, the Commission dealt with the procedural objections and again declared the DRC communication admissible. No state has the right to intervene in the internal or external affairs of another state, it declared. The alleged "grave and massive violations of human and peoples' rights committed by the armed forces of the Respondent States in its eastern provinces" were attendant upon the occupation of those provinces and could not be ignored by the Commission.

Accordingly, the African Commission found in favor of DRC and against Rwanda, Uganda, and Burundi in general and on most of the specific allegations. The majority of the findings confirmed dealt with the illegality of the occupation of eastern DRC, the alleged massacres and deportations, and the burial of Congolese in mass graves in Rwanda. The seizure of Inga dam and the illegal exploitation of Congolese minerals were condemned.

Finding 79 endorsed DRC's allegations regarding sexual violence. The Commission found the "killings, massacres, rapes, mutilations and other grave human rights abuses committed while the Respondent States' armed forces were still in effective occupation of the eastern provinces of the Complainant State reprehensible" and inconsistent with their obligations under the Geneva Conventions. Raping of women and girls is "prohibited under Article 76 of the first Protocol Additional to the Geneva Conventions of 1949," and offends against both the African Charter and the Convention on the Elimination of All Forms of Discrimination Against Women. The Commission found Rwanda, Burundi, and Uganda in violation of Articles 60 and 61 of the African Charter.[9] The Commission did not conduct its own investigation, so it either adopted or failed to adopt the claims made by DRC. In particular, it failed to endorse the Congolese position that sending HIV-positive troops into eastern DRC was intentional, and that Congolese women and girls were infected with an aim of ethnic cleansing (creation of "Tutsiland").

This question of intent to spread AIDS, which echoes a claim made against the Hutu *"génocidaires"* in 1994, is implausible. The crimes committed first in Rwanda, then in eastern DRC, are horrible enough without this additional twist.

An "Epidemic" of Sexual Violence?

Rape has been a weapon in eastern DRC since the Rwandan–Ugandan invasions of 1996 and 1998. All sides in the wars that have raged since then have used it to humiliate and intimidate their victims, and their families and communities. Not all cases of rape can be explained in this manner, however; perhaps not even a majority. Reports from eastern Congo make it clear that there were several types of rapes, committed by different types of perpetrators. Gwendolyn Lusi of Goma-based Doctors on Call for Service (DOCS) identified six categories of rape according to the identity of the perpetrators.

Most often, the crime of rape is committed during an attack on a village by the Interahamwe, the core of which is made up of fighters responsible for the Rwanda genocide of 1994. Hunted by the Rwandan army and the RCD (i.e. Congolese allied with Rwanda), they "survive through pillaging unprotected villages. During an attack, the men of the village are killed, the houses ransacked and burned, food is taken, and the girls and women are raped. The age of the woman is of no consequence for these beasts." Lusi's version is at once believable (such attacks happen and her organization has treated the victims) and incomplete: there is no suggestion that the Rwandan occupation forces and their Congolese allies or pawns who are hunting these "beasts" themselves commit rape in the course of their operations.

Lusi's second category of rape comprises "young girls who have to carry the foodstuffs stolen from the village to the bandits' camp. This road ends for many in death; if the gang decides not to keep the girl as a slave, she is shot on the spot."

A third category of victims (Lusi continues) comprises girls "taken by the regular military personnel in the 'safer' towns.

Because of the lack of discipline in the military camps, the lack of goods and of basic necessities, these young men are in the habit of grabbing everything they encounter on their path," including girls returning from the fields or from the market. This apparently refers to violence by the RCD.

Lusi's fourth category is the victim of armed robbery. "When the bandits, armed and often in military uniform, break into a house to ransack it, the wife or the daughters of the owner are often raped." Her fifth category is "the classic rape," often committed by a local man, known by the woman, and sometimes a member of the family or household. Lusi's sixth and final category comprises rapists of children: "Sometimes that man is HIV positive, and he has heard the false rumour that sex with a virgin guarantees healing from AIDS. Of course it heals nothing, and it most certainly exposes the young girl to infection, and the lesions of the first sexual encounter are an open door for the virus."[10]

Lusi's classification is almost a mirror image of the Congolese government white paper, according to which the Rwandan army and its RCD allies or proxies were responsible for massive rape. She absolves the Rwanda–RCD forces of use of rape as a weapon.

A clearer picture of the war against women within the second Congo war emerges from research carried out in South Kivu province by two Congolese women's organizations and International Alert, and published as *Women's Bodies as a Battleground*.[11] On the basis of 492 interviews, the team was able to develop a profile of women and girls who had been raped: their ages ranged from 12 to 70 years old; and most of the victims were women farmers and women of childbearing age. The consequences of these attacks were disastrous in two respects: first, women farmers are the driving force behind the subsistence economy, and so attacks on them have increased poverty within the community; and, second, victims of childbearing age have developed serious reproductive health problems.

The majority of the victims were married women, representing 59.1 percent of the sample, followed by widows (18.5 percent), single women (17.7 percent), and divorced women

(4.7 percent). The authors point out two possible reasons for the predominance of married women: first, the tendency of rural girls to marry at a young age; and, second, the possibility that unmarried girls left the countryside for the relative safety of town, while married women remained in rural areas with their husbands. Almost all the widows in the sample said their husbands had died during the previous years of fighting.

The ethnic identities of assault victims in South Kivu suggest a war against women from which no one was safe. More than a third of the victims were Bembe and more than a quarter were Shi. The authors note that the Bembe and Shi live near the border with Burundi and Rwanda, respectively. The high incidence of attacks on these two ethnic groups could also be because they were especially resistant to the invaders or seen as such. The Bembe had been involved in a conflict with the Kinyarwanda-speaking Banyamulenge since the 1960s. Shi led the resistance to the Rwandans, although some of them were collaborators. As for the ethnopolitical identities of the rapists, the South Kivu research partly confirms Lusi's generalization in that 27 percent were identified as Interahamwe (Rwandan Hutu) and 26.6 percent as FDD (Burundian Hutu). In third position, however, was the invaders' proxy, the RCD. Nine rapists were identified as members of the Rwandan army (RPA), some of whom may have been Banyamulenge from South Kivu.

The *Women's Bodies* team dealt with the question of intent by asking whether the attacks seemed to have been planned. Seventy percent of the respondents said that this had been the case. The rapes and looting committed around the Kahuzi-Biega National Park (near Kalehe) by the Interahamwe, beginning in 2000, are described in these terms:

> They arrive in a band in the afternoon or after nightfall, over-running the whole village, barging into the houses in small groups and terrorizing the people . . . one lot rape the girls and women while the others pack up the goods to take away. And at the signal for departure, the attackers pick out from among the inhabitants the ones who are going to carry the booty. They

leave the village straight away. That makes you think there has been a certain amount of planning behind it all.[12]

The women sometimes reported on grievances that their attackers expressed against the victims while abusing them. For example, if they accused the woman of having collaborated with the Mayi-Mayi, then the women realized that they were dealing with members of an opposing force, which in this case was the RCD, the RPA, or sometimes even the FDD of Burundi. The women credited foreign forces – the Interahamwe and RPA of Rwanda and the FDD of Burundi – with some of the cruelest and most degrading abuse.

Culture of Violence and Impunity

There has been a great deal of violence in DRC since the late 1990s, much of it directed against women and girls. This violence is often instrumental: that is, intended to achieve political aims. Mass rapes in DRC often aim at collective punishment or ethnic cleansing: the driving out of unwanted people. Some cases of rape seem to be acts of revenge, directed against the woman, her husband, or her family.

Some instances of sexual violence do not conveniently fit into the "rape as a weapon" framework, however. The public health study discussed above revealed that the incidence of rape in Equateur province (northwest DRC) in 2007 was nearly as high as in the eastern war zones.

Even where armed groups are making rational use of rape as a weapon, there must be some kind of cultural support for this activity, some set of ideas that makes it thinkable. The literature suggests three possibilities, not mutually exclusive. These are a culture of rape, a culture of violence, and a culture of impunity.

A "culture of rape" (in Martha McCaughey's words) is "a culture that accepts gender-motivated attacks as normal, natural and even sexy – a culture whose models of masculinity, femininity and sexuality sustain and rationalize men's violence against women."[13]

A "culture of violence" is a broader concept, rooted in the political economy. Rather than explaining sexual violence in terms of characteristics of the perpetrators, one might follow the lead of the African American writer bell hooks. She explains sexism in "gangsta rap" in terms of "white supremacist capitalist patriarchy."[14] There is a comparable problem in understanding sexual violence in DRC. Should one demonize the culture of young Congolese and Rwandan males in the eastern war zone, or try to understand that their sexual violence (like gangsta rap) "does not appear in a cultural vacuum, but, rather, is expressive of the cultural crossing, mixings, and engagement" of their culture with the values, attitudes, and concerns of other Central Africans and of the so-called "international community"? Their violence might be interpreted in the context of Congo's economy of plunder.

The concept of "culture of impunity" was introduced into DRC by international governmental and nongovernmental organizations and adopted, in the first instance, by the country's vibrant civil society groups. At its core is the behavior of violators of rights, behavior that reflects a well-founded belief that they will not be held accountable for their actions. Such lack of accountability is a key element in the widespread theft, killing, and sexual violence in DRC. There are courts in DRC, both military and civilian. However, these are relatively few in number, the judges are poorly trained and poorly paid, and the verdict often goes to the higher bidder. Even those offenders who are charged are rarely found guilty. This dysfunctional justice system sustains a high level of impunity and expectation of impunity, for sexual violence as for other offenses.

The Armed Forces and Sexual Assault

The Congolese Armed Forces (FARDC) reportedly are responsible for much of the sexual violence in the eastern provinces, and for that reason their culture deserves special attention here. These forces are the descendants of the Force Publique of Leopold's Congo Free State, instrument of the violent conquest of the Congo basin. The colonial administration maintained control over these men through harsh discipline. That control was lost in the mutiny that followed independence in 1960, and has never been fully restored.

Violence against women figures prominently in Nancy Hunt's analysis of Free State violence in the rubber-collecting areas of Equateur province. Hunt draws on the testimony before the Commission d'Enquête set up by the Free State in response to what it called the "anti-Congo campaign," as well as memories collected in the 1950s by Belgian missionaries, and the contemporary report and diaries of British/Irish diplomat Roger Casement, to render visible and audible the survivors of the violence unleashed by the Anglo-Belgian India Rubber Company (ABIR) through its private security force.[15] Such private security forces may have been more violent and less disciplined than the Force Publique *per se*.

The Congo Reform campaign of E. D. Morel, starting in 1904, made famous some of the images of mutilation (amputated hands of male workers, in particular), but this only served to further silence the voices telling of murder, rape, and forced incest, among other crimes. Sexual violence "was intrinsically more reproductive and transgressive in its nature."[16]

Conquest and primary resistance went on for decades. Some "revolts" – for example, among the Mongo of northern Kasai – were provoked by abuses committed by private guards of the cotton companies, including sexual abuse of local women and girls. Throughout the colonial period, resistance continued, shifting in form in response to the form of Congolese involvement in the colonial political economy. Belgian officers maintained strict discipline over their troops so that the violence and threat of violence remained focused on the revolt or other disobedience of the population.

During the last years of colonial rule, the colonial state lost its monopoly over coercion; political violence (including sexual assault) increased sharply. Large-scale ethnic cleansing occurred around Luluabourg (the present Kananga), and hundreds of thousands of Luba fled to their "home" area, which many of them had never seen. Five days after independence, the army (former Force Publique) mutinied against its Belgian officers. The discipline of the colonial army melted away. The violence of the mutineers, including reported rape of Belgian women, was used to justify the intervention of Belgian troops, setting off the Congo Crisis of 1960. No mention was made of rape of Congolese women. In August 1960, troops of the newly named Congolese National Army (ANC) were accused of "genocidal" violence against Luba villagers in Kasai. Within a few months, the country had two rival national governments and two secessionist provinces, each with its own army. Most political parties had violent youth wings. During the Mobutu years, the Congolese army remained "an army of mutineers" (in Mobutu's own words), unreliable as a military force and brutal toward civilians.

Under Mobutu, the Congolese/Zaïrian state exercised an approximate monopoly of coercive power, although the army proved extremely weak. The political liberalization of the early 1990s meant the re-emergence of multiple political parties, many of which were equipped with "youth wings" reminiscent of those of the 1960s. Some of the local forces engaged in ethnic cleansing, including sexual violence.

The anti-Rwandan Mayi-Mayi (or Maï-Maï) militias draw on a tradition of local defense, using the magical protection revived by the Lumumbist "Simba" of the 1960s. Like the Simba, the Mayi-Mayi fighters were supposed to abstain from sexual relations in order to preserve the effectiveness of their magic. Several of the rape victims questioned by the *Women's Bodies* team expressed regret that the Mayi-Mayi of South Kivu were not following their own principles; this attitude reflects role conflict in that the women sympathized with the Mayi-Mayi as defenders against foreign invaders but not as sexual predators.[17]

The foreign invaders – the Hutu of the FDLR, CNDD, and FNL, as well as the Tutsi-led regular armies of Rwanda and Burundi – brought with them to DRC a culture of ethnically focused sexual violence. The most atrocious attacks were justified – according to their reported statements – by acts of violence committed by others against their own communities. The sense of entitlement on the part of the Rwandans and on the part of the Congolese is key to understanding this violence.

Trauma and Trauma Healing

The invasions of DRC (in 1996 and especially in 1998) constituted a massive large-group trauma for Congolese, and, as Vamik Volkan maintains, such trauma tends to generate or reinforce a "political ideology of entitlement and violence."[18] The victimized group suffers humiliation and a sense of helplessness. Because members of the traumatized group cannot successfully complete certain psychological tasks (mourning, healing, rebuilding), they transmit these tasks to the children of subsequent generations, along with the conscious and unconscious shared wish that these descendants will resolve them.

The political ideologies of entitlement and violence often focus upon a "chosen trauma" that is passed from generation to generation, according to Volkan. The ideologies of the Hutu and Tutsi in Rwanda are excellent examples. The Hutu ideology focused on the supposed conquest of their community by the Tutsi, four hundred years before, while the Tutsi focused on the European conquest and the consequent division of the Rwandans into antagonistic Hutu, Tutsi, and Twa communities. Hutu and Tutsi deny the reality of the "chosen trauma" of the other (which is not difficult to do, since each version is a gross oversimplification of known history).

The colonial conquest of the Congo was the chosen trauma of the Congolese, a humiliation passed on to subsequent generations. The Rwandans were new conquerors, "neo-Belgians" in the eyes of Congolese, reviving the sense of humiliation. Many Congolese supported Laurent Kabila because he opposed the Rwandans (ignoring the fact that he had been carried to power by the same Rwandans).

There is nothing particularly African about recourse to quasi-historical entitlement to justify rape. In Bosnia, rape and murder were justified by assimilating late twentieth-century Bosniaks to the Turks of the fourteenth century.

Foreign journalists were astonished to hear Serbs talking about "Janissaries" (Ottoman troops recruited in the Balkans and converted to Islam).

At the individual level, trauma resulted not just from the rape but also from issues such as guilt, shame, humiliation, lost dignity, and broken families, since many women were raped in front of their husbands, brothers or in-laws, or even their children.[19] A case study illustrates these issues. Kubota (not her real name) was 19 years old and a virgin when several militiamen raped her in front of her father and brothers. After the rape, she was taken into the forest, where she served as a sexual slave for a year. She became pregnant and her main concern was how to give birth in the bush, where there is not a single medical facility. She was worried that she was going to die. When she reached her full term, as she could not give birth normally, one of her rapists, who had no medical training, decided to perform a Caesarean section on her. He used a razor blade to open her abdomen so that he could retrieve the baby. During the C-section a battle broke out and Kubota was abandoned. The following day, she woke up and found herself in the middle of nowhere as all the militiamen had left. She dragged herself to the nearest place where she could see a sign of life. Before the International Red Cross rescued her, local people treated her for almost two weeks with traditional herbal remedies. The Red Cross took her to a gynecologist, who carried out four surgeries. Although these operations limited some of the damage that Kubota had suffered, she could never expect to have her own biological child.

Kubota told the interviewer she wished she had died since her life had become meaningless. Even after she recovered from the surgeries, she stayed in the hospital; she did not know where to go and she did not know anyone in town. She would never go back to her community because her father and brothers had been forced to watch her being raped. She could no longer face them. She would never get the chance to marry since everyone in the village knew her story.

Kubota may have suffered from "survivor's guilt," a condition in which a person perceives herself to have done wrong by surviving a traumatic event. She complained of anxiety and depression, social withdrawal, sleep disturbance and nightmares, and loss of drive – all of which are symptoms of Post-Traumatic Stress Disorder.

While Kubota's baby died, other rape survivors have one or more children in their care. Often, these children are not accepted in the village. In some instances, villagers even killed such babies because of their supposed Tutsi features, associating them with the "enemy."

Kubota's story is unique, yet broadly similar to the narratives of thousands of raped women in DRC. It shares many elements with the story of Salima in Lynn Nottage's play *Ruined*, although Salima was married and her husband, Fortune, supposedly a soldier, was attempting to bring her home. Salima commits suicide, and her last words are: "You will not fight your battles on my body anymore."[20]

The social context also needs to be taken into account here as this complicates the individual struggle. The extended family, which might have provided some support to an errant member in the past, has been severely weakened. The social services that Congolese had come to expect during the last "welfare state" years of colonial rule had withered from neglect under Mobutu. The Rwandan invasion reinforced the sense that DRC could no longer protect its citizens against violence. Congolese already were traumatized by structural violence before the full-blown horrors of war compounded this, displacing it in their minds. Large-scale rape has created a third layer of trauma, and treating its victims will be a complex process as they are living among other traumatized people in a society that is itself traumatized.

Social problems dominate psychological and personal problems because of the ostracism that rape entails, as evidenced by the case of Kubota. Many people perceive victims of sexual assault as responsible for the trouble because they live in a patriarchal society in which issues of dignity and honor are very important. Women are defined as mothers and/or wives. Having a child outside of wedlock is another issue as the victim of rape often ends up pregnant. When a woman had been sexually assaulted and this is widely known by community members, she often is abandoned by her husband. Not only she has to suffer from the traumatic experience and its psychological effects; more importantly, she has to face community members, who, instead of empathizing with her, often look down on her, as she has lost a great part of her identity as a woman. She is "ruined" as a wife and mother. Similarly, the male survivor of rape demonstrably was unable to protect his household and himself.

The values orienting the behavior of the rape survivor, the members of her or his family, and the community are "traditional" (i.e. long-standing), yet these values have been modified under the pressure of violence, both structural and physical. The Congolese state is unable to protect its subjects, just as the head of the household is unable to protect his family members.

Third parties – Western Europeans and Americans, for the most part – often introduce trauma-healing strategies into DRC. As they do so, they bring in their own worldview regarding trauma issues. The main weakness in these interventions is the failure to understand cultural issues that have a great impact on how rape survivors live with their trauma. Many Congolese women are tired of the multitude of visitors or potential helpers. They are called by some of these NGOs to evaluate their suffering and at times are asked intimate details of their lives. Some of the victims complain of being used as advertising materials for these organizations with little in way of return: just a business card so that they can contact the visitor in the event that they need help.

Congolese victims of sexual violence live in war-torn communities. As Luc Reychler observes, "War engenders a mental environment of desperation in which fear, resentment, jealousy, and rage predominate. Consequently, building peace requires not only attention to the hard layers of the conflict but also to the softer layers of the deep conflict. These softer layers of the conflict would include reconciliation at the psychological and emotional levels."[21] Unfortunately, these softer layers of conflict did not start with the full-blown outbreak of violence in DRC; rather, they stem from the shadow state and its inability to honor the social contract, which Congolese tend to believe in, despite little supporting evidence in their daily lives.

Enabling rape survivors to transcend their trauma and regain control of their lives is problematic, given the sociopolitical environment. Once treated, the survivors run the risk of being re-traumatized simply by living in a traumatized environment comprising people who have lost any hope in the future, and whose personhood was taken by the collapse of the social contract as well as war-related violence. How can victims of sexual violence, as a special category of the Congolese population, bounce back and recover their personhood, in an environment failing to offer structural support to ease their reintegration?

International NGOs apparently do their best to help women on the trauma-healing journey. However, there are many women (probably the majority of rape survivors) who are suffering from trauma and other medical problems resulting from rape who do not report or talk openly about this for fear of the community reaction. This is why NGOs should work hand in hand with community organizations and concentrate on community problems and perceptions that impede women's medical and psychological help. The rape stigma encourages silence, while vocalization can be helpful in the trauma-healing process. As for male rape survivors, the work has not yet begun.

Trauma Healing on Three Levels

As we have just noted, many Congolese, particularly those who have gone to school, believe in the social contract. That is, they believe that the state should provide for their security and wellbeing in exchange for their loyalty. They also believe in the myth of the yoke, attributing all of their misfortune to foreign invasion. They will need to get beyond this myth, and take responsibility for their own futures. This is particularly the case for Congolese women.

Most Congolese have no direct experience of living in a state that honors the social contract or even tries to do so. This is not merely a consequence of the war. The disastrous Congo crisis of 1960 meant that the first elected government under Lumumba was unable to take up the responsibilities it was inheriting from the colonial government and to fulfill the promises it had made during the campaign. Mobutu, who took power by a *coup d'état* in 1965, promised a transformation of the relationship between the citizens and the state. According to the N'Sele Manifesto (drafted by Tshisekedi and other graduates, along with Mobutu), democracy and wellbeing were to be fulfilled within a national movement that was not a single party. Instead, Mobutu transformed the Mouvement Populaire de la Révolution (Popular Movement of the Revolution, MPR) into a single-party dictatorship. Tshisekedi and other deputies eventually defied Mobutu and created an illegal second party, the UDPS, which was committed to democracy and social progress. The Sovereign National Conference of 1991–2 again promised democracy and wellbeing (and elected Tshisekedi as prime minister), but Mobutu thwarted the applications of the decisions of the Conference.

The Mobutu regime had reduced state service delivery virtually to zero in the 1980s. By the mid-1990s, the weakness of the shadow state made possible the invasions of 1996 and 1998. The invasions and their sequels, including pillage, killing, and rape, led to a Hobbesian "war of all against all" in much of the country.

Hugo van der Merwe and Tracy Vienings argue that trauma should be dealt with on three levels. For the healing of trauma on the national level, bodies such as truth and reconciliation commissions can be effective "if their aims are structured to uncover truth and deal with perpetrators." On the community level, "there are many creative ways in which communities deal with the past. Rituals and ceremonies that symbolically pay tribute to the suffering of the past, or that remember those who have died and the loss the community has suffered, are successful in dealing with community traumas."[22] DRC has attempted some healing at the national and provincial levels. (See the discussion of the 2010 Bukavu–Mwenga ceremonies, below.) Individual trauma healing is largely practiced through psychological one-on-one counseling, and this has obvious limitations when a large number of people have been traumatized and few counselors are available.

If there is anything positive to be said about the epidemic of sexual violence in DRC, it concerns the response of Congolese women and of their allies (Congolese and international) in the medical community. The first major action of the 1996 war was an attack on the Protestant hospital at Lemera, in South Kivu. Patients and staff were massacred, including wounded men from the FAZ and the major Burundian rebel movement, the CNDD. A Congolese gynecologist, Dr. Denis Mukwege, had begun a program at Lemera to treat women war victims. He escaped the massacre in late 1996, and then restarted his clinic at another Protestant hospital at Panzi, in the suburbs of Bukavu. Ever since, Panzi and Mukwege have been the main care providers for victims of sexual assault in South Kivu, including surgical repair of fistulas.[23]

In Goma (capital of North Kivu), DOCS, which we referred to above, and which was founded in 1994 by Drs. G. Paul Groen from the USA and Kasereka Lusi, husband of Gwendolyn Lusi, from Congo, provides similar services to rape victims. DOCS has added a new organization, HEAL Africa, to deal with a broader range of services, including medical education. The DOCS/HEAL Africa hospital was destroyed in the volcanic eruption of 2002, but has since been rebuilt.

Laudable as the efforts of Drs. Mukwege, Groen, Lusi, and their colleagues are, it is even more encouraging to note the extent to which the women of eastern DRC have organized to combat the scourge of sexual violence and to assist the survivors to get back on their feet. The first organizations were very small and worked on the local level. In 2002, however, a number of these small organizations joined together in North Kivu under the label of the Synergie des Femmes pour les Victimes des Violences Sexuelles (Women's

Synergy for Victims of Sexual Violence, SFVS). Pooling the resources and the experience of the small groups, SFVS has been able to become an effective defender of women's rights. It also has been a useful partner for international organizations: for example, the Food and Agriculture Organization of the United Nations (FAO), which has funded projects to support the sale of garden produce and fish.

Bringing together the skills and experience of thirty-five Congolese organizations, SFVS mobilizes women around efforts to end violence against women in North Kivu. It provides medical care to victims of sexual violence; offers psychological counseling; raises community awareness of the destructive effects of sexual violence against women; provides legal support; and gives victims opportunities to participate in income-generating activities.

To address the psychological effects of sexual violence, SFVS has held numerous seminars and trained dozens of counselors in psychological trauma counseling, family mediation, and other skills, and has established twenty "listening houses" to welcome victims of sexual violence. Tasked with identifying victims, passive and active listening to them, and assisting in their reintegration into society, counselors form an essential part of SFVS's work in North Kivu. One wonders, however, whether the short training sessions are adequate to prepare the counselors to deal with the multi-level trauma they encounter.

Aiming to increase the awareness of the public, the authorities, and the military of the pervasiveness of sexual violence in eastern Congo, SFVS regularly broadcasts messages on radio and television, organizes conferences and discussions on Congolese law on rape and on the societal effects of rape, and puts up public educational posters.

As a means of providing both group therapy and economic self-sufficiency, SFVS helps women and girls reintegrate into society by providing them with socio-economic skills, including dyeing techniques, sewing, hairdressing, as well as animal husbandry and farming.

In South Kivu, a similar process led to the emergence of the Bukavu-based Réseau des Femmes pour la Défense des

Droits et la Paix (Women's Network for the Defense of Rights and for Peace) and the Uvira-based Réseau des Femmes pour un Développement Associatif (Women's Network for Associative Development) – who were co-sponsors of *Women's Bodies as a Battleground*, which we cited above. Like their counterpart in North Kivu, these are umbrella groups linking a large number of grass-roots women's groups to international supporters.

The resistance of Congolese women did not go unnoticed by the perpetrators of sexual assault; as a result, sexual assault has become a weapon not only in the battlefield (i.e. in the villages that are captured by one armed group after another), but also in the cities. Justine Masika Bihamba of SFVS and her family have been targeted by the DRC military because of her work on behalf of women.[24] SFVS counselors have regularly been threatened and attacked because of their work. Justine was away from home on September 19, 2007 when six army soldiers forced their way into her house. They tied up her six children at gunpoint, and assaulted two of them. Justine's 21-year-old daughter pleaded with the soldiers to take what they wanted but not to hurt anyone. One of the soldiers replied that they had not come to steal anything, but rather were on a "well-defined mission" ("une mission bien déterminée"). The group searched the house. One soldier kicked Justine's 24-year-old daughter in the face, breaking her tooth. He then tried to rape Justine's 21-year-old daughter and sexually assaulted her with a knife.

Justine returned home during the attack and immediately telephoned the authorities. In a search of the neighborhood with the military police, Justine and her children identified the soldiers involved in their attack as bodyguards of a high-ranking army officer. The military police refused to arrest the men and claimed that there was no evidence against them.

Just over a week after the attack, on September 27, Justine lodged a legal complaint against the soldiers. In the following weeks and months, senior military and civilian authorities promised her that justice would be done. Years later, however, the men had still not been brought to trial. Eventually, in 2012, Justine brought the matter to a head. She gave an interview to the BBC, praising the conviction of Thomas Lubanga by the International Criminal Court and calling for the transfer of Bosco Ntaganda to the same court.[25] Following the interview, she received death threats by telephone and was forced to move out of her house in Goma.

Conclusion

A great many Congolese, including many women, have died during the war that began in the mid-1990s and has still not ended. Much of the killing has been "gendercidal": that is, targeted killing of young males. After the events in the former Yugoslavia and in Rwanda, this is not really surprising. However, the majority of the Congolese deaths are only marginally related to the wars; they are more validly attributable to the collapse of social services that began under Mobutu and that continues unabated under Joseph Kabila. This means that restoration of order – desirable in itself – will only slowly reduce the very high death toll among Congolese.

So too with rape and other sexual violence; one must avoid oversimplification. Hundreds of thousands of Congolese women and girls, but also many men and boys, have been raped. The incidence of male rape is even harder to estimate than that for women, since the shame associated with such attacks is so great. For some Congolese male survivors of rape, the day of the attack is "the day they made me into a woman."[26]

Rape has been a weapon of war in eastern DRC, which means that the restoration of order probably will have a favorable effect on the toll of sexual violence, but surely will not end it. Civilians have carried out many of the rapes, not soldiers or members of various militias.

The high tolls of death and rape conceal important differences as to who is involved, meaning that the effort to substantially lower either toll will have to be multifaceted. The problems of victims and of perpetrators will have to be addressed. A basket of programs, including counseling, training, and microcredit for survivors of rape and murder, will have to be accompanied by speedy trials and severe punishment of perpetrators. Training programs for military and justice system personnel will have to address the rights of civilians and especially those of women. Outsiders – the donor community and the international governmental and nongovernmental organizations – can and must push for change in these crucial areas. Ultimately, however, Congolese will have to adopt and carry out these programs, and as they do, the role of outsiders should be to support the reformers, the defenders of human rights and of women's rights, as they go about their difficult and sometimes dangerous work.

Congolese have begun to commemorate the crimes against women. In October 2010, the Third International Action of the World March of Women was held in Bukavu. More than a thousand women from approximately forty-two countries took part. Participants from all regions of the world discussed with their Congolese counterparts four main topics: peace and demilitarization; the common good and public services; violence against women; and women's work. The debates were complemented by dances and performances of plays on topics such as violence and poverty.

In keeping with the logic expressed by van der Merwe and Vienings, two monuments were dedicated in front of the international crowd. In Bukavu, a memorial grove was planted. Some participants in the international event also traveled to Mwenga, several hundred kilometers away, for the inauguration of a monument to the "Martyrs of Mwenga," fifteen local women who had been tortured and then buried alive. The accusation against them was that they had prepared "medicine" to ensure the invulnerability of the Mayi-Mayi, who were fighting against the Rwandan invaders and their RCD allies or agents. The Rwandan women participating in the Bukavu meeting conspicuously refused to travel to Mwenga. They might have been in danger there; in any case, the Rwandan government was still refusing to acknowledge the validity of any of the charges of atrocities committed by its troops and summarized in the UN Mapping Report. Likewise, the Congolese government was focusing on the accusations against Rwanda and ignoring violence against Luba,

Tutsi, and others, also summarized in the Mapping Report. The commemorative grove and monument will help some Congolese remember the terrible events of the 1990s and 2000s. Whether they will promote healing is less likely, given the continued absence of dialogue within DRC and between DRC and its neighbors.

The war against women is likely to continue, unless a modicum of order is restored to the country, and unless the Congolese address the multiple dimensions of culture that underpin and justify the war against women, summarized above as the culture of impunity, the culture of violence, and the culture of rape. The international community can help, but will have to go beyond the oversimplifications – does your cell phone cause rape? – that characterize much of the international campaigning on behalf of Congo. For one example among many, see the "talking points" published by Amnesty International USA in 2009, supporting passage of HR 4128, the Conflict Minerals Trade Act.[27] Point one noted that fighting had been nearly continuous since the mid-1990s, and millions have died. Point two is that rape, sexual mutilation, and sexual slavery were taking place in epidemic proportions. Both assertions were broadly true. The problem arose with the rapid transition to points three and four, according to which the sale of conflict minerals financed the activities of armed groups and the supply chain for conflict minerals was complex and disrupting it would be difficult. The connection between the sexual violence and the minerals trade was underspecified. In the next chapter, I will examine in detail the problem of "conflict minerals" and their place in the Congolese network of violence, including sexual violence.

5   Congo's "Resource Curse"

The "blood minerals" or "conflict minerals" campaigns of the past two decades have made the Democratic Republic of Congo well known across the globe, highlighting the link between the country's minerals and human rights violations. However, they are only the latest version of a fascination with Congolese natural wealth that dates back to the Portuguese encounters in the fifteenth and sixteenth centuries.

In the nineteenth century, King Leopold II allegedly told a collaborator to avoid displeasing the British, who could easily spoil "a good occasion to get ourselves a slice of this magnificent African cake."[1] Eight decades later, speaking before Leopold's great grandnephew King Baudouin I at the Independence Day ceremony in 1960, Patrice Lumumba promised his fellow Congolese, "We are going to ensure that the lands of our fatherland truly profit to its children."[2] That has been the central question for Congo ever since Leopold created his Free State: Who is going to get a slice? Will the riches of Congo enrich only foreigners, or will the Congolese people get a bit too? To use a more recent formulation, is the "resource curse" inevitable?

For the most part, foreign intervention has been disastrous for the locals, however profitable it may have been for the outsiders. Congo was tied to the global economy first through the Atlantic slave trade, and later through the Indian Ocean slave trade. In the 1850s and 1860s, two separate invasions from the present Tanzania led to the establishment of new states in Katanga and Maniema. Msiri, founder of the Garenganze kingdom of Katanga, was a copper trader in Tanzania before he moved along the supply chain to seize the mines of Katanga. Tippu Tib of Zanzibar set up plantations in Maniema and introduced new crops including rice and lemons; he exported ivory and slaves to the coast. These two states were snuffed out by the Congo Free State of Leopold II, which then incorporated men from the defeated armies into its own armed forces. Leopold focused on pillage of ivory and wild rubber, but major mineral deposits were discovered (especially in Katanga) and construction of the infrastructure needed to exploit them was begun.

Contrary to Hobson and Lenin's theory of imperialism, the colonization of Congo did not arise from the efforts of capitalists in the home country to export excess capital into new markets for their products and to obtain new resources for their industries. Instead, Leopold provided a state framework and mobilized capital to support his efforts, from Belgium and elsewhere. The result was a network of chartered companies and state–private partnerships in which the colonial state maintained substantial ownership but left management in the hands of the private interests. Ancillary services – transportation and even food production – were in the hands of affiliated companies. The organization of the mining sector was far more concentrated and hierarchical than in neighboring Northern Rhodesia (Zambia), for example, founded by Cecil Rhodes. The days of a state–private partnership bringing food across provincial borders to thousands of workers are long gone, but the legacy of the early days survives, both in the use of mining companies as cash cows for current expenses under Mobutu and the Kabilas, and in a preference for state retention of minority ownership of mining companies, old and new.

Under colonial rule, the minerals-dominated economy had defined or shaped four major social fields: (1) the Lower Congo, centered on Kinshasa, the administrative capital (then called Léopoldville); (2) Oriental province, a region of agriculture and mining, centering on Kisangani (Stanleyville);

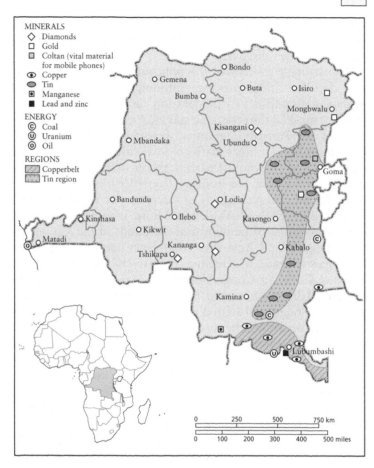

Map 4 Congo minerals

(3) the Copperbelt of South Katanga, around Lubumbashi (Élisabethville); and (4) the diamond mining area of Central Kasai, caught between the gravitational pulls of Kinshasa and South Katanga (Map 4). The colonial state managed the prospection and development of new mines, doling them out little by little so as to protect the existing enterprises. Congolese, who had been following this activity, complained on the eve of independence that whole regions never had been

seriously prospected.[3] This claim has been borne out in recent years, as new and apparently very rich gold and diamond fields have been discovered.

The struggle to control the political economy dominated the decolonization process, although political ideology (radical nationalism vs. "moderation" and centralism vs. federalism) masked the economic stakes. A coalition of nationalists led by Patrice Lumumba, favoring a strong central government and a break with colonial rule, faced off against federalist and secessionist parties, the most extreme of which was the pro-settler, pro-business Confédération des Associations Tribales du Katanga (Confederation of Katanga Tribal Associations, CONAKAT) led by Moïse Tshombe. Following the assassination of Lumumba at the hands of the Katangans (with Belgian and American connivance) and the ouster of Katanga's secessionist regime by ONUC (Opération des Nations Unies au Congo/United Nations Operation in the Congo), Tshombe returned briefly as prime minister of the reunified Congo and settled the *contentieux belgo-congolais* (a dispute regarding the assets and liabilities of the colonial state) in 1965. Mobutu took over a few months later, reopened the *contentieux* and even accused Tshombe of treason for having agreed to a settlement too favorable to Belgium.

Mobutu's effort to create a strong state meant bringing the companies (and the churches) under his control. He attempted to use the colonial companies as cash cows, without realizing (or caring) that his failure to reinvest a portion of proceeds meant that the cash cows were drying up. Mobutu's system of warlord rule also encouraged the development of smuggling networks. One of these linked Laurent Kabila's Hewa Bora "liberated zone" in Fizi territory (South Kivu), where gold and other valuable resources were extracted by forced labor, to Dar es Salaam via Kigoma. As president, Joseph Kabila has emulated Mobutu's "warlord" economic policy, to which, like Laurent Kabila before him, he has added a game of awarding and then withdrawing contracts for mineral rights, each time collecting side payments.

Mobutu's economic "reforms" targeted Belgian companies. American businessmen were exempted. Rather than allowing Congolese businessmen to take control of their own destiny, Mobutu transferred assets to an incompetent and parasitical political elite. "Zaïrianisation" and "radicalization of the revolution" disorganized the economy. Agricultural exports plummeted. Mobutu lived off revenue extracted from the country's minerals. During the 1980s and early 1990s, Western governments and the international financial institutions advocated policies to improve management of public resources and maximize confidence in the private sector. They attempted to reorganize tax and customs collection, reduce price controls, streamline the budget, and improve infrastructure. But for such reforms to be possible, Mobutu would have had to forgo his private access to state wealth. Instead, he diverted aid to his personal accounts, along with proceeds from the sale of diamonds. To defend his control over national resources, he financed a small army within the army and bought loyalty from a small political elite. Public services collapsed under Mobutu: from 1972 to 1992, government spending on social services dropped from 17 percent to 0 percent, while government spending on the presidency increased from 28 percent to 95 percent.

The privatization of Congo's mining parastatals began under Mobutu's prime minister Kengo wa Dondo in 1995. The idea was that to curb the downward spiral of the economy, one had to relaunch the formal mining sector, which, owing to exogenous factors (such as economic recession and price fluctuations on the commodity market) and bad governance, had nearly come to a standstill. Joint-venture agreements were reached with "junior" mining companies, or exploration companies. State-owned Gécamines transferred rights to the Tenke and Fungurume copper–cobalt deposits to a partnership with the Swedish–Canadian Lundin group. Another joint venture brought together Gécamines, Union Minière of Belgium, and the group headed by Belgian national George Forrest to develop the Kasomba copper–cobalt mine. The Australian junior Anvil Mining was awarded exploration rights over a vast concession held by a smaller parastatal, Sodimico (Sodimiza). In the Kivus, the assets of the parastatal

Sominki were transferred to a Canadian junior, Banro Resources Corporation. In Orientale province, the parastatal Okimo (Office des Mines de Kilo-Moto) ceded a huge gold mining concession to the Barrick Gold Corporation (of Canada) and a smaller one to the Belgian–Canadian Mindev.

Kengo's efforts produced no positive results, since the first Congo war began almost immediately thereafter. During the war all belligerent parties negotiated alterations to the existing contracts and new joint-venture agreements. The business of awarding mining contracts, or access to mining sites and resource trade routes, served war purposes and private interests of domestic and foreign belligerents, and of businessmen and politicians who were linked to what the UN experts called "elite networks."

The World Bank began supervising the DRC government's mining policy in 2001. DRC resumed the privatization of the mining parastatals begun by Kengo, in return for a resumption of lending. The central assumption was that economic growth should and could be promoted by attracting foreign investors. The Bank's accomplishments included restructuring of Gécamines, the promulgation of a new, supposedly more "investor-friendly" Mining Code in 2002, and the preparation of a new Mining Registry (Cadastre minier). The restructuring of Gécamines included dismissal of 10,000 employees, with insignificant severance pay and little prospects of finding another job.

Critics pointed out that the Bank's top-down approach lacked true participation. They accused the Bank of neglecting the role of natural resources in fueling conflict, despite the guidelines of its own Conflict Prevention and Reconstruction Unit. Also, the Bank has been criticized for neglecting DRC's lack of institutional capacity to regulate the free-market system that the privatization introduced.

The position of the World Bank and IMF as trustees over the Congolese economy was seriously challenged in 2007, when China and DRC took a "giant leap of faith," in the words of American journalist Howard French.[4] The Chinese offered to lend billions of dollars to the cash-strapped Congolese government in what amounted to a barter agreement.

The Chinese would build much-needed infrastructure (roads, railroads, universities), and in return the Congolese would provide them with an equivalent amount of minerals. The formula was a familiar one: that is, a joint venture between Gécamines and the China Enterprise Group, which includes firms working in railroads, mines, and metallurgy. The international financial institutions reacted very negatively as this deal would greatly increase DRC's international debt, which they had been working to bring under control. Politically, it gave Kinshasa "room to maneuver" in its dealings with the global economy. After lengthy negotiations, the Congolese agreed to scale back the amount of the loan, eliminating three billion dollars' worth of infrastructure projects; if the Chinese got access to the same amount of minerals while providing a smaller loan, this was rather a good deal for them.[5]

China's collaboration with Congo soon ran into some typical Congolese problems. A Congolese parliamentary commission reported that of the $350 million in signing bonuses or "entry fee" that the Chinese consortium agreed to pay for signing the $6 billion swap deal, some $23 million had gone missing. The chair of the commission attributed the loss to the collusion of some senior officials of Gécamines with "local justice officials in Lubumbashi." The missing sum was nearly half of Gécamines' share of the "entry fee."[6]

Apart from the mining concession, the agreement with the Chinese included several smaller projects. One of these, for the production of biofuels, was estimated to be worth $1 billion. The Chinese planned to use 3 million hectares for oil plantations in four Congolese provinces (Equateur, Bandundu, Kasai Oriental, and Orientale). In 2008, the Congolese offered 250 hectares of fertile land for the project. Further discussions failed to bridge the gap, and according to the DRC Ministry of Agriculture, "nobody talks about it anymore." Most of the infrastructure projects, presumably intended to allow Kabila to claim he had fulfilled his campaign promises of 2006, had not materialized either.

In 2011, on the eve of national elections, Gécamines moved to offer its shares to investors, but a huge, secretive sale of assets threatened to undermine the planned offering. Israeli businessman Dan Gertler (a leading player in Congo minerals for a decade) was able to buy stakes in two mining projects without a sales price being announced. This was contrary to the interests of Gécamines, in that investors might be reluctant to buy the company's stock if it did not disclose its revenue from selling properties. One of the two former Gécamines properties, Mutanda Mining, supposedly is worth more than $3 billion. The sale of Gécamines stock was intended to bring in capital to boost output at the big copper company after years of underinvestment and political corruption. But it is hard to see how that goal was advanced by a separate sale of several of the most prized sub-units.

According to the terms of an agreement between the World Bank and the DRC government, sales and prices of Congo's natural resource assets were supposed to be made public. The head of the audit board of the National Assembly's Economic and Financial Committee complained, "Now that they're becoming a private company they don't tell us anything. . . . They must make management transparent and justify what the Congolese state has gained from the sale of all these assets."[7]

The partial privatization of Gécamines symbolizes so much that has gone wrong in the mining sector since the 1990s, including corruption and short-term profit-seeking. Some of the individual sell-offs and joint ventures will be discussed below.

Greed and Grievance in Central Africa

Paul Collier of the World Bank has written that grievance-based explanations of civil wars do not make much sense.[8] Greed, which expresses itself in plunder, is a more satisfactory explanation. My rejoinder is two-fold: (a) the Congo wars are not primarily civil wars, but external aggression passed off as civil war; and (b) of course the Rwandans, Ugandans, and others pillaged DRC, but that does not mean that one can dismiss the Rwandan Tutsi grievance against Hutu *génocidaires* on Congo soil as merely an excuse.

The overthrow of Mobutu reflects the convergence of political interests between the United States, Rwanda, Uganda, and Angola, but economic concerns were present as well. The RPF may have calculated that its war in DRC could be self-financing; certainly it discovered the means of making money from the war. Once Rwanda had sent the AFDL into Congo in 1996, Laurent Kabila (a former gold smuggler) knew exactly where to go to seize gold and other stockpiled wealth. Only after the war had dragged on for a decade and millions of Congolese had died did Rwanda refocus on its main motive in 1996: that is, to defeat or destroy the Hutu *génocidaires* of 1994, by now reorganized as the FDLR. Similarly, Zimbabwe's primary motivation in backing Laurent Kabila may have been political, but its leaders spent considerable time and effort in attempting to profit from joint ventures with Congolese firms.

François Grignon explains that rather than being dealt with directly during negotiations to end the Congo wars, "economic interests were integrated into the peace process and became a virtual 'hidden script' whereby Congolese belligerents cooperated with each other and their foreign governmental patrons to protect and disguise their own and their patrons' economic interests."[9] In 2000, the United Nations began investigating the link between the illegal exploitation of Congolese minerals through these networks and the ongoing fighting in the country. A series of reports by panels of experts laid out compelling evidence for exploitation of Congo's minerals by various armies and armed groups. However, no action was taken against firms or governments implicated in such abuse.

In 2006, then Senator Barack Obama introduced legislation authorizing at least $52 million per year in 2006 and 2007 for programs to provide humanitarian, security and democracy-building assistance in DRC. Signed into law at the end of 2006, the Obama Bill (PL 109–456) also stated that it was the policy of the United States to make all efforts to ensure that the government of DRC was "committed to responsible and transparent management of natural resources across the country" and attempted "to hold accountable individuals who illegally exploit the country's natural resources." DRC was to implement the Extractive Industries Transparency Initiative by enacting laws requiring disclosure and independent auditing of company payments and government receipts for natural resource extraction. President Bush signed the bill into law. However, neither George W. Bush nor Obama himself did much to implement its provisions.[10] (See also Chapter 6, pp. 189–91 on the Obama Bill.)

Finally, in 2010, President Obama signed into law "conflict minerals" legislation that had been promoted by the Enough Project, Global Witness, and other NGOs. To ensure its passage, the legislation was incorporated into the Dodd–Frank financial reform legislation. When the Obama administration embraced the conflict minerals legislation, and the Kabila government saluted this "notable initiative," one could only wonder what was in the current version of the "hidden script." It soon became clear that the Congolese government was defining "armed groups" so as to exclude any former armed groups integrated (however loosely) into the Congolese army (FARDC). This would include the Tutsi-led CNDP as well as some of the Mayi-Mayi militias. US Secretary of State Hillary Clinton spoke strongly of the need for transparency in the minerals trade, so that the link between sale of Congolese minerals and the violence of armed groups could be broken. It remained to be seen whether an effective certification system could be implemented in eastern DRC and whether the United States would insist on independent verification of the certification process in Uganda, Rwanda, and other neighboring countries that had been re-exporting Congolese minerals.

Conflict minerals – or the "3 Ts" plus gold, as the Enough Project called them – have dominated the public discussion on Congolese minerals. We shall examine the unfolding campaign to certify these products as "conflict free," before turning to minerals that are equally as important for the future of Congo, including cobalt, diamonds, and petroleum.

Conflict and "Conflict Minerals" in DRC's Hybrid War

During the second Congo war (1998–2003), the government controlled a zone from the Atlantic Ocean to Katanga, including two of DRC's greatest sources of wealth, Katanga's Copperbelt and Kasai's diamond fields. Kinshasa also controlled the first petroleum-producing wells, on- and offshore in Bas Congo. Uganda occupied much of the northern provinces of Orientale and Equateur. Mineral riches were concentrated in Orientale. Ituri district, which borders on Uganda, includes the famous Kilo-Moto gold mines, while the provincial capital Kisangani is a major hub of trade in diamonds and other exports. Rwanda controlled most of the former Kivu (North Kivu, South Kivu, and Maniema), with gold, tin, tantalum, and other resources. Rwanda's zone extended into northern Katanga and northern East Kasai, giving it access to additional tin, tantalum, and diamonds.

Congolese have reacted to the pillage of their country by blaming it all on Rwanda, Uganda, and their backers. Many claim that Rwanda has no gold, cassiterite (tin ore), or coltan (tantalum/niobium ore) of its own and that the large quantities exported after 1996 therefore derived entirely from eastern DRC. As in so much of the rhetorical combat surrounding the Congo wars, this is overstated. Rwanda possesses gold, cassiterite, wolframite (tungsten ore), and coltan. However, as of 1993 (the eve of the genocide), these resources remained largely undeveloped and contributed little to the Rwandan economy, which remained dependent on coffee (85 percent of export earnings) and foreign aid.

Shortly after the invasions of eastern Congo, Kagame and his associates began importing gold, cassiterite, and other valuable minerals from eastern DRC, and then re-exporting them as Rwandan products. At the same time, the Rwandan leaders pushed to develop their own mines. The government even brought representatives of the Dutch and American embassies to Gitarama to "inspect" a coltan mine, as though the presence of a small operating mine would prove that the vast amounts of coltan exported from Rwanda had or could have originated within its own borders.

An elite network exported minerals and other wealth (including timber and coffee) from each of the three zones: Congolese, Ugandan, and Rwandan. As pointed out by the UN experts panel on "Illegal Exploitation of Natural Resources and Other Forms of Wealth of the Democratic Republic of the Congo," the three networks varied in composition, and included Congolese, foreign Africans, and non-Africans of many nationalities (including Lebanese, Israelis, Indians, Pakistanis, Americans, Britons, and Belgians).

Colette Braeckman's map showed the flow of Congolese resources to neighboring states, as of 2003. Gold from Manono (Katanga), Lodja (East Kasai), and Kindu (Maniema) flowed to Kigali, Rwanda. (Lodja probably should have been shown as a source of diamonds rather than gold.) Diamonds from Kisangani also exited via Kigali. Kampala received diamonds from Bafwasende and gold from Isiro and Bunia.[11] The relationship between partition and pillage was direct. Rwanda controlled North Katanga, East Kasai, and Maniema through its proxy the RCD-Goma. Yangambi, Bumba, and Aketi were controlled by Bemba's MLC, aligned with Uganda. Bafwasende was controlled by the RCD-N, a split-off from the RCD led by the bureaucrat-turned-warlord Roger Lumbala.

Since the map represented the whole of Congo, no attempt was made to represent the myriad points of mineral extraction in North and South Kivu and in Ituri. Most of these minerals flowed out through Rwanda, although Mbusa Nyamwisi's RCD-ML controlled the northern portion of North Kivu (Beni-Lubero) and part of Ituri, and presumably exported most of its minerals through Uganda. Since Braeckman's book was published in 2003, many of these supply chains have continued to function, although various sources of gold, coltan, and other minerals have changed hands.

The RCD, formed by Rwanda and Uganda to put a Congolese face on the second war, "pursued a largely extractive approach by collecting taxes and exploiting natural resources." It consolidated its power structure in "the most strategic areas (urban centres and mining sites) of eastern DRC in order to have access to pre-war structures and networks of economic exchange."[12] The RCD established direct military control over the more lucrative mining sites. It also imposed taxes at the border, at mining sites, at airports, and at checkpoints on roads.

Inspired by the rise in world coltan prices in 2000, the RCD-Goma granted a tax monopoly on all coltan exports originating from mining areas under its control to a company named SOMIGL (Société Minière des Grands Lacs/Great Lakes Mining Company). This arrangement was short-lived because it failed to generate the expected income to the rebels.

To secure its dominance over the exploitation and trading of local resources, the RCD rebels "depended on the willingness of individuals and groups to align with them, in return for protection of their economic interests." This strategy soon revealed several shortcomings. One effect was what Koen Vlassenroot and Timothy Raeymaekers call "the militarization of pre-war networks of patronage." The rebel leadership could not prevent local RCD commanders from keeping some of the revenue from so-called "taxes."[13]

Lacking the means of organizing local production, the invaders and "rebels" attempted to exploit the producers so as to generate revenue and exercise social control. In order to do so, they were forced to negotiate with local Congolese entrepreneurs who held a monopoly on the access to vital economic resources, including mining, agriculture, and trade. For the entrepreneurs, "connection with the rebels was a necessary condition to continue or expand their activities and to increase the predictability of commercial activities in terms of logistics and revenues."[14] In the "grand nord" of North Kivu (Lubero – Beni – Butembo), the rebels of the RCD-K-ML were weak and the businessmen were strong, to the extent that the local Nande business elite became recognized as a legitimate regulatory authority of the Congo–Uganda border zone.

The formal end of the second Congo war in 2003 was supposed to lead to reunification of the country, but important areas, especially in the east, remained out of control of the central authorities in Kinshasa, who lacked the ability to police them, collect taxes, and perform other tasks of statehood there. Pillage continued.

Tackling the Supply Chain

The argument of the Enough Project is not merely that the sale of conflict minerals perpetuates the Congolese war by permitting various armed groups to buy weapons. Beyond that, because the "3 Ts" (tantalum, tungsten, and tin) and gold are used in the manufacture of mobile phones, games consoles, and other consumer electronics, consumers supposedly have the means of putting an end to conflict in DRC by pressuring the electronics manufacturers.[15] (The same argument motivates the Congo Conflict Minerals Act of 2009, which became US law as part of the Dodd–Frank financial reform law of 2010 – see above.) This is too simple. Even if one's cell phone contains material from eastern DRC, it does not necessarily constitute leverage for doing something useful about violence in that region.

Enough breaks down the supply chain of the four minerals into six steps:

1 The mines: A gold rush with guns.
2 Trading houses: Looking the other way.
3 Exporters: Minerals enter international markets.
4 Transit countries: Origins obscured.
5 Refiners: Minerals to metals.
6 Electronics companies: Conflict minerals in your phone.

The conflict mineral supply chain began at one of eastern DRC's many mines (step 1). Of thirteen major mines, armed groups supposedly controlled twelve. The FDLR controlled some of the mines. Other mines were managed by units of the Congolese army, in violation of Congo's mining laws, which prohibit the presence of the army in the mines. The soldiers, many of them ex-militia fighters recently integrated into the army, were illegally "taxing" miners, abusing the population – particularly the women and girls – and paying workers very poor wages. (In 2009–10, the FDLR was driven out of some mining areas, and the army, especially ex-CNDP units, took its place.)

Armed groups controlled the mines in different ways. At some mines the FDLR forced people to work, while at others their relationship to the local population was more strictly commercial. Robert, a local youth leader and civil society activist told Enough, "Overall, mine workers get very little from mining; in the armed areas it is only worse."

Step 2 is really two steps. Buyer-transporters bring the ore from the mines to trading houses, usually located in Bukavu or other cities. The trading houses in turn sell the material to firms that export the minerals. The buyers knew which of their purchases came from armed groups and thus were subsidizing the ongoing violence, yet they made the purchases and passed the goods along the supply chain.

Trading houses purchase and process the minerals. Exporters (step 3) pay the majority of these traders in advance for the minerals they will buy. The majority of the transporters and trading houses were operating in violation of Congo's mining laws, without proper licenses and registration. The government charged $500 for licenses, which the association of traders said was a prohibitively high price to pay. Supposedly only one in ten transporters in Bukavu was officially registered with the government. However, knowledgeable people, including government inspectors, said that such dealerships and transporters were widely known: there were approximately 100 trading houses each in Bukavu and Goma.

Armed groups controlled much of the transport from the mine to the buying house. They either took a large percentage of the profit from transporters – up to $40 per sack – or transported the minerals themselves. Enough estimated that the armed groups generated approximately $75 million from mineral transport in 2008, out of the total of $180 million earned by armed groups from the mineral trade.

The minerals were sent mainly by road, boat, or plane to the transit countries of Rwanda, Uganda, and Burundi (step 4). Some lots of minerals were legally exported, with taxes paid to the Congolese government, while others were smuggled. Either way, conflict minerals formed a major portion of the trade. Vast inconsistencies in the statistics recorded by neighboring countries attest to the scale of the smuggling. Uganda officially produced less than $6 million worth of gold in 2007, yet exported over $74 million worth of it. Rwanda produced $8 million worth of tin ore, but officially exported at least $30 million of it.

The crucial link in the supply chain, in terms of traceability, is refining (step 5). Metal processing companies take the Congolese minerals and smelt or chemically process them. In 2008, tin was the most lucrative conflict mineral in eastern Congo. Ten main smelting companies, almost all based in East Asia, processed over 80 percent of the world's tin. For tantalum, four companies based in Germany, the United States, China, and Kazakhstan made up the overwhelming majority of the chemical processing market. For tungsten, there were several processing companies in China, Austria, and Russia. The main destination for Congolese gold has been Dubai, in the United Arab Emirates. Uganda has begun refining Congolese gold. After the ore is refined into metal, it becomes impossible to distinguish tin or tantalum that originated in Congo. This is why it is essential that these companies document the source of their minerals and make their records subject to independent audits.

Finally, the refiners sold the minerals to the electronics companies (step 6), collectively the single largest consumer of the minerals from eastern Congo. The processed metals usually went through several sub-stages here: first to circuit board and computer chip manufacturers, then to cell phone and other electronics manufacturers, and finally to the mainstream electronics companies such as Intel, Apple, or Nintendo. Because these companies did not have a system to trace, audit, and certify where their materials come from, all cell phones, computers, and game consoles might contain conflict minerals from DRC.

Other industries with a significant stake in conflict minerals included tin can manufacturers, industrial tool and light bulb companies for tungsten, and automobile, aerospace, and defense contractors, as well as the banking and jewelry industries for gold.

The American conflict minerals legislation directly addressed the final stage, imposing on companies under US jurisdiction a requirement to certify to the Securities and Exchange Commission (SEC) that their products did not contain conflict minerals from DRC or adjacent countries. This was an exercise in "naming and shaming" in that no penalty was specified for companies unable to demonstrate that their products were conflict-free. Clearly, the manufacturers took the problem seriously and lobbied first the Congress to defeat the bill, and then the SEC to water down the requirements. The electronics companies did not maintain a united front, however: Motorola declared its intention to demonstrate a conflict-free supply chain, perhaps seeking a competitive advantage over other manufacturers.

To end the abuse of the population associated with illegal mining would require major changes within DRC. Even though the Congolese government hailed Dodd–Frank as a "noble initiative," it is far from evident that the government would want to carry out these changes, and whether it would be able to carry them out if it wanted to. First, it would have to eliminate the illegal military involvement in the minerals trade. It would have to investigate and sanction military personnel, shown to have been illegally involved in the minerals trade, to collude with armed groups, or to have intimidated state mining officials or police. Right away, one sees a problem. Kagame got rid of Kabila's *bête noire* Laurent Nkunda in exchange for Bosco Ntaganda, another Congolese Tutsi general, also accused of war crimes. Ntaganda has been accused of playing a major role in the illegal exportation of gold. Kabila reportedly relied on support from Ntaganda and the CNDP during the elections of 2011, and then turned against this awkward ally early in 2012. Kabila's attempt to transfer the Tutsi officers out of the eastern conflict minerals zone set off the so-called "M23 mutiny."

A problem of definition will have to be resolved before minerals can be certified. Under Dodd–Frank, the State Department is to produce maps showing which mines are under the control of armed groups. What is an armed group? The FDLR would qualify. What about the various Mayi-Mayi groups? While they are out in the bush fighting against all comers, they certainly would qualify as armed groups. Would this be the case for the Mayi-Mayi units that have been integrated into the FARDC? What about the same units if they desert from the FARDC? The Congolese government has said that of course FARDC units are not "armed groups" in terms of the legislation. Sorting this out promises to be difficult.

Apart from its response to the Dodd–Frank legislation from the United States, the DRC government should be fully implementing UN Security Council Resolution 1856 (2008), which requires all states "to take appropriate steps to end the illicit trade in natural resources, including if necessary through judicial means." It should submit to the UN Sanctions Committee the names of individuals and entities in DRC alleged to have conducted illicit trade of natural resources with armed groups in the east of the country.

Whether in terms of the Security Council resolution or Dodd–Frank, the Congolese government should provide effective state oversight of the mining sector. Accurate and centralized trade statistics should be kept that cover the quantity and type of minerals extracted from each mining site, transported by airfreight and other transport companies close to the mining sites, and purchased by buyers, trading houses, and exporters. Aside from providing reliable data on production and trade, and greater possibilities for effective surveillance of the trade, these records would allow accurate identification of all mining sites at which artisanal mining occurs.

Protection of the civilian population in mining areas, and protection of the lives and livelihoods of the several million Congolese earning a living from artisanal mining, will require a substantial effort on the part of the central authorities. The regulation, documentation, and policing required might well be beyond the capacity of the Congolese state in the near future.

Dodd–Frank clearly states that the SEC measures will have to cover imports not just from DRC but from contiguous countries as well, including Tanzania, Burundi, Rwanda, and Uganda.

Tanzania has its own gold industry in the area south of Lake Victoria, and a small refinery there, in the town of Mwanza. It also has a long history of serving as a conduit for gold smuggled out of South Kivu, including the gold from Kabila's "Hewa Bora" enclave. Tanzania asked to be given an extra year to conform to the certification requirements of Dodd–Frank.

Uganda only had two operating gold mines, although small deposits have been found here and there across the country. A Russian firm, Victoria Gold, opened a small refinery in Kampala in 2010; the manager admitted that most of the gold initially would come from DRC but claimed that none would be "conflict gold."

In 2011, Rajesh Export Ltd. of India announced that it was set to establish a gold and diamond processing refinery in Rwanda. The company would establish its continental headquarters in Rwanda because of the "favorable investment climate." Rwanda has small amounts of gold but no known diamonds. It seems likely that most of the gold and all of the diamonds processed and exported by Rajesh will originate in DRC, regardless of what the certificates may say.

In 2011–12, Rwanda made two symbolic gestures apparently designed to show that it was no longer engaged in pillage of Congolese minerals. First, it turned over to DRC several tons of minerals confiscated within Rwanda. Then it arrested four high-ranking military officers (including three generals) on charges of "indiscipline" for having engaged in business dealings with civilians in DRC. No mention was made of business dealings with military personnel in Congo. One of the four officers reportedly had previously headed the "Congo office" at the Rwandan presidency, which coordinated the pillage of minerals. Like the earlier episode involving the inspection of the tantalum mine near Gitarama, the Rwandan moves seemed to reflect a belief that its interlocutors were gullible.

One direct consequence of passage of the "conflict minerals" legislation was President Kabila's announcement that he was banning export of minerals from the two Kivus and

Maniema. The Canadian company Banro immediately announced that it had obtained an exception for its mining activity (in South Kivu and Maniema), allowing it to continue mining and exporting gold. The company also apparently has been allowed to displace local populations, including many artisanal miners, as it developed its concessions on an industrial model. Banro recently handed over to the local community at Luhwinja a new primary school, for 600 pupils. This was the latest in a series of schools, training centers, and other social services for populations living near Banro's Twangiza and Namoya gold mines. The total amount being spent on these activities, through the Banro Foundation, presumably represents a very small amount of the profit being derived by Banro from its Kivu–Maniema mining.

Each of Banro's four mines was located just a few kilometers from territory controlled by the FDLR, according to Hans Romkema of the Netherlands-based Conflict and Transition Consultancies. The FDLR did not control any of the mines. Rather, it controlled the territory around the mines, controlled the local population, and collected taxes. When it came under pressure from government forces, the FDLR responded by attacking villages, killing both government troops and civilians. To keep working, Romkema suggests, Banro had to make deals with both the Congolese government and whatever militia controls the territory in which their mine is located. Someone must have passed the message to leave the miners alone.[16]

When Kabila suspended mining activity in the Kivus and Maniema, Geminaco claimed an exception for a gold mine at Omate, in Walikale territory, North Kivu. This was rather different from Banro's situation in South Kivu. The mining company apparently had obtained control of the mine by ousting the previous owners. General Gabriel Amisi Kumba, the head of Congo's ground forces, allegedly enabled the mining company to take over the mine in exchange for a 25 percent share. In 2012, Kabila put General Amisi in charge of the campaign to put down the M23 mutiny; the failure of the FARDC to crush M23 despite its numerical superiority was attributed to Amisi's incompetence or even his complicity with his former associates in the army of the RCD.

Clearly, the campaign led by Enough, Global Witness, and others has affected the marketing of conflict minerals from eastern DRC. Without this campaign, the US Congress would not have passed legislation requiring due diligence on the part of minerals processors and electronics manufacturers doing business in the United States. Presumably the Kabila government would not have suspended the exportation of minerals from the Kivus. However, this "progress" does not mean that the violence in the Kivus has diminished. The NGO campaign leading up to Dodd–Frank was successful through its oversimplification of a complex issue. The suggestion is that the consumer who buys the cell phone or games console could end the killing and rape in eastern DRC by demanding a conflict-free electronic apparatus, or simply by not buying the apparatus.

The relationship between conflict minerals and sexual violence, in particular, however, is far less direct than the NGOs suggest. Although rape has been a weapon in eastern DRC, much of the sexual violence is not directly linked to minerals. Armed groups that are not participants in the trade in "conflict minerals" commit rape and also, increasingly, it is committed by civilians. For this reason, it is unlikely that drastic reduction of the trade in conflict minerals would end large-scale sexual violence. Moreover, armed groups in North and South Kivu have been fighting to control a variety of resources beyond minerals, including grazing land and timber for charcoal to be sold in Rwanda. They also are fighting for the less tangible resource of control over local administration and its ability to collect taxes and provide jobs.

Minerals in the Former Government Zone

The "3 Ts" and gold, important as they are to Congolese in the eastern war zone and to the international electronics manufacturers, are not the most valuable or important of Congo's minerals. The extreme attention given to the so-called "conflict minerals" has permitted major changes in the ownership of other assets, often through opaque transactions, to pass unnoticed.

It is important to distinguish the importance of mining to the DRC economy from the importance of DRC to the world minerals industry. DRC played a globally significant role in the production of cobalt and diamonds in 2008. The DRC share of world cobalt production amounted to 45 percent in that year. The Congolese share of industrial diamond production was 30 percent and of gem-quality diamonds, 6 percent. DRC was estimated to possess some 48 percent of the world's cobalt reserves. Cobalt's use in jet engines accounts for its prominent place on the US government's list of "strategic materials": that is, a commodity whose lack of availability during a national emergency would seriously affect the country's economic, industrial, and defensive capability.

The American copper mining company Phelps-Dodge won the biggest prize in the scramble for Gécamines properties and for Congolese minerals in general, namely the huge copper–cobalt deposits at Tenke-Fungurume (in the Katanga Copperbelt). With the apparent help of the US embassy, the company was able to navigate through the mess about wartime contracts and secure majority ownership of Tenke-Fungurume.

The UMHK had discovered the Tenke-Fungurume deposits in 1918, but did not exploit them because the appropriate technology did not exist. In the late 1960s, after Mobutu nationalized the UMHK, two international consortia struggled for the right to develop the deposits. The Société Minière de Tenke-Fungurume (Tenke-Fungurume Mining Company, SMTF, involving British, South African, and other interests) won the struggle, over a Belgian-led group. After several years of economic and political struggle, and hundreds of millions of dollars invested, SMTF walked away and the ore deposits remained untouched by industrial mining for another thirty years (although local people began artisanal mining).

In 1996, after the Rwandan-led invasion, but before Laurent Kabila had taken over in Kinshasa, Swedish businessman Adolf Lundin secured rights to Tenke-Fungurume from

Mobutu. Lundin renewed his claim once Kabila had become president, but was unable to re-launch mining at the Katanga site at that time. A parliamentary commission found that Lundin Holdings made its first payment toward the Tenke concession – nearly $50 million dollars – in 1997. The deposit allegedly was paid into the account of Kabila's Rwanda-based Comiex.

During negotiations with the transitional (1 + 4) regime in 2005, Lundin obtained vast reductions in the entry fees and shares to be retained by the local partner under the original agreement concluded in 1996. In 2005, the DRC negotiators agreed to reduce the Tenke-Fungurume fee from $250 million to $50 million (which was an additional payment to the $50 million that Lundin paid in 1997), and reduce their country's ownership share from 45 to 17.5 percent. The reduction in DRC's share represented the surrender of revenues from 5 million tonnes of copper – worth at least $30 billion – over the life of the mine.

The World Bank had mandated a moratorium on new mineral contract negotiations pending a legal review of existing contracts, and the Tenke-Fungurume contract apparently was flagged as problematic. However, the US government seemed to have ignored the ban and helped to push through a renegotiated deal with the transitional government in order to obtain more favorable terms, and a more solid legal footing than the project originally possessed, given its antecedents under Mobutu. The US Embassy lobbied the DRC government to sign a new agreement whereby Phelps-Dodge became the senior partner of Lundin at Tenke-Fungurume.

Despite calls to delay commitments until the pending contract reviews were completed, the Tenke-Fungurume deal received a further seal of approval in the form of sizable investments from international public financial institutions: $250 million from the US Overseas Private Investment Corporation, 100 million euros ($136 million) from the European Investment Bank (EIB), and another $100 million from the African Development Bank (which is funded by African and other governments). The EIB said it regarded the project as highly significant from an economic and developmental point of view and that environmental and social issues connected with the project had been carefully analyzed. Critics within DRC and outside noted that the local population had been provided with information in French on the impact of the project, which most of them could not read. Many people had been relocated to make way for the project without replacement housing being provided. (In 2010, the EIB announced it would not fund the first phase of Tenke-Fungurume.)

After what a South African business journalist called "Tenke arm wrestling," the Tenke-Fungurume contract was revised to increase the stake of Gécamines (i.e. the Congolese state) to 20 percent. Freeport's share in the joint venture was reduced to 56 percent, and that of Lundin to 24 percent. Gécamines was awarded the post of deputy managing director and Tenke-Fungurume agreed to buy various goods and services from the company. The journalist called the revised contract "legalized daylight robbery" but added that DRC remained volatile "and inflamed with serious questions about the ability of President Joseph Kabila to hold onto power for much longer." If he were to be ousted, who knew what a successor regime might come up with as terms for a fair contract?[17]

Tenke-Fungurume began producing copper in 2009, but its problems were not over. On two occasions in 2010, hundreds of artisanal miners looted the Tenke offices, set fire to trucks and stole copper cathodes waiting for export. The head of a local miners' trade union explained, "Tenke has rights but the problem is that they are not engaging with the people and there are no jobs – the miners just want to be able to work." The company said it was "seeking opportunities to defuse tension" in cooperation with local authorities.[18]

Congo's uranium is a "strategic mineral" of a different sort. Uranium from the Shinkolobwe mine in Katanga was used to build the first atomic bombs. The UMHK ceased mining at Shinkolobwe in 1959 and sealed the shaft with concrete in 1961. However, anarchic mining continued on the site. In 2004, eight people were killed and thirteen injured in a partial collapse of artisanal workings. Since the end of the

Cold War, the US concern has been that hostile forces such as North Korea or al-Qaeda could get their hands on Shinkolobwe's uranium.

The Congolese NGO Association Africaine de Défense des Droits de l'Homme (African Association for Defense of Human Rights, Asadho) denounced the illicit artisanal exploitation of the uranium mine and warned of dangers to the miners and to surrounding populations. Despite the mine having been officially closed, mining continued with the complicity of Congolese military personnel, who allegedly charged a fee to miners entering the mine. Asadho warned also of the lack of transparency in the awarding of a contract to the French nuclear power firm AREVA.

The Congolese government responded by arresting Golden Misabiko, Katanga provincial president of Asadho, and charging him with threatening state security and defamation. He was tried swiftly and sentenced to four years in prison and eight additional months of suspended sentence. Released on bail, Misabiko fled to South Africa, thereby removing from the scene one of Congo's most vociferous defenders of human rights.[19]

Diamonds are found in and around kimberlite pipes near Mbuji-Mayi (East Kasai) and Kundelungu (Katanga) and in alluvial deposits across a vast swathe of east-central Congo. Under colonial rule, diamonds had been mined mainly near Mbuji-Mayi (then known as Bakwanga) and Tshikapa. By the 1980s, alluvial deposits were being exploited near Lodja (300 kilometers north of Mbuji-Mayi) and there were reports of diamonds in Equateur and Orientale provinces, and southern Bandundu, along the Angolan border. Because of their value on the international market and their small size, diamonds have long been smuggled out of Congo. Smuggling increased greatly in the 1960s, shortly after independence.

During the Congo wars, diamonds became a "conflict mineral": that is, a target of armed groups and a means of financing their operations. Mbuji-Mayi and Tshikapa remained in the hands of the Kinshasa government and helped to finance its war effort, but the Rwandan and Ugandan armies fought for control of the city of Kisangani, an important center for the diamond trade. The US Geological Survey estimated that between half a million and one million Congolese worked as artisanal or small-scale diamond miners in 2007, with another 100,000 employed in diamond trading. The logic of the Kimberley Process – that is, voluntary public–private cooperation to restrict the export of "blood diamonds" – could not be used in DRC because internal controls were so weak that no one could determine where the exported diamonds actually originated.

The recent fortunes of the diamond company Minière de Bakwanga (Bakwanga Mining, MIBA) illustrate changes since the colonial period as regards DRC's most important export product. MIBA (as Forminière) was one of the key elements in the mixed public–private business world of colonial Congo, and in 1960 the company was at the center of the secession of "South Kasai," the predominantly Luba-Kasai area in the former Kasai province.

Over the years, the MIBA concession has been the site of numerous deaths of artisanal miners. Massacres took place at the localities of Katekelayi and Luamela near Mbuji-Mayi in 1979; Mobutu's security forces apparently killed large numbers of artisanal miners who had been digging for diamonds on MIBA land. Such conflicts, pitting industrial mining companies against the "everyday resistance" of artisanal miners, have occurred many times since then, since the rights of local people and those of large companies (including partially state-owned companies such as MIBA) have yet to be reconciled. Artisanal diamond miners were killed in 2002, 2003, 2006, and probably other years as well. Amnesty International protested to the UN Security Council in 2002 that the guards hired by MIBA – who included Congolese and Zimbabwean troops – were untrained for police work and used violence indiscriminately.[20]

First Mobutu and then the Kabilas treated MIBA as a cash cow, without reinvesting in infrastructure. Under Laurent Kabila, MIBA suffered a major decline. Its gemstone output in 1998 was 6.8 million carats but declined sharply to 5 million carats in 1999 and was expected to be no more than

3.5 million carats in 2000. Large gemstones almost disappeared from DRC exports, which suggests that they were being stolen and smuggled out of the country.

Laurent Kabila had wasted no time helping himself to the company's rich coffers. In April 1997, MIBA's top management instructed the Belgolaise Bank of Brussels to transfer $3.5 million from MIBA's account to Kabila's company Comiex in Kigali, via the City Bank of New York, noting it as "MIBA's contribution to the war effort." More "voluntary" contributions followed in quick succession. The firm was forced to give $2 million in cash to the state presidency budget during 1998.[21]

MIBA also had to provide housing and transportation to the provincial governor and military commanders, and to divert its trucks and bulldozers from their normal work sites to carry out extension work on the Mbuji-Mayi airstrip. Power shortages were causing havoc to MIBA's diamond crushing and washing units. This was because the company's hydro-power station at Lubilanji was also forced to provide electricity to the city of Mbuji-Mayi in order to make up for the inability of SNEL, the national electricity company, to fulfill this task. By the end of 1998, MIBA had problems repaying a $3.2 million loan from the Central Bank. In May 1999, a parcel containing the entire production for the month (400,000 carats worth $10 million) was seized at Kinshasa airport on Laurent Kabila's orders.

MIBA workers complained that the Kabilas treated Kasai Oriental as a "rebel" region. Consignments of fuel, maize, and fish imported from Southern Africa for the workers were being seized on a regular basis without explanation or compensation by the Katanga authorities during their transit to Kasai Oriental. Laurent Kabila, himself a Katangan, did not move a finger to punish the thieves.

The workers also denounced the transfer of MIBA assets to new international companies Sengamines and Oryx, saying that Kabila was sacrificing their future. The UK government and press expressed concern that the operation might finance the exploitation of "conflict diamonds," since one of the shareholders was the Zimbabwean army. British hypocrisy was evident, since the main offenders in the area of conflict minerals were their protégés, Uganda and Rwanda.

As MIBA was declining, new forces were rising in the diamond sector, notably the Israeli Dan Gertler, who reportedly paid $20 million to Laurent Kabila in return for the right to export 88 percent of DRC's diamonds. Some saw Gertler manipulating President Joseph Kabila, but others describe the Israeli as a front man for Kabila in the minerals sector. Presumably, the relationship was mutually beneficial. (From his initial position in diamond marketing, Gertler moved into metals and petroleum. He apparently is a speculator, with little interest in long-term development of such properties.)

Each of the stories of mining companies surviving or beginning operations in the former Kinshasa-controlled zone is unique, yet they share common elements. Mobutu's "warlord" approach to the economy has been modified by the Kabilas. The surviving colonial parastatals – Gécamines, MIBA, and so on – serve as cash cows, but have become virtually obligatory joint-venture partners for foreign investors in DRC mining.

The Future of Congo's Oil

No list of Congolese "conflict minerals" would be complete without petroleum. While the exploitation of oil has not financed rebels or led to the death of thousands of civilians, there continue to be tensions over oil between DRC and two of its neighbors, Angola and Uganda, leading to fatalities. Along the Atlantic Coast, Joseph Kabila's Congo is contesting the role of Angola as regards the offshore border between the two countries as well as the arrangements regarding exploitation of oil and distribution of oil products agreed in the aftermath of the two invasions of DRC in the 1990s. The Angolans have defined their offshore rights (offshore from Angola per se and from Cabinda) so as to deny DRC any exclusive zone, despite its 24 kilometers of shoreline. Supposedly, oil from new wells developed in an offshore Zone of Common Interest extending from the 15 kilometer coastal zone in a 10 kilometer strip to the 375 kilometer (200 mile) limit would be shared between the two neighbors. However, no agreement has been signed. In the meantime, as Congolese see it, Angola has achieved its status as the leading oil exporter of sub-Saharan Africa, partly at their expense.[22]

At the opposite end of the country, where the DRC–Uganda border bisects Lake Albert, two neighbors have been involved in a struggle that has involved deaths of oil company personnel and of Ugandan fishermen. The border between the two countries is inadequately delimited at Lake Albert and the Semliki River, north of the lake. Uganda has authorized drilling on its side of the border and soon should be a significant oil exporter. On the Congo side, concessions initially granted to two of the same small exploration companies have been withdrawn, and re-awarded to companies connected to a nephew of South African president Jacob Zuma. Anti-Kabila websites had a field day with this story, claiming to discern the shadowy figures of Kabila associates Dan Gertler and Augustin Katumba Mwanke, and perhaps Kabila himself, behind the curtain. At a minimum, the Congolese state was acting as a speculator rather than a regulator, as the International Crisis Group put it.[23]

Tullow Oil and Heritage Oil had negotiated rights to two blocks of territory on the Congolese side of Lake Albert. This was during the "1 + 4" days when DRC had one president and four vice-presidents. The two oil companies negotiated their deal with the deputy minister of energy and hydrocarbons, Nicolas Badingaka. The minister, Salomon Banamuhere, was traveling in the interior of the country at the time. Badingaka represented the forces loyal to Vice-President Jean-Pierre Bemba, while his "boss" Banamuhere followed Kabila. Since Tullow and Heritage already held concessions on the Uganda side of Lake Albert, DRC may have feared that its eastern neighbor would come to dominate the oil industry in the Lake Albert area. (Bemba's MLC had been launched by Uganda as a rival to Rwanda's RDC.)

While the two exploration companies were able to bring in major companies, including ENI of Italy, as partners in Uganda operations, ongoing uncertainty on the Congo side

delayed the process of finding major partners. Zuma Khulu-
buse claimed that he and his associates in the hitherto
unknown firms Caprikat and Foxwhelp were going to develop
the concessions themselves, but this appeared unlikely. Major
oil companies from France, the United States, and China were
likely suitors.

Oil deposits may exist further south, between DRC and
Rwanda and between DRC and Tanzania. The Congolese
government initially agreed to allow oil exploration in the
Virunga National Park (a UNESCO World Heritage Site,
home to some of the world's last mountain gorillas) but
withdrew the authorization in the face of a wave of international protest.

There apparently are further oil deposits in DRC's Cuvette
Centrale (central basin) and a Brazilian firm has proposed
building a pipeline from the oil wells to the port of Matadi,
near the mouth of the Congo River. Work would begin on
this project by 2015, according to the Ministry of Oil. This
project may or may not prove feasible; it does have the advantage of not involving any of DRC's neighbors.

Conclusion: Who Will Get a Slice?

Conflict minerals in North and South Kivu have drawn most
international attention, but DRC's mineral problems are
nationwide and center on its weak and corrupt government.
The British NGO the Catholic Fund for Overseas Development (CAFOD) has publicized the dangers associated with
AngloGold Ashanti's activities in Ituri district, and in particular its tailings retreatment project (tailings being the materials
left over after after extraction of valuable minerals from ore).
The project apparently would create fewer jobs than the
number of people displaced. The risk to the drinking water
from pollutants in the tailings and from the chemicals used
to treat the tailings is understated, according to CAFOD.[24]

The Congolese NGO Asadho denounced the illicit artisanal exploitation of the uranium mine at Shinkolobwe with
the complicity of Congolese military personnel. Government

action against Golden Misabiko of Asadho seems to have been meant as a warning to human rights activists not to interfere in the commercial activities of the soldiers. It will be difficult to ensure the safety of miners or the certification of "conflict minerals," whether from Katanga, the Kivus, or anywhere else, unless the NGOs are permitted to perform their task as whistle-blowers.

Braeckman's "new predators"[25] presumably included Rwanda, Uganda, and other African participants in the Congo wars and the pillage that followed the invasions. The United States and Britain were predators in their own right (assisting Freeport and AngloGold Ashanti, respectively), but also enablers as regards Rwanda and Uganda. As the NGO Human Rights First has explained, a

> third-party enabler of genocide or other crimes against human-ity is any government, commercial entity, or individual that directly or indirectly provides to the perpetrator resources, goods, services or other support that help sustain the commis-sion of atrocities. An enabler knows or should know both about the atrocities and how its goods or support are likely to contribute to the commission of these crimes.[26]

The United States and the United Kingdom clearly are enablers according to the Human Rights First definition. They also provide political cover, which may not be covered by that definition. Both the United States and the United Kingdom have a long history of attempting to suppress international reports unfavorable to their allies/clients.

The invasion of Zaïre/Congo in 1996 opened the door for outsiders to move into the vast mineral-rich country. Some of the first were relative small fish, the Swede Lundin and the Mauritian/British Jean-Raymond Boulle, and they success-fully played the role of pilot fish, eventually being bought out by much larger companies with the deep pockets required to invest in the Copperbelt. American government backing helped the American copper giant Phelps-Dodge (now part of Freeport-McMoRan) take over Lundin's Tenke-Fungu-rume project. Other governments also helped their businesses navigate Congolese waters. AREVA got a contract to develop the uranium mine at Shinkolobwe, thanks in part to strong backing from French President Nicolas Sarkozy. Similarly, South Korean President Lee Myung-Bak arrived in Kinshasa at the head of a delegation including representatives of the Korean National Oil Corporation and of POSCO steel (the world's largest steel company). The oil company is to launch a joint venture with the Congolese company Cohydro, including a barter component, while the steel company is to explore Congo's iron resources (presumably the ones that prompted the ill-fated Maluku steel factory in the 1970s). The Korean package also included a loan to DRC. In short, it resembled the Chinese approach, with barter of minerals for infrastructure at the center.

Many of the deals reached during the war years or thereafter seem to have been disadvantageous to DRC and the Congolese population, to say the least. The lack of transparency is worrisome. Against that, one should weight the possibility that the sheer number of partners – American, Chinese, South African, Canadian, Australian, French, South Korean, Brazilian, and other nationalities – may mitigate against foreign dependency. There still remains much to be done, notably as regards environmental impact and the rights of artisanal miners and other local people.

The common thread in these and other cases is the government of DRC, which is a "vast, organized scam" according to Pierre Englebert. The politicians and administrators get rich by "keeping their state dysfunctional" and "promote violence to serve their interests."[27] The Congolese minerals sector seems to be reviving after years of decline. What remains to be seen, however, is who will get a slice of Congo's magnificent cake. Will Congo's riches be remarkable for the misery they generate? Will they continue to finance rebellion and disorder? Will the proceeds be frittered away by a state that acts as a speculator, with no long-term vision? Or will they finally benefit Congo's children, as Patrice Lumumba hoped in 1960?

6 | The Responsibility to Protect _____

As we noted in the Introduction, the Congo has been a hot spot, off and on, since the nineteenth century, and shows few signs of cooling off any time soon. The country's riches continue to attract the interest of foreigners, from within Africa and from beyond. The state remains extremely weak, both in terms of its ability to impose order within and its ability to defend its frontiers and its people. The combination of great riches to be had, and a weak state largely incapable of repelling invaders, means that future wars are likely. The Congolese people will continue to need protection, from their own government and from other, stronger states, until they can protect themselves.

Over the past century, international rules and norms have developed so that atrocities such as those that took place under King Leopold's Congo Free State should be prevented, or at least punished. Clearly, however, the rules and norms have not been enforced or internalized: the atrocities that have occurred in DRC since the mid-1990s are on the same scale as those of the 1880s and 1890s. In this chapter, we shall examine the interaction of change on the level of rules and norms and on the level of behavior, attempting to determine who has the responsibility to protect Congolese civilians, and who is exercising it.

"Humanitarian intervention" has been invoked since the beginning of the Congolese state, although the expression is more recent than the behavior. Leopold II exploited humanitarianism, in the form of the campaign against the Arab slave trade, as one of the public justifications for his intervention in Central Africa. At the Berlin Conference of 1884–5, the "international community," in the form of fourteen European powers plus the United States, spent most of its time and energy on the principles by which some of its members could acquire territory in Africa; however, it also devoted the second chapter of the General Act of Berlin to banning the slave trade from the "Conventional Basin of the Congo."[1] Presumably some participants believed in the mission of protecting the local people from slavery, but the cynical manipulation of the issue set a pattern that has endured.

When forced labor took the place of Afro-Arab slavery in Leopold's Free State, and state monopolies flourished at the expense of the promised free trade, millions of Congolese died. The Catholic Church largely accepted Leopold's claim to be bringing Christian civilization to Central Africa, but a number of Protestant missionaries denounced the abuses. The Congo Reform Association turned the humanitarian impulse against the Free State, asking for action to end the violence.

Forced by the reform campaign to annex the Free State, Belgium preserved and reinforced Leopold's tripartite system of domination by the colonial administration, the state-chartered capitalist corporations, and the Catholic Church. The transfer of sovereignty from the Congo Free State to the Belgian Kingdom occurred before World War I, in an era in which the notion of international responsibility remained extremely vague. The "international community" accepted the legitimacy of Belgian rule and paid little attention to Belgian repression of a series of revolts, often provoked by forced cultivation and the imposition of taxes.

The decolonization of Congo took place in the context of the Cold War and of Third World reactions to it (the Bandung Conference, the All-African Peoples' Conference, and the like). Belgium gambled on the possibility of a neo-colonial transition to a nominally independent state in which elected Congolese institutions would coexist with the "colonial trinity" (administration, companies, Church). Once the Force

Publique soldiers had mutinied against their white Belgian officers, however, the "international community" faced the first in a series of Congo crises. The "Responsibility to Protect" was not evoked in 1960. When the Force Publique mutinied, Belgium sent in "metropolitan" troops, ostensibly to protect Belgian civilians from murder and rape at the hands of the mutineers. President Kasa-Vubu and Prime Minister Lumumba appealed for help against "external aggression." The UN Security Council responded by asking Belgium to withdraw and authorized the sending of ONUC.

The ONUC mandate was to ensure the withdrawal of the Belgian forces, to assist the government in maintaining law and order, to maintain the territorial integrity and political independence of Congo, to prevent civil war, and to expel mercenaries. This mandate was unclear as to priorities among the various elements of the mandate, however. Nowhere was there an explicit reference to the responsibility to protect civilians. The UN eventually used two provisions – the right of UN personnel to travel freely and to defend themselves – to suppress the Katanga secession, thereby maintaining the territorial integrity of Congo. If that was not done earlier, the reason for the delay was political rather than legal.

The Cold War context weighed heavily on decision makers, including UN Secretary-General Dag Hammarskjöld. Congolese political scientist Georges Nzongola-Ntalaja writes that Hammarskjöld "interpreted the UN mandate in accordance with Western neocolonialist interests and the US Cold War imperative of preventing Soviet expansion in the Third World."[2] This led to a bitter dispute between Lumumba and Hammarskjöld, which (in Nzongola-Ntalaja's opinion) led to the US- and Belgian-led initiatives to assassinate the democratically elected prime minister who had invited in the UN.

Hammarskjöld declared that the killings of Luba civilians in eastern Kasai by Congolese army troops had "the characteristics of the crime of genocide, since they appear to be directed toward the extermination of a specific ethnic group, the Baluba tribe."[3] This was a misuse of the term "genocide," since there was no clear intention to exterminate the Luba-Kasai. It is best understood as ethnic violence, possibly a war crime, an attack on civilians in the context of a campaign against the secessionist movement led by Kalonji and other Luba-Kasai leaders. Nevertheless, the Hammarskjöld attack weakened Lumumba's position. The UN restored order, ended the Katanga secession, and consolidated the Congolese government, in line with its mandate. However, some of the UN accomplishments were called into question as soon as it withdrew its forces. The nationalist bloc, on its heels since the murder of its leader Lumumba, came roaring back and quickly took control of half the national territory. Nationalist "rebels" killed many Congolese, particularly those seen as enemies of Lumumba and profiteers of independence. In turn, the central government and its backers killed many Congolese seen as rebel sympathizers.

Using Western (white) hostages as a pretext, the United States and Belgium decapitated the Lumumbist "People's Republic of the Congo" in 1964. America's man Mobutu took power a year later and remained there for more than thirty years. During the first twenty-five years of Mobutu's rule – corresponding to the second half of the Cold War – the West tolerated misrule by its Cold War ally, much as it did with Suharto in Indonesia.

Mobutu's armed forces proved incapable of defending the national frontiers but carried out massive reprisals against Congolese civilians suspected of collaboration with invaders or rebels. In 1971, many civilians were killed when government FAZ troops burned their houses during reprisal operations following incursions by Laurent Kabila's PRP into villages of South Kivu. In 1977, following "Shaba I" (the invasion of southern Shaba or Katanga by the Angola-based FLNC) the FAZ counter-offensive with support of Moroccan troops produced a terrible repression of the civilian population of southwest Katanga, suspected of collusion with the invaders. The FLNC was Lunda-led and most of the civilian victims presumably were Lunda as well, yet no one to my knowledge called the repression genocide. An insurrection in southern Bandundu, led by someone claiming to be the resurrected Pierre Mulele (who had been executed by Mobutu's forces in 1968 for his role in the Lumumbist "Simba" rebellion), was repressed at a cost of 500 lives. Punitive action against illegal miners near Mbuji-Mayi in 1979 cost over 100 lives (see Chapter 5). None of these cases of disproportionate use of force by government against its own civilians attracted much international attention. The Carter administration, which had proclaimed human rights its top foreign policy priority, apparently accepted Mobutu's explanation that Cuba backed the FLNC, and on that basis provided "non-lethal" assistance to the FAZ during "Shaba II."

Mobutu was slow to adjust to the ending of the Cold War, a new situation in which he would be subject to greater scrutiny. Following violence against students from his home province of Equateur at the University of Lubumbashi, his men carried out a punitive expedition on the campus. "Radio Trottoir" (the Congolese rumor mill) soon referred to the killing of several dozen students. The Zaïrian opposition picked up the rumors in order to push Belgium into adopting a firmer attitude toward the Mobutu regime. On May 22, 1990, the Belgian daily *Le Soir* claimed that the disturbances at Lubumbashi had resulted in a "massacre" of more than fifty people. The same day the prime minister of Zaïre, Lunda Bululu, and the governor of Shaba, Louis Alphonse Koyagialo, denied this claim. Three days later, Belgium suspended aid and asked for an international commission of inquiry. While it has never been possible to establish the precise number of casualties, it seems that observers, the media, and the Belgian authorities, which apparently wanted to seize the opportunity to get rid of Mobutu, overstated the toll.

Violence became commonplace. Starting in 1991, soldiers rioted in Kinshasa and other major cities, in part over issues of pay. The situation grew more and more dangerous for Congolese civilians. The UN Mapping Report of 2010 found that the most serious violations of human rights and international humanitarian law between March 1993 and June 1996 happened in Katanga, North Kivu, and Kinshasa.[4] The violence in Shaba-Katanga, directed against Luba-Kasai, was attributed to two sets of factors. On the one hand, there were long-standing grievances of "authentic Katangans" against what they saw as outsiders who had come in to take jobs and mineral resources that belonged to the locals. On the other hand, Mobutu's rule in Kinshasa was being challenged by the opposition alliance headed by Étienne Tshisekedi, himself a Luba-Kasai. In this context, Mobutu found it useful to fan the flames of ethnic hatred against the Luba. Once Tshisekedi had been evicted from the premiership in 1993, Mobutu did not need the Katangans anymore; he deployed his security forces to suppress the youth wing of the Katangan party, the Union des Fédéralistes et des Républicains Indépendants (Union of Federalists and Independent Republicans, UFERI), which had been attacking the Luba-Kasai.

Similarly, in North Kivu, Mobutu alternated between playing the ethnic card and intervening to restore calm. The victory of the RPF in Rwanda followed by flight of some 700,000 mainly Hutu Rwandans into North Kivu shattered the unity of the Banyarwanda of Kivu; members of the Tutsi minority were victimized by other groups and in some cases by the authorities. Mobutu reacted in contradictory fashion, aggravating the situation. In August 1995, for example, FAZ soldiers forcibly repatriated several thousand Rwandan refugees (presumably Hutu) from the Mugunga camp (near Goma) and handed them over to the Rwandan authorities. In the first half of 1996, in contrast, members of the Zaïrian security forces forcibly expelled to Rwanda an unknown number of Tutsi living in Goma and in the territories of Rutshuru, Masisi, and Lubero. Members of the security forces also pillaged many Tutsi homes.

When the Rwandan army crossed the border and attacked the refugee camps in Kivu, Mobutu's FAZ pillaged the local area and then fled. Clearly they felt no responsibility to protect civilians. Thus unopposed, the Rwandan army began a systematic campaign against Congo's Hutu inhabitants. As the UN Mapping Report suggests, this campaign might have involved genocide. At the time, however, the international community tried to ignore these atrocities, despite the beginning of an agreement to assume collective responsibility for mass violence against civilians.

Responsibility to Protect, Globally and in DRC

The concept of Responsibility to Protect (R2P) emerged around 1990, as the Mobutu regime was melting down. This idea connects a state's responsibilities toward its population and the responsibility of the "international community" in case a state fails to fulfill its responsibilities. One important aim is to provide a legal and ethical basis for "humanitarian intervention": that is, intervention by external actors (preferably the international community through the UN) in a state that is unwilling or unable to prevent or stop genocide, massive killings, and other massive human rights violations. Supporters of R2P view it as a method of establishing a normative basis for humanitarian intervention and its consistent application. Detractors argue that by justifying external breaches of state sovereignty, R2P encourages foreign aggression by stronger states. The DRC case seems to support the latter contention, at least in the short run.

The R2P concept was strengthened by the failure of the international community to protect civilians in Rwanda in 1994. There was plenty of blame to go around. Extremists in the Hutu government apparently were willing to do anything, even commit genocide, to hang onto Rwanda. The Tutsi invaders of the RPF apparently were more concerned to seize power – perhaps even shooting down the president's plane – than to save their fellow Tutsi from genocide. The French apparently were more concerned with backing "their" Rwandans than with the interests of Rwanda as a whole. General Roméo Dallaire, force commander of the UN Assistance Mission for Rwanda, later charged that Kofi Annan, Director of Peacekeeping Operations for the UN, had been overly passive in his response to the imminent genocide, holding back UN troops from intervening to settle the conflict, and from providing more logistical and material support. Ten years later, Annan conceded, "I could and should have done more to sound the alarm and rally support."[5]

While the contending Rwandan parties, the French, and the UN all share in the blame for the Rwandan catastrophe, the United States bears a heavy burden of responsibility. In failing to protect civilians, President Bill Clinton violated his own public commitment. Running for president in 1992, Clinton had declared, "If the horrors of the Holocaust taught us anything, it is the high cost of remaining silent and paralyzed in the face of genocide." Two years later the same man remained silent and paralyzed in the face of genocide. As an American army officer wrote, the United States was alone in possessing the political and military power to organize and lead an intervention "to stop the slaughter – yet America took no action."[6] Instead, the Clinton administration decided not to act, "a startling decision in retrospect given the expressed principles of the administration and the almost unbelievable scale of the unfolding tragedy." This was despite the fact that the administration knew in detail that a systematic program of mass murder was in progress during the period April–June 1994.

The US Embassy in Kigali continued to function for three weeks after the genocide began, and continued to inform Washington. Then all American personnel were evacuated, abandoning Rwandan personnel to their fate. A Defense Intelligence Agency report released on May 9 described an organized, ongoing "genocide" against Tutsi. Major American newspapers gave front-page coverage to events in Rwanda, although some of the articles framed the violence in terms of "civil war" rather than "genocide." There is no basis to the later claim by Clinton that he or the US government in general had been uninformed.

The United States performed contortions to avoid pronouncing the word "genocide," implicitly acknowledging its international obligation to act should genocide be taking place. The Clinton administration policy on peacekeeping and humanitarian interventions (formalized as Presidential Decision Directive 25) required "a showing that US interests were at stake, a clear mission goal, acceptable costs, Congressional, allied and public support, a clear command and control arrangement, and an exit strategy." These requirements, drawn up in the aftermath of the Mogadishu fiasco, were not published until May 3 (four weeks after the genocide began) but had been fully vetted by concerned agencies.

PDD 25 "would provide the pretext for inaction that would guide the Clinton administration throughout the crisis."[7]

The only action on the part of the Clinton administration was to limit or defeat the efforts of others to act against the genocide. At the United Nations, Ambassador Madeleine Albright worked to kill General Dallaire's request for reinforcements and instead brokered the immediate pullout of most of the United Nations Assistance Mission for Rwanda (UNAMIR) force. Richard Clarke of the National Security Council pooh-poohed Dallaire's requests for reinforcements and asserted the infeasibility of any UN military operation to fly into Kigali. Less ambitious proposals such as jamming radio broadcasts of genocide propaganda were stymied by bureaucratic delay.

In 1999, a UN panel investigating the 1994 genocide in Rwanda reported that the incompetence of the United Nations, coupled with the political paralysis of the United States and other major powers, led to the failure to stop the murder of as many as 800,000 Rwandans. "The United Nations failed the people of Rwanda during the genocide in 1994," the panel concluded. The report was highly critical of Kofi Annan, who was head of the United Nations' peacekeeping department in 1994, but it also blamed members of the Security Council, including the United States, for failing to provide the world body with the political support and material means to prevent the genocide.[8]

As UN secretary general (succeeding the pro-French Boutros Boutros-Ghali of Egypt), Annan pushed hard to make "Responsibility to Protect" an official policy of the United Nations. However, on the next important occasion to exercise that responsibility, in DRC, the UN and the international community in general again failed.

Rwanda and the other invaders of 1996 came into a country already at war (as the UN Mapping Report makes very clear) and initiated a new round of massacres. Most of the deaths resulted from attacks on civilians carried out by armed groups, rather than clashes between two armed groups. The most egregious abuses apparently were attacks on Rwandan Hutu refugees, and some Congolese Hutu, carried out by the AFDL and the Rwandan army. These were widely reported in the press, but UN efforts to investigate were thwarted at the time by President Kabila, then under heavy Rwandan influence.

In 2000, after many thousands of Congolese and others had died, the UN Security Council authorized the creation of a "panel of experts" to investigate the illegal exploitation of Congolese resources and the apparent link between such exploitation and human rights abuses, including mass violence. The series of reports on this topic, and then on the violation of the UN arms embargo, provided the basis for action against governments, firms, and individuals involved in such illegal activities. Such actions perhaps could have protected Congolese civilians by reducing the level of violence. No such actions were taken, however, in large part because the American, British, and other governments protected themselves and their companies, accused of violations.[9]

The scope of the humanitarian crisis in DRC was highlighted in 2000 when the International Rescue Committee published the results of a survey purporting to show that 1.7 million "excess" deaths had occurred in the five provinces most affected by the war.

Subsequent reports raised the total of excess deaths past 5 million. These reports increased the pressure on Rwanda and Uganda and their international backers to take steps to protect civilians in eastern DRC; they may have led the UN Security Council to put MONUC into eastern Congo and then to broaden its mandate to include civilian protection.

The international community moved haltingly to assume its responsibilities in DRC, to restore peace but also to protect civilians. Under the Pretoria agreement of December 2002, it created an international committee to oversee the situation, the CIAT, comprising representatives of the five permanent members of the UN security council, six other governments (Angola, Belgium, Canada, Gabon, South Africa, and Zambia), and three international organizations (the African Union, the European Union, and the UN mission in Congo, MONUC). The CIAT was supposed to oversee the work of the institutions of the transition, and in particular the

Independent Electoral Commission. Inevitably, it focused on keeping the electoral process on track and was less concerned with violence against civilians.

MONUC began as an observer mission but was expanded to cover peacekeeping. In 2004, it was given a series of more specific mandates, the first of which was "to deploy and maintain a presence in the key areas of potential volatility in order to promote the re-establishment of confidence, to discourage violence, in particular by deterring the use of force to threaten the political process, and to allow United Nations personnel to operate freely." A second major mandate was "to ensure the protection of civilians, including humanitarian personnel, under imminent threat of physical violence." Given conditions in eastern DRC, this could have included many thousands of people. Since some of the major perpetrators of such violence were members of the Congolese armed forces, the mandate placed MONUC in an impossible situation, in which it was expected to cooperate with the FARDC in its efforts to restore the authority of the state, except insofar as the FARDC itself was the source of the imminent threat of physical violence against civilians.

The United States, implicated in the Congo wars from the beginning, was very slow to assume direct responsibility for civilian protection. In 2003, as the second Congo war was ending (officially), the state-sponsored US Holocaust Memorial Museum first put DRC on its "warning list." The museum cited five elements of concern, including the relationship of the Congo crisis to the 1994 Rwandan genocide, the scale and effects of violence against civilians, mass sexual violence against women, continued fighting in the east, and the role of ethnicity in the perpetuation of violence. This *faux naïf* report warned against something that had been going on for years, but it did serve to give greater visibility in Washington to the scale of the killings in DRC.[10]

As we noted in the previous chapter, the American Congress finally addressed the Congo problem in a comprehensive fashion in 2006, in the form of the "Obama Bill" (S. 2125) or Democratic Republic of the Congo Relief, Security, and Democracy Promotion Act of 2006 (enacted as Public

Law 109–456). The "Obama Bill" cited the IRC on mortality and Amnesty International on sexual violence. It expressed the sense of Congress that the Congolese government "should exercise control over its armed forces, stop the mass rapes by its armed forces, and hold those responsible accountable before an appropriate tribunal . . . [and] should establish expert teams to assess the health, counseling, and social support needs of such victims." It noted that the international community was providing substantial funding for these needs, "but this assistance cannot continue in perpetuity." The secretary of state "should withhold assistance if the government of the DRC is not making sufficient progress towards accomplishing the policy objectives." Clearly, the Congolese government did not make much progress toward accomplishing these objectives, but the secretary of state did not withhold assistance.

Symmetrically, the Obama Bill authorized withholding of assistance under the Foreign Assistance Act of 1961, other than humanitarian, peacekeeping, and counterterrorism assistance, for "a foreign country determined by the Secretary to be acting to destabilize the DRC." Multilaterally, the United States should use its influence to strengthen the UN mission (MONUC), put an end to recruitment and arming of child soldiers, strengthen the arms embargo, allow for more effective protection of Congolese resources, and "press countries in the Congo region to help facilitate an end to violence in the DRC."[11] Rwanda and Uganda were destabilizing DRC, although the loopholes for humanitarian, peacekeeping and counterterrorism would have allowed substantial aid to continue. The United States took no action.

President George W. Bush signed the "Obama Bill" into law at the end of 2006, but the effects were minimal. A year later, the Government Accountability Office (GAO) found that the US government was spending substantial sums in DRC but was not doing much to accomplish the key objectives of PL 109–456 or even to assess its progress. It also cited the UN experts on Congo's natural resources "serving as an incentive for conflict between neighboring countries' militias and armed domestic factions. . . . For example, the UN has reported that profits from Congolese coltan have financed a large part of Rwanda's military budget and that gold smuggled into Uganda continues to finance militias."[12]

When Obama was elected president in 2008, one might have expected rapid attention to DRC. Indeed, rapid attention was forthcoming, but the "Obama Bill" remained in cold storage. Some provisions clearly were unacceptable at high levels of the administration.

Obama's secretary of state Hillary Clinton not only visited Kinshasa but (reportedly against the advice of her aides) also visited Goma, where she met with rape victims. Clinton had been well briefed, and was able to present the links between several major issues. She denounced the epidemic of sexual violence and linked it to impunity. She called for measures to stop the trade in conflict minerals that funds the militias that are responsible for killing, mass displacement, and the epidemic of sexual violence. And so that the United States would not be accused of being all talk and no action, she pledged more than $17 million in new funding to prevent and respond to gender and sexual violence. Almost $3 million would be dedicated to recruiting and training police officers, particularly women, "so that they understand their duty to protect women and girls, and to investigate sexual violence." Women and front-line workers would be given mobile phones to report abuse and to receive information on treatment and legal options. Clinton said also that she had raised the issues of sexual and gender-based violence with government officials (presumably including President Kabila and Prime Minister Adolphe Muzito), making the case for an end to impunity.

Unfortunately for Secretary Clinton and for the Congolese who might eventually gain protection from the increased US aid, international media coverage of the Clinton visit was heavily skewed toward her supposed "gaffe." In Kinshasa, Secretary Clinton took part in a "town meeting" or question-and-answer session at Collège Saint-Joseph (St. Joseph's School), organized by the NGOs Search for Common Ground and COJESKI (Collectif des Organisations des Jeunes Solidaires du Congo-Kinshasa/Collective of Organizations and Youth Associations in Congo-Kinshasa). Clinton was accompanied by former professional basketball star Dikembe Mutombo, whose hospital she had visited. The audience was made up mainly of university students. They asked about exploitation of DRC's natural resources, about sexual violence, about climate change, and about the nature of the proposed partnership between the United States and DRC. Secretary Clinton answered these questions easily. Mutombo joined on a few points.

Then things began to heat up. A law student named Oteke said that none of the Congolese students could deny that when Laurent-Désiré Kabila returned to Congo, "we all had at least some hope of a better future," but that hope was dashed. Oteke said he had just read a book that showed the involvement of the United States in the conflict in eastern Congo. He was concerned about the death of Laurent Kabila, and its possible origins in the United States. So could Clinton reassure him, "if I become president tomorrow of this country, will I be autonomous and independent and work for the interest of my compatriots, or . . . will I be killed if I refuse to follow what I am being told?"

The audience applauded, but Clinton simply replied that she could not excuse the past and would not try to do so. Many countries, including many in Europe and many in Africa, "have interfered with the development and the potential of the Congolese people." We all (including Congolese) face a simple choice, Clinton concluded: "Will I be dragged down by the past, or will I decide to do something that will give me the chance to have a better future?" Clinton's response set off lively discussion on Congo-related websites. Her suggestion that the Congolese should forget the past, a suggestion that she would never think to make to the Israelis or the Rwandans, became emblematic of the US double standard in Central Africa. In the US media, however, the Clinton–Oteke exchange was largely ignored in favor of another:

QUESTION: [Via interpreter] . . . Mrs. Clinton, we've all heard about the Chinese contracts in this country, the interferences from the World Bank against this contract. What does Mr. Clinton think through the mouth of Mrs. Clinton, and what does Mr. Mutombo think on this situation? Thank you very much.

SECRETARY CLINTON: Wait, you want me to tell you what my husband thinks? My husband is not the secretary of state. I am. So you ask my opinion? I will tell you my opinion. I'm not going to be channeling my husband.

The student later explained that he had been attempting to ask about Mr. Obama's opinion, not Mr. Clinton's opinion. Secretary Clinton's testy response was reported by the Drudge Report under the headline, "Snap." Andrea Mitchell referred to a "bad hair day." A "tide of trivialization" swept away the message Clinton was trying to get across.[13]

The American positions being presented by Secretary Clinton were contradictory in several respects. The United States had played an active role in the elimination of Lumumba. Thirty-six years later, it helped the Lumumbist Laurent Kabila to become president. Two years after that, it assisted an attempt to overthrow the same man. Then Kabila was assassinated in murky circumstances, and the United States and its protégé Rwanda may have participated. Oteke's question was reasonable. The second question, concerning the opinions of Mrs. Clinton, Mr. Clinton, Mr. Obama, and/or Mr. Mutombo, dealt with the proposed deal whereby DRC agreed to award China the right to develop a copper and cobalt mine in exchange for roads, railways, hospitals, and universities built by Chinese state firms. The Paris Club of creditors and the IMF opposed the deal. In the cloud of smoke produced by Secretary Clinton's response about channeling, neither the Congolese students nor the rest of us learned what she thinks about this deal.[14]

The American contribution to the seemingly endless conflict in the Great Lakes region consists of a long series of efforts to avoid accountability for the human rights abuses committed by the United States itself and by its Rwandan and Ugandan allies over the years. From the Gersony report of 1994,[15] blocked before it took final form, to the Garretón report of 1999,[16] to the appendices of the UN experts' reports[17] and the UN Mapping Report of 2010,[18] the US government (under several different presidents) has rather consistently attempted to suppress evidence of human rights violations. Another consistent pattern is the adoption of legislation that is not implemented, most notably the Obama Law.

Neither Bush nor (initially) Obama took any public action against Rwanda and Uganda for their massive human rights abuses in DRC. Instead, the latter governments were encouraged to undertake joint operations with the FARDC to root out the FDLR and LRA, respectively. Both campaigns turned out badly, leading to reprisals against Congolese civilians, many of who were killed, raped, or displaced.

In this context – the American and other governments recognizing the links between Congolese minerals, foreign governments, and violence in Congo's mining zones, but little action being taken to break those links – concerned senators and members of Congress launched similar bills in both houses of the US Congress. House Resolution 4128, the Conflict Minerals Trade Act, was designed "to improve transparency and reduce trade in conflict minerals" from DRC.

The "findings" – background information justifying the action section of the House bill – avoided assigning responsibility for the wars and resulting casualties. The conflict in 1996–7 was labeled a "civil war," whereas the one that began in 1998 "resulted" in intervention. Reading this, no one would understand that Rwanda and Uganda invaded DRC twice, with US support.

The second finding included similar blame-avoiding language:

> Despite the signing of a peace agreement and subsequent withdrawal of foreign forces in 2003, the eastern region of the Democratic Republic of Congo has continued to suffer from high levels of poverty, insecurity, and a culture of impunity, in which illegal armed groups and military forces continue to commit widespread human rights abuses.[19]

The "military forces" mentioned were mainly the armed forces of DRC (FARDC), which had incorporated many units of the illegal armed groups at the urging of the international community. This incorporation, and the assigning of high ranks to former rebel officers, has promoted the culture of impunity and made further mutinies and further abuse of civilians more likely.

As was noted in the previous chapter, the conflict minerals bill eventually became law by being attached to "Dodd–Frank" (PL 111–203 of 2010), a long and complicated bill on reform of American financial institutions. Section 1502 of Dodd–Frank requires companies under US jurisdiction to demonstrate to the Securities and Exchange Commission that products they make or sell do not use "conflict minerals": that is, gold, tin, tantalum, or tungsten from DRC, the proceeds of which might support armed groups. The United States would attack the problem of impunity by providing training to Congolese security forces, including training on human rights, and would help to reform the justice system.

Was this finally an important step toward protection of the suffering people of eastern DRC, or just a feel-good measure for Americans? The process of ensuring that exports to the United States or to world markets in general are "conflict-free" would take several years. It might make it less likely that another war of plunder occurs in eastern DRC. It was unlikely to do anything for the many thousands of Congolese being raped or displaced from their homes owing to continued fighting. By 2012, the Dodd–Frank law itself was in difficulty, with the Securities and Exchange Commission facing heavy lobbying from the US Chamber of Commerce and other groups opposed to regulation of the banking sector.

The real test of Dodd–Frank as a means of stopping or damping down conflict was still to come. Would DRC be able to develop and put in place a plausible system for certification of so-called "conflict minerals," and would the neighboring states develop systems that would make it clear that exports of the "3 Ts" plus gold were from their own sources, and did not include Congolese illegal exports being "laundered"? Until these things happened, then no useful consequences would occur as far as protection of civilians was concerned.

End of the Tunnel or More of the Same?

By 2010, the United States apparently had achieved most of its foreign policy objectives in the Great Lakes region. It had brought about satisfactory if not good relations between DRC, Rwanda, and Uganda. It also kept Rwanda, Uganda, and Burundi as significant contributors to its international "war on terrorism" through their roles as peacekeepers in Darfur and Somalia.

A closer look, however, suggested that the *Pax Americana* in Central Africa was a house of cards. The DRC military clearly was still too disorganized and too violence-prone to be called on for help in the war on terrorism, whether Islamic or other. The FARDC remained unable to protect the country's borders and its citizens. The LRA, numerically insignificant, continued to roam free over vast expanses of northeastern DRC and adjacent areas of the Central African Republic and South Sudan, murdering and mutilating civilians. The FDLR continued to terrorize people in mining zones of North and South Kivu, and to battle the Congolese army. The Congolese army – which in many instances meant the Tutsi-led units of the former CNDP incorporated into the FARDC – also abused the population. Caught between the FDLR, the Mayi-Mayi, and the FARDC, the population could only hope that the UN forces (now known as MONUSCO) would protect them. Too often, however, MONUSCO was unwilling or unable to do so.

Real peace and security for the people of the region were far off. Events in 2012 made it clear that relative peace for DRC depended on good relations with Rwanda. Kabila apparently had reached an agreement with Kagame according to which the two states would stop supporting one another's armed opposition groups. In return for Rwanda's arrest of Congolese Tutsi General Laurent Nkunda, who had been supported by Rwanda, the Congolese government would take military action against Rwandan Hutu opposition forces operating on Congolese soil. Rwanda detained Nkunda in January 2009 and place him under house arrest in Kigali. In return, Congo permitted Rwandan troops to cross the border and take part in joint operations with the Congolese army (FARDC) against the Rwandan Hutu of the FDLR, which had been allied with Congo to that point. DRC also agreed to reintegrate into the FARDC the CNDP, minus Nkunda. By the end of 2010, the civilian CNDP had been recognized as a political party and allowed to join the "Alliance for the Presidential Majority," Kabila's coalition.

Following the brief joint operation "Umoja Wetu" (Our Unity) in January and February 2009, the FARDC continued the campaign against the FDLR with UN help. The ex-CNDP men acted as spearheads of Operation Kimia II ("Kimia" or "Kimya" means quiet in Swahili). Assessments of the success of the operation vary. For some, it disrupted the FDLR and led many of its men to abandon their weapons and return home. For others, the FDLR withdrew when attacked, then returned to abandoned positions as soon as the FARDC had moved on. What is clear is that the toll in civilians killed, raped, and displaced was very high. Responsibility to Protect seemed to have been lost in the shuffle.

Kabila's decision to reconcile with Kagame was politically costly for him, and costly for Congolese civilians. Leading members of his party, the PPRD, opposed the reconciliation, and especially the invitation to bring in Rwandan troops under Umoja Wetu. Several were forced to resign, including the president of the National Assembly, Vital Kamerhe of South Kivu. Kamerhe later ran for president, opposing Kabila. During and after the election campaign of 2011, a number of prominent Kamerhe supporters were murdered or kidnapped, apparently by Kabila forces, including ex-CNDP elements. Soon afterward, the so-called "M23" mutinied against the Kabila government, leading to another round of death, rape, and displacement of civilians in North Kivu. This mutiny, and especially the evidence of Rwandan sponsorship of M23, proved to be the final straw for the Americans.

As M23 was staging its mutiny and rolling back Kabila's army, the Obama administration announced that it was implementing a decision, announced in 2011, to establish an interagency board charged with prevention of atrocities, including genocide. Obama advisor Samantha Power, author of a devastating critique of America's role in Rwanda in 1994, was put in charge of the council. In April 2012, President Obama spoke at the Holocaust Museum in Washington. Without using the words "Responsibility to Protect," he affirmed, "Preventing mass atrocities and genocide is a core national security interest and a core moral responsibility of the United States of America."[20]

Secretary Clinton followed that up in July when she also visited the Holocaust Museum and delivered a more specific statement of American policy, explaining what the administration means when it says "never again." The examples chosen were uncontroversial, at least to an American audience: Khmer Rouge massacres of educated Cambodians, Saddam Hussein's massacres of Kurds, Sudanese villages wiped out by government-supported militias. Clinton referred to Rwanda without assuming any responsibility: "I remember being in Rwanda with my husband when I was first lady, listening to story after story from survivors about the loved ones they lost and the horrors they had endured." The United States acted too late in Bosnia, she conceded, but had intervened with its NATO allies in Kosovo. Under Obama, the United States and allies had taken action against Libya's Muammar Qadhafi (who was threatening Benghazi), Côte d'Ivoire's Laurent Gbagbo (who now faced trial at the International Criminal Court), and the LRA.

Why intervene in these cases and not others? Clinton continued: "The fact is that there is no one-size-fits-all solution. Every situation requires a tailored and careful response." The administration was placing new emphasis on prevention, and seeking to expand the range of partners contributing to this cause.[21]

Apart from the LRA case, publicized by the Christian NGO "Invisible Children," and embraced by the Obama administration, Clinton dealt with DRC only in terms of the Civilian Response Corps (deployed there, as well as in South Sudan, Sri Lanka, and Kyrgyzstan), and in terms of rape as a weapon of war. The neighboring countries – Rwanda and Uganda – were not mentioned. Soon after Clinton's Holocaust Museum speech, however, the United States endorsed the report of the UN Group of Experts on M23 and withheld a small but symbolically important amount of military aid to Rwanda. The message Obama and Clinton may have wanted to send was undercut a few weeks later, however, when the British government decided that Rwanda was being sufficiently cooperative on M23 to release half of the aid funds it had suspended. Only in December 2012, when President Obama telephoned President Kagame, was an unambiguous message delivered to Rwanda.[22] It remained unclear, however, whether the new, more comprehensive American approach to responsibility to prevent and protect was going to protect any civilians.

Justice and Protection

Secretary Clinton (and her boss, President Obama) may have wanted the Congolese to forget past crimes and look to the future. Clearly, however, matters cannot be left there. Ending impunity is important in itself, but also as a means of deterrence, and in this sense it constitutes a major element of civilian protection. The protection of civilians in eastern DRC will have to include some measure of punishment of offenders, yet politics and the relationship with Rwanda in particular have gotten in the way.

Punishment of war crimes is primarily the responsibility of the national justice system, but international courts can judge cases where national courts are unable or unwilling to do so. The International Criminal Court began functioning in 2004, and initially addressed itself to the situation in DRC (later turning to the Central African Republic, Uganda, and Sudan). The first indictments concerned Ituri district (in the former Ugandan occupation zone), where the court indicted Thomas Lubanga, Germain Katanga, Mathieu Ngudjolo, and Bosco Ntaganda. The first three, all local Ituri warlords, were turned over to the tribunal by the Congolese government. The fourth indictee, Bosco Ntaganda, had been sent by Rwanda to assist Lubanga. The Congolese and Rwandan governments used Ntaganda to overthrow General Nkunda and bring the Tutsi-led CNDP over to the side of Kabila. The new civilian president of the CNDP, Philippe Gafishi, was maintaining a parallel state administration in part of the Rwandophone zone of North Kivu. Ntaganda and his men constituted a parallel military structure within the FARDC. It seemed likely that these men reported directly to officials in Kigali, giving Rwanda a foothold in Congolese territory. The Rwandans bore a share of responsibility for the ongoing pillage and rape in the "*petit nord*" (i.e. southern North Kivu) even before the mutiny of Rwandophone troops of the so-called "M23." It would seem that the failure to send Ntaganda to the International Criminal Court is a joint failure on the part of the Congolese and Rwandan governments.

The presidential and legislative elections in DRC at the end of 2011 set off a surge in political violence. Violence in Kinshasa drew considerable media attention. Less attention went to electoral violence in North Kivu. Rutshuru was among a handful of areas nationwide where the election results had to be thrown out; there were numerous reports of intimidation of villagers by FARDC (ex-CNDP) soldiers, who wanted them to vote for Kabila. Hundreds of thousands of people remained in camps for "internally displaced persons"; some of them were attacked, raped, and even killed by armed groups who attacked the camps.

The United Nations mission (MONUSCO, formerly MONUC) remains the only source of protection for civilians in DRC, even though it is not very effective in this role. President Kabila asked the UN to withdraw MONUSCO by June 2011. At the time, legislative elections were scheduled for July 2011, to be followed by presidential elections in October. Withdrawal of MONUSCO, in particular its civilian staff, would have reduced the number of independent observers during the election period, as well as lessening civilian protection. By 2012, in contrast, Kabila was urging reinforcement of MONUSCO to help him survive the M23 challenge.

The conflicts in North Kivu and others do not confirm the assessment of Jeffrey Herbst and Greg Mills that the Congolese state does not exist.[23] There is a state, but it apparently is too weak to be able to fulfill its responsibilities of protecting its borders (particularly against aggressors who enjoy international support) and of protecting the citizens within those borders. The problem of incapacity is compounded by a lack of will to exercise sovereignty.

The international community has not been helpful in protecting civilians in DRC. However, the release of the UN Mapping Report on human rights violations in DRC between 1993 and 2003 caused an enormous commotion in mid-2010. The Rwandan government rejected the report and tried to argue that it supposedly reflected bias against Rwanda (presumably calculating that most people had not read the report and would not know that it dealt with alleged violations committed by the governments of Angola, Burundi, DRC, Rwanda, and Uganda, and provincial authorities in Katanga in the case of ethnic cleansing of Luba-Kasai). The Ugandans rejected all of the charges against them (perhaps hoping that the rest of the world had forgotten that the World Court found against Uganda in a case filed by DRC, for similar offenses). Both Rwanda and Uganda threatened to withdraw their peacekeepers from Sudan (Darfur) and Somalia, respectively. Both governments, however, subsequently backed down on these threats; it is not known what they may have been promised regarding punishment for these transgressions.

Almost at the same time, it became known that more than 300 civilians had been raped in 2010 in Walikale territory, North Kivu, by an alliance of the FDLR (Rwandan Hutu), dissident Congolese Tutsi (apparently deserters from the FARDC), and local Mayi-Mayi (comprising "autochthonous" people of Walikale territory). The rapists or their commanders seem to have calculated that these outrageous acts would increase their bargaining position in negotiations over control of Walikale's political institutions and its mineral wealth. These rapes demonstrated that political violence was a current reality and that as in 1993–2003 the civilian population, female and male, adults and children, paid the price of the quarrels of the "leaders." The United Nations mission was present in the area but seemingly unaware of the assaults until afterward. The central government did nothing to prosecute those allegedly responsible. Indeed, Ntabo Ntaberi, alias Sheka, head of the Walikale

Mayi-Mayi, was allowed to stand for election in November 2011. (He was not elected.)

"Africa's world war" supposedly ended in 2003, but a decade later the killing persists. The "rape capital of the world" continues to produce horrendous incidents of mass sexual violence. The pillage of Congo's minerals ("conflict minerals") is ongoing, although the Dodd–Frank legislation (still not implemented) has begun to reshape the supply chains. The elections of 2011, meanwhile, meant to show that the country had moved beyond violence and chaos, were so badly organized and so violent, that the demonstration was quite the contrary.

For years, Congolese and other advocates of Congo spoke and wrote about the need to "break the silence." This cliché faded from use, since there is no shortage of attention to DRC and its problems, from the international media and international organizations, both governmental and nongovernmental. Instead, as we saw in Chapter 4, there is a cacophony of voices, each proclaiming that the "real" problem in Congo is its pet cause: the failed state, the invasion of Congo by its neighbors, the vastness of the country and the supposed impossibility of governing it, the curse of its mineral wealth, the culture of impunity, and others. Having identified the real problem, many observers and campaigners have proceeded to identify a cure, ignoring all the complicating factors. If "conflict minerals" cause the killing and mass rape, then the magic bullet remedy is the certification of minerals. If Congo is too vast and too chaotic to govern, then the remedy lies in partition of the territory. Each of these diagnoses is simplistic; intervening variables are ignored, as are likely negative consequences. Conflict minerals campaigners do not tell us how certification of minerals would stop killing and rapes. They may have things backwards: peace might be a prerequisite for an effective certification program. Nor do advocates of partition explain how two or three successor states would be free of the infirmities of the present state; if experience elsewhere is any guide, partition might lead to greater violence (see South Sudan).

Instead of silence, we have witnessed a competition to impose a dominant narrative on the society. In Rwanda, the

RPF victory led to a concerted campaign to convince Rwandans that they (or their ancestors) had lived together harmoniously in the pre-colonial era, only to be divided into hostile ethnic communities by the nefarious colonizers. The Hutu version of history – 400 years of Tutsi oppression – was heard no longer within the country, although of course it was repeated in the refugee camps in surrounding countries, and found easy acceptance among Congolese victims of Rwandan aggression.

In DRC, in contrast, the myth of Congo as a "Bantu" society dovetailed with the myth of the yoke, according to which all the country's ills were due to outsiders. This worldview is complementary with the Rwandan Hutu version of history. This ideological convergence helps to explain the perpetuation of the conflict in eastern DRC. Beyond the pillage of Congolese minerals by Rwanda and Uganda, and the callous treatment of Congolese civilians by their armed forces, there is an important identity dimension to the conflict.

DRC remains a hell for the Congolese for a variety of reasons, many of which are deeply rooted. The culture of rape in DRC is rooted in part in the inequality of women and girls; another deeply rooted element is tacit acceptance of violence against civilians as a legitimate strategy of war. The culture of impunity for murder, theft, and sexual violence overlays the culture of rape and makes it more difficult to punish sexual violence and to provide reparations to survivors.

The protection of Congolese civilians is the responsibility, first and foremost, of the Congolese state. Since the last years of the Mobutu dictatorship, the state has progressively divested itself of most of its social service functions. It has become less and less capable of defending the country's borders, or of protecting civilians within those borders. Worse than that, much of the violence against Congolese is the work of state institutions, including the Congolese armed forces (FARDC), the National Police, and the National Intelligence Agency (ANR). The donor community recognizes this yet does not take it into account in an effective manner. For example, the US government proceeds to train a battalion of the FARDC, ignoring the experience of units trained by outsiders (including the United States) since the 1960s.

The changes (plural) that will be required, to provide a relatively secure, relatively just environment for the Congolese, will have to come from the Congolese themselves. They will have to stop promoting the "myth of the yoke," according to which all their problems come from outside, even though this myth is partly valid. They will have to assume responsibility for their own affairs. Outside assistance doubtless will be required, but the Congolese must set the terms on which that assistance takes place.

Over fifty years after independence, Congo has survived, despite recurrent attempts to carve it up. However, the Congolese state cannot or does not provide protection to its citizens. The international community has provided a measure of protection, notably through MONUC and MONUSCO, but this cannot go on forever. Old Congo hands, remembering 1964, when the withdrawal of the UN force ONUC was followed by uprisings that nearly swept out the central government, prophesy disaster were the international community to withdraw. However, history does not repeat itself. Congolese civil society is much stronger now than it was in the 1960s, and is interlaced with a variety of donors that provide not only financing but also assistance in making their operations more rational and effective. There is no equivalent of the nationalists of 1964; the opposition forces are divided. Congolese women's organizations have their own international support networks, and thus are capable of acting autonomously vis-à-vis the male-dominated state. Moreover, the African community, through the Great Lakes summits and SADC, has recently shown signs of becoming involved in a helpful way.

The great unknown, however, is the FARDC (armed forces), source of much of the abuse of civilians but also perhaps a threat to the central government should the government attempt to rein in the military. In short, DRC remains a hot spot, simmering on. There is a perennial danger of a flare-up, producing another major conflagration.

Notes

Introduction: Congo, a Perennial Hot Spot

1 Les Roberts, *Mortality in Eastern DRC: Results from Five Mortality Surveys in Eastern DRC by the International Rescue Committee* (Bukavu: International Rescue Committee, 2000); UN Official Calls DR Congo "Rape Capital of the World," BBC News, April 28, 2010: *http://news.bbc.co.uk/1/hi/8650112.stm* (accessed October 18, 2012); Enough Project Team with the Grassroots Reconciliation Group, *A Comprehensive Approach to Congo's Conflict Minerals*, Strategy Paper, April 24, 2009: *http://www.enoughproject.org/publications/comprehensive-approach-conflict-minerals-strategy-paper* (accessed October 18, 2012).

2 O.-P. Gilbert, *L'empire du silence, Congo 1946* (Brussels, 1947); Antoine Tshitungu Kongolo and Catherine Labio, "Colonial Memories in Belgian and Congolese Literature," *Yale French Studies*, 102, Belgian Memories (2002), 79–93.

3 Johannes Fabian and Tshibumba Kanda Matulu, *Remembering the Present: Painting and Popular History in Zaïre* (Berkeley: University of California Press, 1996), painting 5 and interview, 22–3.

   Tshibumba painted *Diego Cao et le Roi du Congo* in 1973 or 1974. The European anthropologist Johannes Fabian acquired his copy in 1974. Diogo Cão arrived at the mouth of the Congo River in 1482. On a second visit in 1485, he met Africans on the left bank of the Congo mouth and learned from them that Mbanza Kongo was the residence of an important ruler. Not until his third visit (1487) did he meet that ruler, Nzinga Kuwu. Nzinga later was baptized João, thereby sharing the name of the Portuguese king. The King of Kongo in Tshibumba's painting may be Nzinga or a symbolic representation of Kongo rulers over the centuries.

Welsh-born Henry Morton Stanley first visited Central Africa, on behalf of the *New York Herald*, to locate the Scottish missionary and explorer David Livingstone, which he did near Lake Tanganyika in 1871. On a second trip, three years later, he crossed the continent, reaching the Lualaba (Upper Congo River) in what is now Maniema province, DRC, and then descending the Lualaba and Congo proper to the Atlantic Ocean, at which he arrived in 1877.

Hired by King Leopold II, Stanley returned to the Congo in 1879, and played a major role in developing infrastructure, including the rail link between the mouth of the Congo River and the site of the present Kinshasa.

Francis Dhanis, a Belgian military officer, volunteered for service in the Congo Free State, and went out for his first term in 1887. He led the Free State forces in the war against the Arab-Swahili traders (1892–4) and in an expedition to the Upper Nile (1896–7).

Omer Bodson was a Belgian officer, serving under the British officer William Stairs, sent to bring Katanga under Free State control in the 1890s (see p. 7 below).

4   John Thornton shows that the area around the capital Mbanza Kongo became wealthy and densely populated owing to plantations worked by slaves, before declining as the coastal province of Soyo grew under the influence of the Atlantic trade. See *The Kingdom of Kongo: Civil War and Transition, 1641–1718* (Madison: University of Wisconsin Press, 1983) and *Africa and Africans in the Making of the Atlantic World, 1400–1650* (Cambridge: Cambridge University Press, 1992). On the "king of the Americans," see Wyatt MacGaffey, "Kongo and the King of the Americans," *The Journal of Modern African Studies*, 6 (1968), 171–81.

5   Adam Hochschild, *King Leopold's Ghost: A Story of Greed, Terror, and Heroism in Colonial Africa* (New York: Houghton Mifflin Company, 1998), p. 5; Nancy Rose Hunt, "An Acoustic Register, Tenacious Images, and Congolese Scenes of Rape and Repetition," *Cultural Anthropology*, 23:2 (May 2008), 224–5.

6   Michela Wrong, *In the Footsteps of Mr. Kurtz: Living on the Brink of Disaster in Mobutu's Congo* (London: Fourth Estate/ New York: HarperCollins, 2001), 58–9.

7   Vamik D. Volkan, "Transgenerational Transmission and Chosen Traumas: An Aspect of Large-Group Identity," *Group Analysis*, 34 (March 2001), 79–97.

8   T. O. Ranger, "Connexions between 'Primary Resistance' Movements and Modern Mass Nationalism in East and Central Africa: II," *The Journal of African History*, 9:4 (1968), 631–41.

9   Crawford Young, *The African Colonial State in Comparative Perspective* (New Haven: Yale University Press, 1997), 244; Bruce J. Berman, "The Perils of Bula Matari: Constraint and Power in the State," *Canadian Journal of African Studies*, 31:3 (1997), 556–70.

10 Mahmood Mamdani, *Citizen and Subject: Contemporary Africa and the Legacy of Late Colonialism* (Princeton, NJ: Princeton University Press, 1996).

11 Jean-Claude Willame, *Patrice Lumumba: La crise congolaise revisitée* (Paris: Karthala, 1990), 470.

12 Patrice Lumumba, "Speech at Proclamation of Independence," in *Lumumba Speaks: The Speeches and Writings of Patrice Lumumba, 1958–1961*, ed. Jean Van Lierde, trans. Helen R. Lane (Boston: Little, Brown and Co., 1972), 222; reprinted with commentary in *Milestone Documents in World History*, Vol. 4 (Dallas: Schlager Group, 2010), 1624–6.

13 William Reno, "Shadow States and the Political Economy of Civil Wars," in Mats Berdal and David M. Malone, eds., *Greed and Grievance: Economic Agendas in Civil Wars* (Boulder, CO: Lynne Reinner, 2000). See also Georges Nzongola-Ntalaja, *The Congo from Leopold to Kabila: A People's History* (London: Zed Books, 2002), Chapter 6.

14 An example of such a simplistic approach was the Facebook posting of "Students against Conflict Minerals" calling on activists to visit the Facebook page of computer manufacturer Dell and post this message: "Really, Dell? When you stand behind the US Chamber of Commerce, you stand for child labor and rape in eastern Congo. Free your supply chain of Congo conflict minerals. Step up for Dodd-Frank 1502. Say NO to the Chamber's push to derail strong SEC regulations" (downloaded October 10, 2011). The following day Panasonic was targeted, and then Acer. For a convincing reply, see Laura

Seay, "Do We Have the Congo Rape Crisis All Wrong?" *The Atlantic* (online), May 24, 2011: *http://www.theatlantic.com/international/archive/2011/05/do-we-have-the-congo-rape-crisis-all-wrong/239328/* (accessed October 29, 2012).

15 Mahmood Mamdani, *When Victims Become Killers: Colonialism, Nativism, and the Genocide in Rwanda* (Princeton, NJ: Princeton University Press, 2001).

Chapter 1 Congo as a Playing Field

1 Herman J. Cohen, "The Agony of the Congo," *American Diplomacy*, 5:3 (Summer 2000): *http://www.unc.edu/depts/diplomat/AD_Issues/amdipl_16/cohen_agony.html* (accessed October 26, 2012).

2 Dena Montague, "Stolen Goods: Coltan and Conflict in the Democratic Republic of Congo," *SAIS Review*, 22:1 (Winter–Spring 2002), 103–18.

3 Georges Nzongola-Ntalaja, *The Congo from Leopold to Kabila: A People's History* (London: Zed Books, 2002), 226.

4 Gérard Prunier, *Africa's World War: Congo, the Rwandan Genocide, and the Making of a Continental Catastrophe* (Oxford and New York: Oxford University Press, 2009), 47.

5 United Nations, "Report of the Panel of Experts on the Illegal Exploitation of Natural Resources and Other Forms of Wealth of the Democratic Republic of the Congo" (New York, 2001): *http://www.un.org/News/dh/latest/drcongo.htm* (accessed October 19, 2012).

6 The Fashoda Syndrome derives from Franco-British competition to control the Upper Nile. A French expedition under Major Jean-Baptiste Marchand left Gabon in 1896, heading for the Nile. Simultaneously, a British force under General Sir Herbert Kitchener advanced southward from Egypt. The French reached Fashoda (the present Kodok, in Upper Nile province, South Sudan) in July 1898 and occupied an abandoned Egyptian fort. The British arrived in September. Neither the Frenchman Marchand nor the Briton Kitchener was ready to give up his claims to the position, but rather than fight they agreed that the Egyptian, British, and French flags should fly over the fort. Anxious to gain British support against Germany, the French foreign minister ignored public outcry and instructed Marchand to withdraw from Fashoda. The two governments agreed in

1899 that the Nile–Congo watershed should mark the frontier between their respective spheres of influence. Fashoda was largely forgotten in the English-speaking world but festered on in French political culture as a symbol of having been deprived of African land that should rightly have been theirs.

7 Herman J. Cohen, "Africa's Surrogate Wars: The Most Significant Challenge to African Stability and US Security Interests in Africa." Presented to National Defense University Symposium, Africa: Vital to U.S. Security?, November 15–16, 2005.

8 Wayne Madsen, *Genocide and Covert Operations in Africa (1993–1999)* (Lewiston, ME: Edwin Mellen Press, 2000), 94.

9 Prunier, *Africa's World War*, 140–2.

10 Johannes Fabian and Tshibumba Kanda Matulu, *Remembering the Present: Painting and Popular History in Zaïre* (Berkeley: University of California Press, 1996), 49–50, 298–306; D. de Lannoy, Mabiala Seda Diangwala, and Bongeli Yeikelo Ya Ato, *Tango ya Banoko, "Le Temps des Oncles"* (Brussels: CEDAF/ASDOC, 1986) (*Cahiers du CEDAF, 5–6*).

11 Ludo De Witte, *The Assassination of Lumumba*, trans. Ann Wright and Renée Fenby (London: Verso, 2002), p. 38. Mineral-rich Katanga province provided nearly half of the gross domestic product of the colony and thus of the revenues of the central administration. Belgian commercial interests, led by the public–private Union Minière du Haut-Katanga and an association of white settlers, supported a coalition of "authentic Katangan" political parties, Conakat (Confédération des Associations du Katanga), and helped to ensure that it formed the provincial government after elections. The result had been essentially a tie between Conakat and a rival coalition led by the Balubakat (Association des Baluba du Katanga). To resolve the stalemate and permit Conakat to rule without coalition partners, the Belgian parliament even amended the *Loi Fondamentale*, which it had just promulgated. A few days after independence, Katanga province seceded, with support of the Belgian government and especially of the king.

12 René Lemarchand, *Dynamics of Violence in Central Africa* (Philadelphia: University of Pennsylvania Press, 2009), 87, 129.

13 Daniel Bourmaud, "France in Africa," *Issue: A Journal of Opinion*, 23:2, Rwanda (1995), 58–62.

14 Kees Homan, "Operation Artemis in the Democratic Republic of Congo," in *European Commission: Faster and More United? The Debate about Europe's Crisis Response Capacity*, May

2007, 151–5: *http://www.clingendael.nl/publications/2007/20070531_cscp_chapter_homan.pdf* (accessed October 23, 2012); Anastase Shyaka, "La Force Multinationale Intérimaire d'urgence en Ituri: 'Artémis'. Quand la géopolitique se sert de l'humanitaire," in Shyaka, ed., *La Résolution des conflits en Afrique des Grands Lacs: Revue critique des mécanismes internationaux* (Butare: Éditions de l'Université Nationale du Rwanda, 2004), 27–46.

15 Chester A. Arthur, State of the Union Address, December 4, 1883, 29–30: *http://www2.hn.psu.edu/faculty/jmanis/poldocs/uspressu/SUaddressCArthur.pdf* (accessed October 26, 2012).

16 Mark Twain, *King Leopold's Soliloquy: A Defense of His Congo Rule*, 2nd edition (Boston: The P. R. Warren Co., 1905), 31 (pagination according to International Publishers, 1970: *http://chss.montclair.edu/english/furr/i2l/kls.html* (accessed October 23, 2012).

17 This was Mobutu's second seizure of power. In September 1960 he had ousted Lumumba with the sponsorship of the CIA. See Madeleine G. Kalb, *The Congo Cables: The Cold War in Africa – from Eisenhower to Kennedy* (London: Macmillan, 1982), 189–96.

18 Sean Kelly, *America's Tyrant: The CIA and Mobutu of Zaïre* (Washington, DC: American University Press, 1993); Elaine Forbes Pachter, "Our Man in Kinshasa: US Relations with Mobutu, 1970–1983. Patron–Client Relations in the International Sphere," doctoral dissertation, Johns Hopkins University, 1987.

19 Colette Braeckman, "Ce que le mapping report ne dit pas," blog, October 1, 2010: *http://blog.lesoir.be/colette-braeckman/2010/10/01/ce-que-le-mapping-report-ne-dit-pas/* (accessed October 23, 2012).

20 Lynne Duke, "US Military Role in Rwanda Greater Than Disclosed," *The Washington Post*, August 16, 1997: *http://www.highbeam.com/doc/1P2-738116.html* (accessed October 23, 2012).

21 In July 2010, MONUC (United Nations Organization Mission in the Democratic Republic of the Congo) was renamed MONUSCO (United Nations Organization Stabilization Mission in the Democratic Republic of the Congo) to assuage nationalistic feelings on the part of the Kabila government.

22 Jeffrey Gettleman, "Firebrand Attracts Votes in Congo, Dismaying West," *New York Times*, December 2, 2011; Hillary

Rodham Clinton, "Supreme Court Decision Confirming Results of the Presidential Election in the Democratic Republic of the Congo (DRC)," press statement, December 20, 2011: *http://www.state.gov/secretary/rm/2011/12/179195.htm* (accessed October 23, 2012).

23 Nzongola-Ntalaja, *The Congo from Leopold to Kabila*, p. 128.

24 Barney Jopson, "IMF-Paris Club Want DRC to Alter China Deal As They Lend," *Afrik-News*, February 23, 2009: *http://www.afrik-news.com/article15339.html* (accessed October 23, 2012).

Chapter 2 African Players on the Congo Field

1 Nick Young, "Uganda: A Pawn in the US's Proxy African War on Terror," *Guardian*, September 25, 2010: *http://www.guardian.co.uk/commentisfree/cifamerica/2010/sep/25/ugandas-proxy-war-on-terror* (accessed October 30, 2012).

2 James Karuhanga, "Rwanda: DRC Foreign Minister Labels FDLR a 'Cancer,'" *The New Times* (Kigali), December 11, 2008: *http://allafrica.com/stories/200812110271.html* (accessed November 2, 2012).

3 In 2009, Rwanda's leading newspaper, *The New Times*, had to be corrected in its reporting on aid dependency. Chris Scott, "President Kagame: Good Aid is Necessary, But Shun 'Bad' Aid Dependency," One Blog, June 11, 2009: *http://www.one.org/blog/2009/06/11/president-kagame-good-aid-is-necessary-but-shun-bad-aid-dependency/* (accessed November 2, 2012). By 2012, Kagame's position had shifted. "Rwanda Launches 'Dignity Fund' to Cut Foreign Aid Dependence," MSN African News, August 24, 2012: *http://african.howzit.msn.com/rwanda-launches-dignity-fund-to-cut-foreign-aid-dependence-1* (accessed November 2, 2012).

4 Filip Reyntjens, *The Great African War: Congo and Regional Politics, 1996–2006* (Cambridge and New York: Cambridge University Press, 2009), 44.

5 Benoit Verhaegen, "Du Congo 1964 au Zaïre 1997: Similitudes et divergences," in *Annuaire des Grands Lacs, 1996–1997* (Antwerp: The Institute of Development Policy and Management, 1997).

6 René Lemarchand and David Martin, *Selective Genocide in Burundi* (Report – Minority Rights Group, no. 20, 1974).

7   The RCD was to split on several occasions, leading to the RCD-Goma, RCD-Kisangani, RCD-ML, RCD-National, and so on.

8   Colette Braeckman, "Ce que le mapping report ne dit pas," blog, October 1, 2010: *http://blog.lesoir.be/colette-braeckman/2010/10/01/ce-que-le-mapping-report-ne-dit-pas/* (accessed October 23, 2012).

9   Ibid.

10 Timothy Longman, "The Complex Reasons for Rwanda's Engagement in Congo," in John F. Clark, ed., *The African Stakes of the Congo War* (New York: Palgrave Macmillan, 2004), 130.

11 Ibid., 130–3.

12 Jason Stearns, "Who Killed Laurent Kabila?" February 6, 2010: *http://congosiasa.blogspot.com/2010/02/who-killed-laurent-kabila.html* (accessed October 30, 2012). Arnaud Zajtman and Marlène Rabaud, *Murder in Kinshasa*, film, 48 minutes, 2011: *http://www.aljazeera.com/programmes/2011/10/2011102713 1838717148.html* (accessed October 30, 2012).

13 John F. Clark, "Museveni's Adventure in the Congo: Uganda's Vietnam?" in Clark, ed., *The African Stakes of the Congo War*, 147.

14 Ibid., 147.

15 The ADF is a Ugandan opposition group, operating on both sides of the Uganda–DRC border in the Ruwenzori area. The group resulted from the merger of a Muslim group (Tabliq sect) and another rebel group, the National Army for the Liberation of Uganda. It chose the Ruwenzori base because the local population (Konjo) were disaffected from the Ugandan government and because the Nande, across the border in DRC, speak the same language. (See Chapter 3, p. 115.)

16 Clark, "Museveni's Adventures in the Congo," 148–9.

17 Ibid., 149–51.

18 Ibid., 151–2.

19 The Independent Team, "Misconduct Splits UPDF, RPA Forces in Congo," *The Independent*, Uganda, June 23, 2009: *http://www.independent.co.ug/index.php/the-last-word/the-last-word/1078?joscclean=1&comment_id=3207* (accessed October 30, 2012).

20 Xan Rice, "US Reveals Plan to Disarm LRA Fighters," *Guardian*, November 25, 2010: *http://www.guardian.co.uk/world/2010/nov/25/us-plan-disarm-rebels-central-africa* (accessed November 2, 2012).

21 Gérard Prunier, *Africa's World War: Congo, the Rwandan Genocide, and the Making of a Continental Catastrophe* (Oxford and New York: Oxford University Press, 2009), 198.

22 Jean-Pierre Chrétien, "The Recurrence of Violence in Burundi: Memories of the 'Catastrophe' of 1972," in J.-P. Chrétien and Richard Banégas, eds., *The Recurring Great Lakes Crisis: Identity, Violence and Power* (London: Hurst, 2008; New York: Columbia University Press, 2011).

23 René Lemarchand, *Dynamics of Violence in Central Africa* (Philadelphia: University of Pennsylvania Press, 2009), 85.

24 "Burundi: Amnesty Calls for an Independent International Investigation of the Gatumba Massacre," Amnesty International, August 19, 2004: *http://www.amnesty.org.uk/news_details.asp?NewsID=15553* (accessed October 30, 2012).

25 I. William Zartman, *Ripe for Resolution: Conflict and Intervention in Africa*, revised edition (New York: Oxford University Press for the Council on Foreign Relations, 1989), 43.

26 Mohammed Ayoob, "Inequality and Theorizing in International Relations: The Case for Subaltern Realism," *International Studies Review*, 4:3 (2002), 27–48.

27 Ibid., 45.

28 Séverine Autesserre, *The Trouble with the Congo: Local Violence and the Failure of International Peacekeeping* (Cambridge and New York: Cambridge University Press, 2010).

Chapter 3   Identity as a Driver of Conflict

1 Kimbanguism is a branch of Christianity heavily influenced by the prophetic tradition of the Kongo people of western DRC. It was founded during the colonial era by Simon Kimbangu, who was arrested by the Belgian authorities and later died in prison. The church is known as the Église de Jésus Christ sur la Terre par son Envoyé Spécial Simon Kimbangu (The Church of Christ on Earth by His Special Envoy Simon Kimbangu, EJCSK). Since Congolese independence, the Church has modified its teachings and rituals and has been admitted to the World Council of Churches (1969). However, it retains several unorthodox beliefs, starting with the idea that Kimbangu was the incarnation of the Holy Spirit. See Wyatt MacGaffey, *Modern Kongo Prophets: Religion in a Plural Society* (Bloomington: Indiana University Press, 1983); Marie-Louise Martin,

Kimbangu: An African Prophet and His Church, trans. D. M. Moore (Oxford: Blackwell, 1975).

2 Kevin Dunn, *Imagining the Congo: The International Relations of Identity* (New York: Palgrave, 2003).

3 Thomas Turner, "Nationalism, Historiography, and the (Re)construction of the Rwandan Past," in Claire Norton, ed., *Nationalism, Historiography and the (Re)Construction of the Past* (Washington, DC: New Academia Press, 2006), 97–111.

4 Josh Kron, "Israel in Africa," *Guardian*, February 8, 2010: *http://www.guardian.co.uk/commentisfree/belief/2010/feb/08/rwanda-jewish-tutsi* (accessed November 2, 2012). The subtitle reads "In Rwanda, 'Jewish' has mysteriously ended up becoming shorthand for 'Tutsi'." The process is not so mysterious as Kron seems to think. The Tutsi supposedly come from Ethiopia, and Ethiopia's monarchs supposedly descend from Solomon and Sheba.

5 Kasper Hoffmann, "Governing the 'Maquis': A Case Study of General Padiri's Maï-Maï Movement," working paper no. 6, Ghent: Conflict Research Group, 2006.

6 Interpretation of constitutional provisions on nationality set off a war between academics. See, *inter alia*, O. Ndeshyo Rurihose, "La nationalité de la population Congolaise (Zaïroise) d'expression Kinyarwanda au regard de la loi de 29 juin 1981," in *Considérations juridiques* (Kinshasa: CERIA/Édition Electronique ASYST, 1992), and Célestin Nguya-Ndila Malengana, *Nationalité et citoyenneté au Congo/Kinshasa: Le cas du Kivu* (Paris/Montréal: L'Harmattan, 2001).

7 APARECO, *Joseph Kabila? From the Hidden Origins of the Sphinx to His Bloody Entry in Power*: *http://www.pdfport.com/view/150659-joseph-kabila.html* (accessed November 27, 2012); also, Mwamba Tshibangu, *Joseph Kabila: La vérité étouffée* (Paris: L'Harmattan, 2005).

8 Karl W. Deutsch, *Nationalism and Social Communication*, 2nd edition (Cambridge, MA: MIT Press, 1966).

9 Didier L. Goyvaerts, "The Emergence of Lingala in Bukavu, Zaïre," *The Journal of Modern African Studies*, 33:2 (1995), 299–314.

10 See results: *http://www.electoralgeography.com/new/en/countries/c/congo/2006-president-election-congo.html* (accessed November 2, 2012). Herbert Weiss suggests an alternative interpretation, according to which Kabila, Bemba and the RCD-Goma all lost in their respective occupation zones:

that is, the people voted against the warlords (personal communication, 2010).

11   Tamuzi Talekwene Tafe Félicien, "Elections et droits de l'homme dans le Bandundu: Rapport de l'observation électorale faite dans la Province du Bandundu," Bandundu, 2012; L'honorable Dieudonné Bakungu Mitondeke derrière Vital Kamerhe. Infocom-Lumen, October 30, 2011.

12   In colonial Congo, "arabization" referred to the adoption of cultural traits from East Africa, notably Islam and the Swahili language. The term was abusively used in Sankuru, where few people spoke Swahili and very few were Muslim.

13   Georges Balandier, *Sociologie actuelle de l'Afrique noire: Dynamique sociale en Afrique central*, 4th edition (Paris: PUF, 1982 [1955]).

14   Stanley's "Ashanti of the Congo" became an ethnic group. See Crawford Young, *The Politics of Cultural Pluralism* (Madison: University of Wisconsin Press, 1976), 171.

15   Thomas Turner, "Batetela, Baluba, Basonge: Ethnogenesis in Zaïre," *Cahiers d'études africaines*, 33:4 (1993), 587–612; Bruce Fetter, "The Luluaburg Revolt at Elisabethville," *African Historical Studies*, 2:2 (1969), 269–77; Auguste Mabika-Kalanda, *Baluba et Lulua: Une ethnie à la recherche d'un nouvel équilibre* (Brussels: Éditions de Remarques congolaises, 1959).

16   Peter Geschiere and Stephen Jackson, "Autochthony and the Crisis of Citizenship: Democratization, Decentralization, and the Politics of Belonging," *African Studies Review*, 49:2 (September 2006), 6.

17   See, for example, Affaire BDK: Yves Kisombe exclu du MLC, March 28, 2008: *http://congodebout.blog.kazeo.com/index/p/2008/03/602007* (accessed November 28, 2012).

18   T. K. Biaya, "Société parallèle, 'Mobutucratie' et nationalisme post-colonial en République Démocratique du Congo," *African Journal of Political Science*, 4:1 (1999), 63–82.

19   A *groupement*, in Congolese administration, is a territorial unit smaller than a collectivity (*chefferie* or *secteur*) but larger than a village.

20   Georges Weis, *Le pays d'Uvira* (Brussels: Académie Royale des Sciences Coloniales, 1959).

21   Koen Vlassenroot, "Citizenship, Identity Formation and Conflict in South Kivu: The Case of the Banyamulenge," *Review of African Political Economy*, 29:93/94 (September/December 2002), 504.

22 Roberto Garretón, Report of the Special Rapporteur on the Situation of Human Rights in Zaïre, E/CN.4/1997/6, January 28, 1997: *http://reliefweb.int/node/29822* (accessed November 5, 2012). Hamitic is sometimes used in place of Nilotic in Congolese political discourse.

23 Richard Kandt, *Kaput Nili – Eine empfindsame Reise zu den Quellen des Nils*, Vol. I (Berlin: Dietrich Reimer Verlag, 1921), 261, cited in Claudine Vidal, *Sociologie des passions: Rwanda, Côte d'Ivoire* (Paris: Karthala, 1991), 23.

24 Koen Vlassenroot and Timothy Raeymaekers, "The Formation of the Centres of Profit, Power and Protection: Conflict and Social Transformation in the Eastern DR Congo," Occasional Paper, Center of African Studies, University of Copenhagen, 2005.

25 Yves Musoni Musana, "La problématique de la cohabitation conflictuelle entre les Banyarwanda et leurs voisins du Congo (RDC): Le cas du Nord-Kivu," thesis, National University of Rwanda, Butare, 2003.

26 Ibid.

27 Stanislas Bucyalimwe Mararo, "Le Nord-Kivu au coeur de la crise congolais," in Stefaan Marysse and Filip Reyntjens, eds., *L'Afrique des Grands Lacs. Annuaire 2001–2002* (Antwerp: Institute of Development Policy and Management, University of Antwerp, 2002), 153.

28 "Zaïre: Forced to Flee: Violence against the Tutsis in Zaïre," Human Rights Watch, 8:2 (A), July 1996: *http://www.hrw.org/legacy/reports/1996/Zaire.htm* (accessed November 5, 2012).

29 Ibid.

30 Ibid.

31 "DRC Congo: ICC-Indicted War Criminal Implicated in Assassination of Opponents," Human Rights Watch, October 13, 2010.

32 International Crisis Group, "No Stability in Kivu Despite a Rapprochement with Rwanda," *Africa Report* 165, November 16, 2010.

33 Christina Clark, "Borders of Everyday Life: Congolese Young People's Political Identification in Contexts of Conflict-Induced Displacement," Households in Conflict Network, Third Annual Workshop, University of Sussex, 2008.

34 Ludo Martens, "La grande biographie imaginaire de Laurent Désiré Kabila. Analyse critique du livre de Erik Kennes *Essai biographique sur Laurent Désiré Kabila*," *Debout Congolais*, March 28, 2004: *http://www.deboutcongolais.info/actualite5/*

art_319.htm (accessed November 27, 2012); Georges Nzon-gola-Ntalaja, *The Congo from Leopold to Kabila: A People's History* (London: Zed Books, 2002).

35 "Joseph Kabila salue les colonisateurs," *La Libre Belgique*, February 10, 2004: *http://www.lalibre.be/actu/international/ article/153344/joseph-kabila-salue-les-colonisateurs.html* (accessed November 27, 2012).

Chapter 4   Congo's War against Women

1   The long history of alleged sex abuse by MONUC/MONUSCO is summarized in "UN Probes Peacekeepers for Sex Abuse in DrCongo [*sic*]," AFP, July 4, 2010: *http://www.google.com/ hostednews/afp/article/ALeqM5g0ELtp4CGui14IC-3WFtypy9ScnyA* (accessed November 27, 2012).

2   Benjamin Coghlan et al., *Democratic Republic of Congo: An Ongoing Crisis* (New York: International Rescue Committee, 2008):   *http://www.rescue.org/sites/default/files/migrated/ resources/2007/2006-7_congomortalitysurvey.pdf*   (accessed November 5, 20120).

3   Adam Jones, "Gendercide and Genocide," *Journal of Genocide Research*, 2:2 (June 2000), 185–211.

4   John Bohannon and John Travis, "How Many Have Died Due to Congo's Fighting? Scientists Battle over How to Estimate War-Related Deaths," ScienceInsider, January 21, 2010: *http:// news.sciencemag.org/scienceinsider/2010/01/post-1.html* (accessed November 5, 2012). The analysts at Simon Fraser also criticize the IRC researchers for having chosen their research sites on the basis of their being "hot": that is, likely to be places where many deaths had occurred.

5   André Lambert and Louis Lohlé-Tart, "La surmortalité au Congo (RDC) durant les troubles de 1998–2004: Une estima-tion des décès en surnombre, scientifiquement fondée à partir des méthodes de la démographie," ADRASS, October 2008. See also: David Aronson, "New Mortality Study Dramatically Reduces Estimates of War Toll," Congo Resources, January 7, 2009: *http://www.congoresources.org/2009/01/new-mortality-study-slashes-estimates.html* (accessed November 5, 2012). Benjamin Litsani, "Des chercheurs belges manipulent des chif-fres," Africa Presse.com, January 5, 2011: *http://www.africa-presse.com/news-1745/* (accessed November 5, 2012).

6 Amber Peterman, Tia Palermo, and Caryn Bredenkamp, "Estimates and Determinants of Sexual Violence against Women in the Democratic Republic of Congo," *American Journal of Public Health*, 101:6 (June 2011), 1060–7. See also Jeffrey Gettleman, "Congo Study Sets Estimate for Rapes Much Higher," *New York Times*, May 11, 2011: *http://www.nytimes.com/2011/05/12/world/africa/12congo.html* (accessed November 5, 2012).

7 Jina Moore, "Congo War Leaves Legacy of Sexual Violence against Women," *Christian Science Monitor*, June 30, 2010: *http://www.csmonitor.com/World/Africa/2010/0630/Congo-war-leaves-legacy-of-sexual-violence-against-women* (accessed November 28, 2012); Elizabeth Dickinson, "How Can We Explain the Rape Epidemic in Congo?" *Foreign Policy* blog, August 9, 2011: *http://blog.foreignpolicy.com/posts/2011/05/11/what_can_explain_the_rape_epidemic_in_congo* (accessed November 5, 2012); Charli Carpenter, "Congo Rape Study: Systematic or Simplistic?" The Duck of Minerva, May 16, 2011: *http://duckofminerva.blogspot.com/2011/05/congo-rape-study-systematic-or.html* (accessed November 5, 2012).

8 See, *inter alia*: *http://www.achpr.org/english/Decison_Communication/Uganda/Comm.227-99.pdf*; *http://www1.umn.edu/humanrts/africa/comcases/227-99.html* (accessed November 5, 2012).

9 Articles 60 and 61 of the African Charter "recognize regional and international human rights instruments and African practices consistent with international norms on human and peoples' rights as being important reference points for the application and interpretation of the African Charter."

10 Gwendolyn J. Lusi, "An Open Wound: The Issue of Gender-Based Violence in North Kivu," *Regards croisés*, August 2004, 8–9: *http://www.pole-institute.org/documents/regard11bis.pdf* (accessed November 6, 2012).

11 Réseau des Femmes pour un Développement Associatif, Réseau des Femmes pour la Défense des Droits et la Paix, and International Alert, *Women's Bodies as a Battleground: Sexual Violence Against Women and Girls During the War in the Democratic Republic of Congo: South Kivu (1996–2003)*, 2005: *http://www.international-alert.org/pdf/sexual_violence_congo_english.pdf* (accessed November 6, 2012).

12 Ibid., 37.

13 Martha McCaughey, *Real Knockouts: The Physical Feminism of Women's Self-Defense* (New York: NYU Press, 1997), p. 56.

14 bell hooks, "Sexism and Misogyny: Who Takes the Rap?" *Z Magazine*, February 1994: *http://race.eserver.org/misogyny. html* (accessed November 6, 2012).

15 Nancy Rose Hunt, "An Acoustic Register, Tenacious Images, and Congolese Scenes of Rape and Repetition," *Cultural Anthropology*, 23:2 (May 2008), 220–53.

16 Ibid., 226.

17 Réseau des Femmes pour un Développement Associatif et al., *Women's Bodies as a Battleground*, 20.

18 Vamik D. Volkan, "Chosen Trauma, the Political Ideology of Entitlement and Violence," January 2004: *http://www. vamikvolkan.com/Chosen-Trauma,-the-Political-Ideology-of-Entitlement-and-Violence.php* (accessed November 6, 2012).

19 Irène S. Turner, "Trauma Healing in the Absence of State Structure: Lessons from the Democratic Republic of Congo," unpublished paper, George Mason University, December 2009.

20 Lynn Nottage, *Ruined* (New York: Theatre Communications Group, 2009), p. 63.

21 Luc Reychler, "Field Diplomacy: A New Conflict Prevention Paradigm," paper presented at the Brisbane conference of the International Peace Research Association, 1996.

22 Hugo van der Merwe and Tracy Vienings, "Coping with Trauma," in Luc Reychler and Thania Paffenholz, eds., *Peace-Building: A Field Guide* (Boulder, CO: Lynne Rienner, 2001), 343.

23 See Eve Ensler, "Dr. Denis Mukwege: We Have Few Heroes in This World. He is One," *Guardian*, October 26, 2012: *http:// www.guardian.co.uk/commentisfree/2012/oct/26/dr-denis-mukwege-heroes* (accessed November 27, 2012).

24 Amnesty International, "Protect Human Rights Defender Justine Masika Bihamba," November 3, 2008.

25 Thomas Lubanga was a warlord of Hema origin, supported first by Uganda and then by Rwanda. He was found guilty by the International Criminal Court of recruiting children under 15 years of age and sending them into battle. Bosco Ntaganda, a Kinyarwanda-speaking Tutsi, born in Rwanda, apparently was sent to Ituri by Rwanda to serve as Lubanga's deputy. He has been indicted by the ICC but as of 2012 had not been arrested.

26 Moses Seruwagi, "Congo-Kinshasa: Unreported Horrors – Male Rape," All-Africa, November 13, 2011: *http://allafrica. com/stories/201111140001.html* (accessed November 6, 2012).

27 For an example, see the Amnesty International USA "talking points" on "conflict minerals": *http://takeaction.amnestyusa.*

*org/atf/cf/%7B74ba1956-0c57-4b8e-9d15-d6ab8ce64cf1%
7D/AI_CMTA_TALKINGPOINTS.PDF* (accessed November
30, 2012).

Chapter 5   Congo's "Resource Curse"

1 Letter to Baron Solvyns, November 19, 1877, cited by Fran-
çoise de Moor and Jean-Pierre Jacquemin, *Notre Congo/Onze
Kongo. La propagande coloniale belge: fragments pour une
étude critique* (Brussels: CEC   [Coopération-Education-
Culture], 2000), 12.

2 Patrice Lumumba, "Speech at Proclamation of Independence,"
in *Lumumba Speaks: The Speeches and Writings of Patrice
Lumumba, 1958–1961*, ed. Jean Van Lierde, trans. Helen R.
Lane (Boston: Little, Brown and Co., 1972), 222; reprinted
with commentary in *Milestone Documents in World History*,
Vol. 4 (Dallas: Schlager Group, 2010), 1624–6.

3 Resolutions of Ankutshu-Anamongo Congress, Tshumbe,
1960, reprinted in *Congo 1960*, Vol. III (Brussels: CRISP, 1961),
7–18.

4 Howard W. French, "The Chinese and Congo Take a Giant
Leap of Faith," *New York Times*, September 21, 2007: *http://
www.nytimes.com/2007/09/21/world/asia/21iht-letter.1.
7595719.html* (accessed November 9, 2012).

5 "Kinshasa's Missing Millions," *Africa-Asia Confidential*, 3:4,
February 2010.

6 Jason Stearns, "Two Huge New Secretive Sales of Congolese
Mining Assets," Congo Siasa Blogspot, July 13, 20110: *http://
congosiasa.blogspot.co.uk/2011/07/two-huge-new-secretive-
sales-of.html* (accessed November 12, 2012).

7 Ibid.

8 For example, Paul Collier, "Economic Causes of Civil Conflict
and Their Implications for Policy." Working paper, Oxford:
Oxford University, 2006; Paul Collier and Anke Hoeffler,
"Greed and Grievance in Civil War," *Oxford Economic Papers*,
56:4 (2004), 563–95.

9 François Grignon, "Economic Agendas in the Congolese Peace
Process," in Michael W. Nest, ed., *The Democratic Republic
of Congo: Economic Dimensions of War and Peace* (Boulder,
CO and London: Lynne Rienner, 2006), 64.

10 S. 2125: Democratic Republic of the Congo Relief, Security,
and Democracy Promotion Act of 2006 (became Public Law

No. 109–456): *http://www.govtrack.us/congress/bill.xpd?bill=s109-2125* (accessed November 12, 2012).

11   Colette Braeckman, *Les nouveaux prédateurs: Politique des puissances en Afrique centrale* (Paris: Fayard, 2003), map (frontispiece).

12   Koen Vlassenroot and Timothy Raeymaekers, "New Political Order in the DR Congo? The Transformation of Regulation," *Afrika Focus*, 21:3 (2008), 43, 44.

13   Ibid.

14   Ibid.

15   Sasha Lezhnev and John Prendergast, "From Mine to Mobile Phone: The Conflict Minerals Supply Chain," Enough Project, November 10, 2009: *http://www.enoughproject.org/publications/mine-mobile-phone* (accessed November 12, 2012).

16   Hans Romkema, "Opportunities and Constraints for the Disarmament and Repatriation of Foreign Armed Groups in the DRC," Washington, DC: Wilson Center, 2001: *http://www.wilsoncenter.org/sites/default/files/MDRPDRCCOFSStudy_Final_ENGL.pdf* (accessed November 27, 2012). John Lasker, "Digging for Gold, Mining Corruption: One of Africa's Poorest and Most Embattled Countries is Prey to Canadian Mining Companies Searching for the Last Great Gold Mine," Canadian Dimension, October 29, 2009: *http://canadiandimension.com/articles/2565/* (accessed November 12, 2012).

17   "D.R. Congo Reaps Bonanza from Tenke Arm Wrestling," Minefund, October 22, 2010: *http://minefund.com/wordpress/2010/10/22/d-r-congo-reaps-bonanza-from-tenke-arm-wrestling/* (accessed November 27, 2012).

18   Katrina Manson, "Illegal Diggers Block Exports at Freeport Congo Mine," Reuters, August 18, 2010: *http://uk.reuters.com/article/2010/08/18/congo-democratic-tenke-idUKLDE67H1O720100818* (accessed November 12, 2012).

19   Human Rights Watch, Annual Report, 2010 (covering 2009), New York, 2010, "Democratic Republic of Congo," p. 104; Amnesty International, "Democratic Republic of Congo Must End Persecution of Human Rights Defenders," February 17, 2010: *http://www.amnesty.org/en/news-and-updates/report/democratic-republic-congo-must-end-persecution-human-rights-defenders-201* (accessed November 27, 2012).

20   Amnesty International, "Democratic Republic of Congo: Making a Killing: The Diamond Trade in Government-Controlled DRC," London, October 22, 2002. AI index:

AFR 62/017/2002: *http://www.grandslacs.net/doc/2454.pdf* (accessed November 27, 2012).

21 François Misser, "Kabila Diamonds Turn to Dust," *African Business*, July 2000.

22 "Angola and Congo Eye End to Border Oil Dispute," Reuters, April 22, 2009: *http://www.defenceweb.co.za/index.php? option=com_content&view=article&id=1734&catid=49:Nati onal%20Security&Itemid=115* (accessed November 12, 2012).

23 International Crisis Group, "Black Gold in the Congo: Threat to Stability or Development Opportunity?" July 11, 2012: *http://www.crisisgroup.org/en/regions/africa/central-africa/dr-congo/188-black-gold-in-the-congo-threat-to-stability-or-development-opportunity.aspx* (accessed November 12, 2012).

24 CAFOD, "Analysis of Proposed Tailings Retreatment Project: Submission to Mining Company AngloGold Ashanti Outlining a Series of Environmental and Social Concerns About a Community Development Initiative Proposed by the Company to Generate Employment in the Mongbwalu Area of the Democratic Republic of Congo," January 5, 2010.

25 Braeckman, *Les nouveaux prédateurs* (see note 11).

26 Human Rights First, "Disrupting the Supply Chain for Mass Atrocities," July 2011: *http://www.humanrightsfirst.org/2011/07/07/disrupting-the-supply-chain-for-mass-atrocities/* (accessed November 12, 2012).

27 Pierre Englebert, "Clinton's Challenge in Congo," *Christian Science Monitor*, August 10, 2009: *http://www.csmonitor.com/Commentary/Opinion/2009/0810/p09s02-coop.html* (accessed November 12, 2012).

Chapter 6 The Responsibility to Protect

1 Sybil E. Crowe, *The Berlin West Africa Conference, 1884–1885*, new edn (New York: Longmans, Green, 1981).

2 Georges Nzongola-Ntalaja, *The Congo from Leopold to Kabila: A People's History* (London: Zed Books, 2002), 95.

3 Andrew W. Cordier and Wilder Foote, eds., *Public Papers: Dag Hammarskjöld, 1960–1961* (New York: Columbia University Press, 1974), p. 167.

4 "Democratic Republic of the Congo, 1993–2003: Report of the Mapping Exercise Commenting on the Most Serious Violations of Human Rights in the Democratic Republic of the Congo

between March 1993 and June 2003," August 2010: *http://www.ohchr.org/Documents/Countries/ZR/DRC_MAPPING_REPORT_FINAL_EN.pdf* (accessed November 12, 2012).

5 Kofi Annan, Remarks by Secretary-General Kofi Annan at the Rwanda Genocide Memorial Conference, March 26, 2004: *http://www.un.org/News/Press/docs/2004/afr868.doc.htm* (accessed November 29, 2012).

6 Richard D. Hooker, Jr., "US Policy Choices During the Rwandan Genocide." Research Paper, National War College, Washington, DC, 2003.

7 Ibid.

8 Barbara Crossette, "Inquiry Says UN Inertia in '94 Worsened Genocide in Rwanda," *New York Times*, December 17, 1999: *http://www.nytimes.com/1999/12/17/world/inquiry-says-un-inertia-in-94-worsened-genocide-in-rwanda.html?pagewanted=all&src=pm* (accessed November 13, 2012).

9 United Nations, "Report of the Panel of Experts on the Illegal Exploitation of Natural Resources and Other Forms of Wealth of the Democratic Republic of the Congo," New York, 2001: *http://www.un.org/News/dh/latest/drcongo.htm* (accessed November 13, 2012).

10 United States Holocaust Memorial Museum, "DR Congo: Overview": *http://www.ushmm.org/genocide/take_action/atrisk/region/dr-congo* (accessed November 13, 2012).

11 S. 2125: Democratic Republic of the Congo Relief, Security, and Democracy Promotion Act of 2006 (became Public Law No. 109–456): *http://www.govtrack.us/congress/bill.xpd?bill=s109-2125* (accessed November 12, 2012).

12 United States Government Accountability Office, Report to Congress, The Democratic Republic of the Congo: Systematic Assessment Is Needed to Determine Agencies' Progress Toward US Policy Objectives. Washington, December 2007. GAO-08-188.

13 "Clinton: I'm Secretary of State, not Bill," NBCnews.com, August 11, 2009: *http://www.msnbc.msn.com/id/32361939/ns/politics-more_politics/* (accessed November 13, 2012). See also Judith Warner, "Hillary Fights a Tide of Trivialization," Opinionator, nytimes.com, August 12, 2009: *http://opinionator.blogs.nytimes.com/2009/08/12/hillary-fights-a-tide-of-trivialization/* (accessed November 13, 2012).

14 Though see Hillary Rodham Clinton,"Town Hall with Search for Common Ground and Congolese University Students," St.

Joseph's School, Kinshasa, Democratic Republic of the Congo," August 10, 2009: *http://www.state.gov/secretary/rm/2009a/08/127173.htm* (accessed November 29, 2012).

15 Robert Gersony, an American consultant working for the UN High Commissioner for Refugees, prepared a report on conditions in post-genocide Rwanda that might interfere with the repatriation of mainly Hutu refugees from Burundi, Tanzania, and Zaïre. He apparently was prevented from presenting a final report because the information on Rwandan army killings within Rwanda was deemed too damaging by the United Nations and/or certain governments. [Robert Gersony], "Summary of UNHCR Presentation before Commission of Experts, 10 October 1994: Prospects for Early Repatriation of Rwanda Refugees Currently in Burundi, Tanzania and Zaïre," Geneva.

16 Roberto Garretón of the United Nations was prevented by Laurent Kabila from conducting an inquiry into alleged massacres of Hutu refugees. See Roberto Garretón, "Report on the Situation of Human Rights in the Democratic Republic of the Congo, Submitted by the Special Rapporteur, Mr. Roberto Garretón, in accordance with Commission Resolution 1998/61," UN Economic and Social Council, Commission on Human Rights, 1991. Once Kabila had broken with the Rwandans and Ugandans, he became much more cooperative.

17 The UN panels of experts on illegal exploitation of Congolese resources and on violations of the arms embargo cited names of violators; often the appendices containing the names were deemed confidential, only to be leaked to the press by elements within the UN.

18 The UN Mapping Report apparently was completed in 2009, but was released only in 2010 after a draft version had been leaked.

19 *Conflict Minerals Trade Act (2009; 111th Congress H.R. 4128: http:// www.govtrack.us/congress/bills/111/hr4128* (accessed November 29, 2012).

20 Barack Obama, "Remarks by the President at the United States Holocaust Memorial Museum," April 23, 2012: *http://www.whitehouse.gov/the-press-office/2012/04/23/remarks-president-united-states-holocaust-memorial-museum* (accessed November 13, 2012).

21 Hillary Clinton, "Remarks at the US Holocaust Memorial Museum Forward-Looking Symposium on Genocide Preven-

tion," July 24, 2012: *http://www.state.gov/secretary/rm/2012/07/195409.htm* (accessed November 13, 2012).

22 "Obama Urges Kagame to End DRC Rebel Support," Voice of America, December 19, 2012: *http://www.voanews.com/content/obama-urges-rwandan-president-to-end-drc-rebel-support/1567859.html* (accessed December 22, 2012).

23 Jeffrey Herbst and Greg Mills, There Is No Congo. Why the Only Way to Help Congo Is to Stop Pretending It Exists," *Foreign Policy*, March 18, 2009: *http://www.foreignpolicy.com/articles/2009/03/17/there_is_no_congo* (accessed November 29, 2012).

Bibliography

Autesserre, Séverine, *The Trouble with the Congo: Local Violence and the Failure of International Peacekeeping*. Cambridge and New York: Cambridge University Press, 2010.

Balandier, Georges, *Sociologie actuelle de l'Afrique noire: Dynamique sociale en Afrique centrale*. 4th edition. Paris: PUF, 1982 [1955].

Bayart, Jean-François, Stephen Ellis, and Béatrice Hibou, *The Criminalization of the State in Africa*. Trans. Stephen Ellis. Oxford: The International African Institute in association with James Currey; Bloomington: Indiana University Press, 1999.

Braeckman, Colette, *Les nouveaux prédateurs: Politique des puissances en Afrique central*. Paris: Fayard, 2003.

Chrétien J.-P., and Richard Banégas, eds., *The Recurring Great Lakes Crisis: Identity, Violence and Power*. London: Hurst, 2008; New York: Columbia University Press, 2011.

Clark, John F., ed., *The African Stakes of the Congo War*. New York: Palgrave Macmillan, 2002.

De Witte, Ludo, *The Assassination of Lumumba*. Trans. Ann Wright and Renée Fenby. London: Verso, 2002.

Deutsch, Karl W., *Nationalism and Social Communication*. 2nd edition. Cambridge, MA and London: MIT Press, 1966.

Duke, Lynne, *Mandela, Mobutu and Me: A Newswoman's African Journey*. New York: Doubleday, 2003.

Dunn, Kevin, *Imagining the Congo: The International Relations of Identity*. New York: Palgrave, 2003.

Evans, Gareth, *The Responsibility to Protect: Ending Mass Atrocity Crimes Once and for All*. Washington, DC: Brookings Institution Press, 2008.

Fabian, Johannes, and Tshibumba Kanda Matulu, *Remembering the Present: Painting and Popular History in Zaïre*. Berkeley: University of California Press, 1996.

Hochschild, Adam, *King Leopold's Ghost: A Story of Greed, Terror, and Heroism in Colonial Africa*. New York: Houghton Mifflin Company, 1998.

Kelly, Sean, *America's Tyrant: The CIA and Mobutu of Zaïre*. Washington, DC: American University Press, 1993.

Kennes, Erik, and Munkana N'Ge, *Essai biographique sur Laurent-Désiré Kabila*.

Tervuren: Institut Africain (CEDAF), 2003.

Khadiagala, Gilbert M., ed., *Security Dynamics in Africa's Great Lakes Region*. Boulder, CO and London: Lynne Rienner for the International Peace Academy, 2006.

Lanotte, Olivier, *Guerres sans frontières en République Démocratique du Congo*. Brussels: GRIP-Complexe.

Lanotte, Olivier, Claude Roosens, and Caty Clément, eds., *La Belgique et l'Afrique Centrale, de 1960 à nos jours*. Brussels: GRIP-Complexe, 2000.

Lemarchand, René, *Dynamics of Violence in Central Africa*. Philadelphia: University of Pennsylvania Press.

Lewis, M. Paul, ed., *Ethnologue: Languages of the World*. 16th edition. Dallas: SIL International. (Online version, 2009: *http://www.ethnologue.com/*.)

Lumumba, Patrice, *Lumumba Speaks: The Speeches and Writings of Patrice Lumumba, 1958–1961*. Ed. Jean Van Lierde, trans. Helen R. Lane. Boston: Little, Brown and Co., 1972.

McCaughey, Martha, *Real Knockouts: The Physical Feminism of Women's Self-Defense*. New York: NYU Press, 1997.

MacGaffey, Janet, *Entrepreneurs and Parasites: The Struggle for Indigenous Capitalism in Zaïre*. Cambridge and New York: Cambridge University Press, 1987.

MacGaffey, Janet, *The Real Economy of Zaïre: The Contribution of Smuggling and Other Unofficial Activities to National Wealth*. Philadelphia: University of Pennsylvania Press, 1991.

Madsen, Wayne, *Genocide and Covert Operations in Africa (1993–1999)*. Lewiston, ME: Edwin Mellen Press, 1999.

Maurel, Auguste, *Le Congo de la colonisation belge à l'indépendance*. Paris: Harmattan, 1992. (1st edition, 1962, published under pseudonym Michel Merlier.)

Mwamba Tshibangu, *Joseph Kabila: La vérité étouffée*. Paris: L'Harmattan, 2005.

Nest, Michael W., ed., *The Democratic Republic of Congo: Economic Dimensions of War and Peace*. Boulder, CO and London: Lynne Rienner, 2006.

Nguya-Ndila Malengana, Célestin, *Nationalité et citoyenneté au Congo/Kinshasa: Le cas du Kivu*. Paris and Montréal: L'Harmattan, 2001.

Nottage, Lynn, *Ruined*. New York: Theatre Communications Group, 2009.

Nzongola-Ntalaja, Georges, *The Congo from Leopold to Kabila: A People's History*. London: Zed Books, 2002.

Prunier, Gérard, *Africa's World War: Congo, the Rwandan Genocide, and the Making of a Continental Catastrophe*. Oxford and New York: Oxford University Press, 2009.

Reyntjens, Filip, *The Great African War: Congo and Regional Geopolitics, 1996–2006*. Cambridge and New York: Cambridge University Press, 2009.

Reychler, Luc, and Thania Paffenholz, eds., *Peacebuilding: A Field Guide*. Boulder, CO: Lynne Rienner, 2000.

Schatzberg, Michael G., *The Dialectics of Oppression in Zaïre*. Bloomington and Indianapolis: Indiana University Press, 1988.

Stearns, Jason K., *Dancing in the Glory of Monsters: The Collapse of the Congo and the Great War of Africa*. New York: Public Affairs, 2011.

Thornton, John, *The Kingdom of Kongo: Civil War and Transition, 1641–1718*. Madison: University of Wisconsin Press, 1983.

Thornton, John, *Africa and Africans in the Making of the Atlantic World, 1400–1650*. Cambridge: Cambridge University Press, 1992.

Trefon, Theodore, ed., *Reinventing Order in the Congo. How People Respond to State Failure in Kinshasa*. London: Zed Books, 2004.

Trefon, Theodore, *Congo Masquerade: The Political Culture of Aid Inefficiency and Reform Failure*. London: Zed Books, 2011.

Turner, Thomas, *The Congo Wars: Conflict, Myth, and Reality*. London: Zed Books, 2007.

Twain, Mark, *King Leopold's Soliloquy: A Defense of His Congo Rule*. 2nd edition. Boston: P. R. Warren Co., 1905.

Verhaegen, Benoit, *Rébellions au Congo*, tomes 1 and II. Brussels and Kinshasa: CRISP and IRES, 1967, 1970.

Weis, Georges, *Le pays d'Uvira*. Brussels: Académie Royale des Sciences Coloniales, 1959.

Wrong, Michela, *In the Footsteps of Mr. Kurtz: Living on the Brink of Disaster in Mobutu's Congo*. London: Fourth Estate/New York: HarperCollins, 2001.

Young, Crawford, *The African Colonial State in Comparative Perspective*. New Haven: Yale University Press, 1997.

Young, Crawford, and Thomas Turner. *The Rise and Decline of the Zaïrian State*. Madison: University of Wisconsin Press, 1985.

Zartman, I. William, *Ripe for Resolution: Conflict and Intervention in Africa*. Revised edition. New York: Oxford University Press for the Council on Foreign Relations.

Index